THE MYTHIC PATH

THE MYTHIC PATH

Discovering the Guiding Stories of Your Past—Creating a Vision for Your Future

---

DAVID FEINSTEIN, PH.D.

STANLEY KRIPPNER, PH.D.

Introduction by Jean Houston, Ph.D.

Foreword to Original Edition by June Singer, Ph.D.

Illustrations by Gayle Gray

A Jeremy P. Tarcher/Putnam Book

Published by G. P. Putnam's Sons   New York

Most Tarcher/Putnam books are available at special quantity discounts for bulk
purchases for sales promotions, premiums, fund-raising, and educational needs.
Special books or book excerpts also can be created to fit specific needs.
For details, write or telephone Special Markets, The Putnam Publishing Group,
200 Madison Avenue, New York, NY 10016; (212) 951-8891.

———————

A Jeremy P. Tarcher/Putnam Book
Published by G. P. Putnam's Sons
Publishers Since 1838
200 Madison Avenue
New York, NY 10016
http://www.putnam.com/putnam

Library of Congress Cataloging-in-Publication Data

Feinstein, David.
The mythic path : discovering the guiding stories of your past—
creating a vision for your future / David Feinstein, Stanley Krippner.
p.   cm.
"A Jeremy P. Tarcher/Putnam book."
ISBN 0-87477-857-3 (alk. paper)
1. Attitude (Psychology)   2. Mythology—Psychological aspects.
3. Self-perception.   4. Attitude change.   5. Self-actualization
(Psychology).   I. Krippner, Stanley, date.   II. Title.
BF327.F446   1997   96-26397 CIP
155.2—dc20

Book design by Chris Welch
Cover design by Lee Fukui
Front cover illustration © by Jose Ortega / SIS
Photograph of David Feinstein by Steven R. Goldstein
Photograph of Stanley Krippner by Bonnie Colodzin
Gayle Gray, the illustrator, is a freelance artist in Ashland, Oregon.

Printed in the United States of America

3   5   7   9   10   8   6   4

This book is printed on acid-free paper. ∞

SUPPLEMENTAL PROGRAMS AND MATERIALS

A three-hour cassette tape program containing the guided imagery and movement instructions presented in this book, accompanied by powerful inspirational and shamanistic music, is offered for $16.95 through Innersource. Please add $2 for shipping and handling per order ($3 for overseas airmail). Call 1-800-835-8332, or send name, address, and phone number with check, money order, or Visa or MasterCard number and signature to Innersource, PO Box 213, Ashland, OR 97520. A free brochure describing other available tapes and books is included with each order or may be requested by mail or phone.

ACKNOWLEDGMENTS

Discussions with Rosie Adams, Dianna Butler, Sharon Doubiago, Richard Evans, Steve Goldstein, Joel Heller, Wendy Hill, Jerry Jud, Steve Kierulff, Don Klein, Ron Kurtz, Danielle Light, Dana Lundin, Bill Lyon, Gene Mallory, Rollo May, Reid Meloy, Stella Monday, Ann Mortifee, Linda Nicholls, Paul Oas, Rod Plimpton, Tiziana de Rovere, Julie Schwartz, Rupert Sheldrake, Katherine Yates, and Carl Young all contributed to our thinking, in ways that are gratefully acknowledged. Dan McAdams provided catalytic suggestions for the first edition of this volume. Peg Elliott Mayo, who has been a constant source of perceptive and buoyant counsel through both editions, has contributed more of substance to this work than is prudent to admit. The astute and patient editing of Connie Zweig and Ted Mason in the original edition, and of Irene Prokop and Alan Rinzler for this revision, have been of immeasurable value. We also recognize and deeply appreciate the anonymous contributions of the many workshop participants, students, and psychotherapy clients with whom we have been privileged to work.

A number of institutions have provided hospitable surroundings and generous support over the years as these ideas have developed, particularly Innersource in Ashland, Oregon; Saybrook Institute in San Francisco; Esalen Institute in Big Sur; and Haven By-the-Sea on Gabriola Island, British Columbia. We would specifically like to express our gratitude to Rita Rohen and the late Richard Price, who arranged for us to be able to write several chapters of the first edition of this book in the beautiful environs of Esalen Institute.

Jeremy Tarcher has been a persuasive and imaginative force in this effort to bring the ideas and methods presented in our seminars and professional writings to a wider audience.

The love, understanding, and inspirational presence of our partners in marriage, Donna Eden and Lelie Krippner, are appreciated beyond words.

To Joel Elkes—pioneer, mentor, friend—
who serendipitously set our collaboration in motion

CONTENTS

———— ❧ ————

Jean Houston, Ph.D.

Some years ago I found myself sitting on the ground in a village in India watching a television dramatization of the Ramayana. The village's one television set was a source of great pride, and all the villagers had come from their fields and houses to be inspired and entertained by the weekly hour in which the many episodes of this key myth of the Hindu world were so gloriously produced. The story tells of Prince Rama (an avatar of the god Vishnu) and his noble wife, Princess Sita (a human incarnation of the goddess Lakshmi), and how they have been betrayed and banished to live in a forest for fourteen years. Nevertheless they are very happy, for Rama is noble, handsome, and full of valor, while Sita is virtuous, beautiful, and completely subservient to her husband. They are, in other words, the archaic ideal of the perfect married couple. Unfortunately, their forest idyll is brutally interrupted when Sita is abducted by the many-headed, multi-armed demon Ravana, who promptly carries her off to his own kingdom of Sri Lanka. Enter the saintly monkey Hanuman, who with his army of monkeys and bears, along with

Rama, is eventually able to vanquish Ravana and his formidable troops of demons and rescue Sita. Rama takes her back, however, only after he is convinced of her virtue and the fact that she not once "sat on the demon's lap."

There is never a minute in the Hindu world when this story is not enacted, sung, performed in a puppet show, a Balinese shadow play, or a stage or screen performance. It is the core myth of the Hindu psyche. And this television series was a lavish treatment, filled with spectacular effects, exotic costumes, thrilling music and dance, and acting appropriate to the playing of the gods. The villagers were as entranced as I, for this was religion, morality, and hopping good musical theater all in one. Furthermore, they were joined together in the knowledge that all over India at that moment hundreds of millions of people were watching this program with the same fascination. Suddenly, the old Brahman lady who owned the television set, and was sitting next to me on the ground, turned to me and said in lilting English, "Oh, I don't like Sita!"

"Pardon?" I was aghast. This was like my Sicilian grandmother saying that she doesn't like the Madonna.

"No, I really don't like Sita. She is too weak, too passive. We women in India are much stronger than that. She should have something to do with her own rescue, not just sit there moaning and hoping that Rama will come. We need to change the story."

"But the story is at least three thousand years old!" I protested.

"Even more reason why we need to change it. Make Sita stronger. Let her make her own decisions. You know, my name is Sita and my husband's name is Rama. Very common names in India. He is a lazy bum. If any demon got him, I would have to go and make the rescue."

She turned and translated what she had just said to the others who were sitting around. They all laughed and agreed, especially the women. Then the villagers began to discuss what an alternative story, one that had Sita taking a much larger part, might look like. It was a revisionist's dream, listening to people whose lives had not changed much over thousands of years actively rethinking their primal story. It was like sitting in a small town in southern Mississippi, listening to Christian fundamentalists rewrite the Bible. Astonished and exhilarated, I sensed that I was experiencing in this village a beginning stage of the re-invention of myth, the changing of the story. No matter that this primal tale was ancient beyond ancient, venerable beyond venerable; it belonged to an outmoded perception of women and their relationship to men and society, and it had to change or go.

The fact of the matter is that we are required to change the story not just in India but everywhere in the world. Patterns of millennia have prepared us for another world, another time, and, above all, another story. At the same time, exponential change, unlike any ever known in human history or prehistory, has confused our values, uprooted our traditions, and left us in a labyrinth of misdirection. Factors unique in human experience are all around us—the inevitable unfolding toward a planetary civilization, the rise of women to full partnership with men, the daily revolutions in technology, the media becoming the matrix of culture, and the revolution in the understanding of human and social capacities. The zeit is getting geistier as the old story becomes ever more antiquated. It cannot address the multiples of experience and complexity of life unknown to our great-grandparents, nor can it heal the many wounds that come with this plethora of experience and its attending chaos. We have become so full of holes that perhaps we are well on the way to becoming holy.

Since the new story, the new mythology, is not yet in place, it is up to us separately and together to carry out the work of reenvisionment. But can one ever really change, or even invent a myth? Go beneath the surface crust of consciousness of virtually anyone anywhere, and you will find repositories of the imaginal world—the teeming terrain of myth and archetype: holy men and wise women, flying horses, talking frogs, sacred spaces, deaths and resurrections, the journeys of the heroes and heroines of a thousand faces. Having taken depth probings of the psyche of many people the world over, I know this to be so.

Myths, after all, contain the greater story that never was but is always happening. Their waters run far deeper than the compelling tales told around ancient campfires to explain the seasons, the weather, and the formidable conflicts found within human societies and the human soul. Myth does serve as a manner of explanation, but it is also a mode of discovery, for myth is the coded DNA of the human psyche. It is the stuff of the evolving self that awakens consciousness and culture according to the needs of time and place. It is the promise of our becoming.

When we undertake to work consciously with the great old myths, a rich and varied world of experience opens to us. We can travel with Odysseus, experience the passion play of Isis and Osiris, wander with Percival in search of the Grail, and die and be reborn with Jesus. Within the spoken or ritually enacted myth we can allow our lives to be writ larger, the personal particulars of our local existence finding their amplification and elucidation in the personal universals of the greater story and the larger characters that myth contains.

Those of us who work with myth, like the authors of this book and myself, find that our clients and students, having entered the realm of the ancient stories and their personae, seem to inherit a cache of experience that illumines and fortifies their own. They soon discover that they too are valuable characters in the drama of the world soul, pushing the boundaries of their own local story and gaining the courage to be and do so much more.

How, then, can we change patterns so deeply woven into the structure of our psyches? Until recent decades, I doubt that one could have done much more than alter certain details. Now, however, in a time of whole system transition, when everything is deconstructing and reconstructing, myth, too, requires its redemption. This is the crisis and the opportunity the authors of this potent work help us navigate. They have embarked on as critical a task as one could attempt at the cusp of the millennium—how to go about changing the dominant myths by guiding people into the realms of the psyche wherein they have the power to change their own essential story. They work on the premise that all over the world, psyche is now emerging, larger than it was. We are experiencing the harvest of all the world's cultures, belief systems, ways of knowing, seeing, doing, being. What had been contained in the "unconscious" over hundreds and thousands of years is up and about and preparing to go to work. What had been part of the collective as the shared myth or archetype is now finding new rivers of unique stories flowing from the passion play of individual lives.

This does not mean the dismissal of traditional myths, but rather that now as the outmoded maps of tradition no longer fit the territory, we must live our lives with the mythic vibrancy of those who inhabited the ancient stories. We are mentored and informed by the ancient myths, and we are also in an open moment, a jump time when myth is re-creating itself from the stuff of personal experience. For the development of the psyche, this is as monumental as when people stopped depending on the meanderings of the hunt and settled down to agriculture and civilization. Just as we are becoming capable of discovering our own personal mythologies, we are becoming required to encounter them. In so doing, we add our own deepening story to that of the emerging New Story and, with it, the new planetary civilization.

What is offered in this book is essentially a technology of the sacred, a high art form as well as a once and future science. It finds its theory and practice in the teachings of the mystery schools of old, in shamanic training and initiations, as well as in the modern laboratories of consciousness research and the cutting edges of psychotherapy. While fiber optics, interactive television, global computer networks, and other information superhighways give us access to the world mind, the authors belong to a small group of artist-scientists who are providing us with the high ways to the world soul.

In my Mother/Father's house are many mansions. Maybe so, but part of our job is to help provide the furniture and set up housekeeping in the rooms of the mansions that heretofore were relatively uninhabited by our conscious minds. As masters of the geography of the inscapes, David Feinstein and Stanley Krippner guide you into a most comprehensive developmental program for discovering the uniquely personal worlds and wonders that lie within. To this end, they have provided an ensemble of state-of-the-art methods to travel and train in inner space. These include guided imagery, dream incubation, working with the Inner Shaman, even rewriting your own history through the emotionally corrective daydream. You will be taken on journeys backward and forward in time, so that you may heal old wounds and transform obstacles into opportunities. New powers are opened as you learn to reframe your story as a fairy tale, finding within your own body the metaphors for conflict and conciliation, discovering power objects, personal shields, and inner allies. Always reminded and reconnected to the myths of generations past, you are luminously led to become a pioneer in the undiscovered continent of the myths of times to come.

Since culture is everywhere being newly reimagined, nothing is more necessary than a rebirth of the self. This book is meant to breach our souls, unlock the treasures of our minds, and, through the divine act of remythologizing, release the purpose, the plan, and the possibilities of our lives. We are regrown to greatness and take our place with Percival and Penelope, with White Buffalo Woman and the Lady of the Lake, with Quetzalcoatl and Bridget and Mr. Spock. And the name of this new character out of myth is You. And the name of the myth is Your Story—reframed in the light of the understanding that has come from this process, and reconceived for the renewal of self and history.

"Thank God, our time is now," the poet Christopher Fry says, "when wrong comes up to meet us everywhere. Never to leave us, till we take the longest stride of soul men ever took." This stride of soul must carry us through every shadow toward an open possibility, in a time when everything is quite literally up for grabs. We can do no less. The psyche requires its greatness, as do the times. This adventure in personal mythology is one very important, very original, and exciting way to greatness, or should I say, responsible living of the life we are given.

The times, they *are* a-changing. Back in that village in India, after the beautiful episode from the Ramayana ended, the next program all of India was watching was the prime-time soap opera of some seasons ago, *Dynasty*! As I looked at the dubious comings and goings of the characters, I didn't know where to hide my head. My hostess saw my embarrassment at the comparative low level of American television and, patting my arm, said, "Oh, sister, do not be embarrassed. Don't you see? It is the same story."

"How can you say that?"

"Oh, yes, indeed," she continued, her head wagging from side to side. "It is the same story. You've got the good man. You've got the bad man. You've got the good woman. You've got the bad woman. You've got the beautiful house, the beautiful clothes, the people flying through the air. You've got the good fighting against the evil. Oh, yes, indeed, it is the same story!"

Thus are myths and metaphors recast, redesigning the human fabric and all our ways of seeing. It is the privilege and the particular challenge of the authors of this remarkable book to witness and assist a new story coming into time through evoking the living content of the life of you who are reading these pages.

These are the times. We are the people.

June Singer, Ph.D.

P ersonal myths are not what you think they are. They are not false beliefs. They are not the stories you tell yourself to explain your circumstances and behavior. Your personal mythology is, rather, the vibrant infrastructure that informs your life, whether or not you are aware of it. Consciously and unconsciously, you live by your mythology. In this remarkable book, the authors challenge you, through the use of ritual, dreams, and story, to become aware of the mythology you are living, to confront it, and in the end to gain some mastery over it. The book is an exercise in the "evolution of consciousness"—your consciousness and the consciousness of the culture in which you are embedded.

To live mythically means to become aware of your personal and collective origins. In the process of learning to do this you will discover, or affirm, that you are not an isolated, independent being, but the end product of the millennia of acculturation and maturation of the human race. Personal mythology is but the flower on the bush: the family myth is the branch, society's conventions form the stem, and the root is the human condition.

Personal myths structure our awareness and point us in the direction that becomes our path. If we are unacquainted with the contents of our personal mythology we are carried by it unconsciously, with the result that we confuse what exists objectively in the world with the image of the world supplied to us by our own distorted lenses. On the basis of an unconscious personal mythology, or a mythology rigidly imposed by our social group, we tend to see only one correct path. We do not see it as *our* way, but as *the* way, and we do not see that it could lead to disaster as easily as to contentment.

The book has its roots in a research project at The Johns Hopkins University School of Medicine in which David Feinstein compared several emerging systems of personal growth therapies with more traditional therapies. He found a common denominator: each therapy, in its own way, attempted to influence how people construct their understanding of themselves and their place in the world. He used the term *personal mythology* to describe this "evolving construction of inner reality" and to emphasize that all human constructions of reality are mythologies.

Stanley Krippner's role in this book has been one of offering inspiration and insight to the primary author. He brings to the collaboration thirty years of pioneering research on human consciousness, particularly his studies of dreams, healing, and altered states. Over the past decade the authors have conducted workshops and developed methods through which people can become aware of the mythologies that have guided them in the past. With that understanding, it is possible to move on to guiding myths that are more vital and viable. The process is systematically arranged and constitutes the major portion of this work. Step by step, the book sets forth a guide to personal transformation through explanation, participatory experiences, and case material. It not only provides the necessary conceptual information, but helps the reader integrate the knowledge through rituals and practices and then apply the new awareness to everyday life.

An approach that delineates five stages of growth is offered. The stages are informed by sources encompassing many schools, all the way from ancient Greek philosophy to the methods and theories of Freudian and Jungian psychology to the practical approaches of contemporary behaviorism and cognitive psychology. None of these systems is applied uncritically, and the authors have managed to integrate a coherent synthesis of a tremendous body of psychological theory into their work.

The first three stages echo the Socratic thesis, antithesis, and synthesis. Stage one involves recognizing and defining one's own personal myth and discovering to what degree this guiding myth is no longer an ally. Stage two requires the identification of an opposing personal myth, one that creates a conflict in the person's psyche. The conflicting myths are brought into focus and examined to see how each is linked to the past. The person will soon recognize that the myths of childhood are rarely appropriate to serve the adult.

Stage three, synthesis, entails conceiving a unifying vision. Here the old myth and the counter-myth are brought into confrontation. They may be personified so that the conflict can be worked out as a drama of the inner life, and so that, as Feinstein and Krippner so nicely put it, it does not have to be played "out on the rack of life." In the process, obstacles to harmony are re-visioned as opportunities for growth.

Stage four begins where many modes of therapy end. It is called "From Vision to Commitment." Here is where the insights are tested and reinforced so that the process envisioned can move from the hypothetical and imaginal realm into the phase of intention and then into action. Stage five entails weaving the new mythology into life. Here a series of practical steps is suggested whereby the inner transformation can be demonstrated in the world. The butterfly emerges from the chrysalis and is (and is not) a new being. From here on, the process continues both as inner work and as living in the world in a new way, more free of the constrictions of unconscious assumptions.

The book's great contribution, it seems to me, lies in the way it facilitates individuals in recognizing the root causes of their difficulties and then taking responsibility for their own healing process. In this age, information is more accessible to more people than ever before, and individuals are better informed about what is needed to gain and maintain a healthy state both physically and psychologically. Consequently the physician, the psychiatrist, and the psychotherapist are no longer held up as the only people who can lead us to better health. In many situations it is possible and also desirable for individuals to take responsibility for their own well-being. This is done through such practices as exercise, good nutrition, and maintaining a variety of interests. Feinstein and Krippner point the way and provide some very good guidance for attending to one's psychological health and development. Each person who reads this book is challenged to undertake the journey in whatever way is appropriate: alone, with a partner, with friends, or in a group committed to a growth process.

At some point along the way, personal myths converge with cultural myths to govern every human activity. There comes a time, as we work on our personal issues, when we realize the degree to which our personal concerns are of limited significance. The independent individual is a myth gone bankrupt. We have always depended on others for our most basic needs: food, shelter, security, and affection. How much more do we need one another to supply all the complex requirements of life today! You are a participant in the creation of whatever will happen next on this planet. In the emerging global village, as Marshall McLuhan called it, allegiances transcend regional and cultural boundaries. Information, business, the arts, the media, the news, all know no national limitations.

We can no longer separate ourselves from the destiny of the planet, be it a global society in which people may live in mutual trust and high productivity, or nuclear annihilation. The next challenge, which Feinstein and Krippner raise in closing, is to apply to the human community the principles derived from observing the way individuals think mythically. Can the methods the authors have presented for dealing with intrapersonal conflict be used in dealing with the cultural myths that foster intergroup and international conflicts? As in any open system, the solution of one series of problems opens the door to working with a set of higher-level problems. That challenge may well lead us to the next step in the evolution of consciousness.

An Invitation

Renew the Dream
That Quickens Your Spirit

———————— ✦ ————————

Renew the Dream

That Quickens Your Spirit

❧

Mythological symbols touch and exhilarate centers of life beyond
the reach of the vocabularies of reason and coercion.

—Joseph Campbell[1]

Your personal mythology is the loom on which you weave the raw materials of daily experience into a coherent story. You live your life from
within this mythology, drawing to yourself the characters and creating
the scenes that correspond with its guiding theme. A great deal of this activity
occurs outside your awareness. To discover and begin to transform your mythology is one of the most empowering choices open to you. A renewed mythology
calls up fresh perceptions, values, and a revitalized sense of purpose.

When carefully examined, personal myths reveal themselves to be every bit
as creative and imaginative as the most enterprising nighttime dream, setting the
standards for success and failure, good and evil, heroism and villainy, while defining for you a unique role in it all. The source of your mythology is also the
source of your motivations, of your imagination, of your emotions, of awareness itself. It is the point at which consciousness springs into being. In his classic
work on the interpretation of dreams, Sigmund Freud wrote of "a tangle of
dreamthoughts which cannot be unraveled. . . . This is the dream's navel, the

spot where it reaches down into the unknown."[2] To explore your guiding mythology, as you are invited to do with this book, is to bring your awareness ever closer to that mysterious, illuminating source.

As you begin to grasp how your personal story evolves within the larger scheme of existence, you engage yourself with the great spiritual quandaries that have always challenged human beings. Just how are we to view the guiding themes that animate our lives, give them meaning, and in the end, determine their quality? In asking such questions, you open yourself to a larger story, a living appreciation of the mysteries and magnificence of the cosmos as it is reflected in you, its microcosm.

Among the most vivid literary accounts of the radical transformation of a person's guiding mythology is in Charles Dickens's *A Christmas Carol*. The spirits of Christmas Past, Christmas Present, and Christmas Yet to Come escort Ebenezer Scrooge on a series of journeys that transfigure his mythology from one narrowly focused on material concerns to one infused with compassion and a sense of wonder. Scrooge did not know that his mythology was in need of change. When the Spirit of Christmas Past explains that its business is Scrooge's welfare, Scrooge "could not help thinking that a night of unbroken rest would have been more conducive to that end."[3] Most of us, in fact, can benefit by bringing focused attention to the deep beliefs that shape our lives. With this book, we invite you to embark on a sequence of interior journeys—also into your past, present, and possible futures—that are designed to inspire a mythology that brings you to new levels of fulfillment. We hope you will come along.

TWO FACTS OF PSYCHOLOGICAL LIFE

One fact of psychological life—the one on which this book is based—is that beneath your conscious awareness, a dynamic, dramatic personal underworld is in constant motion. It is, moment by moment, involved in the enormously creative task of mapping the reality in which you live. You operate according to the map that it creates, yet the influence of this map is largely outside your conscious awareness. Most people are so thoroughly immersed in their personalized version of reality that it is invisible to them, much as fish are the last creatures on the planet likely to discover water. Yet you can cultivate the immensely useful skill of stepping back, examining your lived reality, and recognizing it as a *personal mythology* that you can learn to articulate, assess, and transform. The more effective your guiding mythology, the better equipped you are to meet the challenges your life presents.

A second fact of psychological life is that your personal mythology is continually evolving. It is a map that forever needs to be updated because its territory is always changing. You take a new job, your guiding mythology needs to be modified. You enter a new relationship, your mythology needs to be modified. You reach another stage of psychological maturity, your mythology has been modified. You lose a lifelong partner, your mythology is turned upside down. Your culture's mythology is in chaos, parts of *your* mythology are in chaos. Your culture's mythology is in profound chaos. Out of that chaos, dynamic new myths are vying to be born in your society as well as in your psyche. This book is designed to assist you in midwifing these myths, distilling their wisdom, and incorporating this wisdom into your larger mythology so it may become an ever more trustworthy and life-affirming map.

WHAT IS A PERSONAL MYTH?

Your life resonates to the myths you spontaneously create to explain your past, account for the present, and guide you into the future. Like our ancestors, we are myth-makers. To conceive of oneself and one's world is to create a mythology. While you are not necessarily aware of your underlying mythology, you *can become* aware of the way it serves as a dynamic inner force by examining the significance of your dreams, by making up a fairy tale about your life, or by reflecting on the themes woven into your ways of loving, working, and living in the world. You will be utilizing such methods in this program.

A Lens for Life. The renowned inventor Buckminster Fuller, speaking late in his life with Stanley Krippner, reflected on the consequences of his severely impaired eyesight as a small child. Everything he saw was extremely fuzzy until, at age four, he was given eyeglasses and was astounded by how the world suddenly came into focus. This modern Renaissance thinker speculated that receiving those glasses might have accounted for his lifelong conviction that even if ideas and relationships seemed fuzzy to him at first, they would eventually become clear. That was, for him, a positive, effective, and realistic guiding myth. It organized his experience of the world and directed his actions.

A personal myth is a constellation of beliefs, feelings, images, and rules—operating largely outside of conscious awareness—that interprets sensations, constructs new explanations, and directs behavior. When Buckminster Fuller confronted a baffling question, his mythology explained to him that his confusion would clear once he found the lens that could bring the matter into focus, it directed him to keep looking for that lens, and it provided him with images of how to proceed.

Your personal mythology is a lens that gives meaning to every situation you meet and determines what you will do in it. Personal myths speak to the broad concerns of identity (Who am I?), direction (Where am I going?), and purpose (Why am I going there?). For an internal system of images, narratives, and emotions to be called a personal myth, it must address at least one of the core concerns of human existence, the traditional domains of cultural mythology. According to Joseph Campbell, these include:

1. the hunger to comprehend the natural world in a meaningful way;
2. the search for a marked pathway through the succeeding epochs of human life;
3. the need to establish secure and fulfilling relationships within a community;
4. the yearning to know one's part in the vast wonder and mystery of the cosmos.[4]

Personal myths explain the external world, guide personal development, provide social direction, and address spiritual questions in a manner that is analogous to the way cultural myths carry out those functions for entire groups of people. Your myths do for you what cultural myths do for a society. Your *personal mythology* is the system of complementary as well as contradictory *personal myths* that organizes your experiences and guides your actions. It is the lens through which you perceive the world. Its values and assumptions color all you see.

A Conscious Alliance with Your Evolving Mythology. We use the term *personal mythology* because it is the most useful psychological construct we have found for helping people form a conscious alliance with their deepest sources of wisdom. Like any useful tool, it requires skill to understand and employ effectively. While your personal myths mold your thoughts and behavior, it can be very difficult to pin them down. First of all, they typically operate beneath the threshold of awareness. Second, language and linear analysis do not easily capture their deep roots and dynamic character. Third, personal myths are circular in their effects—a personal myth is a constellation of beliefs, feelings, images, and rules of behavior that influences your experiences, which shape your mythology, which further shape your experiences. . . . Your personal mythology is your map—within the culture's house of mirrors—and the more trust-worthy you can make it, the more capably you will find your way.

Another concrete image for thinking about a personal myth is to view it as a template. Like the seal that stamped a king's insignia into wax, your personal myths imprint your unique way of organizing reality onto your experience. They result in your characteristic styles of perceiving, feeling, thinking, and acting. Myths, in the sense we are using the term, are not the stories you tell, the attitudes you hold, or the beliefs you embrace, although each of these may reflect your deeper mythology. Nor are myths properly judged as being true or false, right or wrong; rather, they are more or less functional for the development of an individual or a group—and even that evaluation is made inevitably according to the dictates of a larger myth.

Personal myths bring together specific elements of psychological life and organize them in distinctive ways. For example, a man whose personal mythology tells him he will be abandoned by anyone he loves might not only perceive rejection in situations where others would not but also unwittingly choose relationships that set the stage for abandonment. The theme of his guiding myth is captured in the country-western title "If You Won't Leave Me, I'll Find Somebody Who Will." He perceives his world, organizes his perceptions, and molds events to correspond with his personal mythology.

Whether fully elaborated into a great cultural myth or still in the raw form of a motif in the inner life of a single mortal, myths operate largely outside consciousness. Once a myth could be described clearly by a tribal culture, Campbell observed, it had already lost much of its power. Just as societies live according to a mythology they often cannot name, individuals live according to a constructed reality—a personal mythology—they often cannot name. This program draws from contemporary psychological practices and ancient spiritual traditions in opening a way for naming the myths operating within you and living in creative partnership with them. The very act of naming a dysfunctional guiding myth is a step toward changing it.

A New Kind of Myth. The ability to reflect on and modify the myths you are living is an aptitude you have that your distant ancestors did not have, and the emergence of this capacity changed the foundations of human consciousness. We are still myth-makers, but viable myths can no longer be based primarily on the prestige of authority, the habits of tradition, or the doctrines of a group. Not only is the modern mind distinguished for having developed and finely honed its abilities for self-reflection, empirical observation, and critical thought, but the media provide immediate feedback, so the myths of social groups are continually being scrutinized. While in its original sense myth was rooted in passion rather than rationality, and has thus been deemed false by modern criteria, contemporary myth-making is based not solely on visceral sources of knowledge; it is subject also to rational logic and empirical standards of validity. Behavioral scientists, who have, like the culture, tended to elevate *logos* over *mythos,* "linear" over "narrative" modes of thought, are beginning to recognize that the two are complementary.[5] Each plays a critical role in effective reasoning. With the integration of both modes of thought, the psychological construction of reality is evolving into an increasingly sophisticated enterprise.

Through myth, observed the historian of religion Mircea Eliade, "the various and sometimes dramatic breakthroughs of the sacred" into the world are expressed most adequately.[6] It is in mythology's embrace of the transcendent or spiritual dimension of experience that a mythically attuned framework exhibits its most distinctive strengths over approaches that are more behaviorally, cognitively, or psychodynamically oriented. To live mythologically, according to Ken Wilber, "means to begin to grasp the transcendent, to see it alive in oneself, in one's life, in one's work, friends, and environment."[7] Many of the procedures introduced in this program invite experiences that can transcend your usual ways of thought and perception and attune you to deeper realities about yourself and your life.

In early times, myth-making connected people and communities with the larger forces of nature. Recalling how the old myths engaged us with a spiritual realm that has been blurred by the psychic pollution of modern life need not trap us in the shortcomings of the older form. Notice whether expressions such as "That's just a myth," and the attitudes behind them, echo in your mind as you begin this journey, where the terms *myth* and *mythology* are treated with deep respect. You need to understand from the outset that "myth" is being used here in a thoroughly contemporary sense that recognizes that the *fundamental task* of the human psyche is to construct a model of reality, a guiding mythology; that this guiding mythology embraces the spiritual foundations of your life as well as the more traditional areas of psychology, such as your feelings and thoughts; and that your success in generating a vital guiding mythology determines, in large part, your success in life. This program will direct your intelligence and your passion toward the perpetual challenge of updating and refining your guiding mythology.

THE SELF-FULFILLING NATURE OF PERSONAL MYTHS

The personal myths that are central in your life tend to be self-fulfilling—you are drawn to live out their underlying themes. If a premise of your personal mythology is that you are bright, you are likely to use your intellectual capacities more effectively than if you believe you are dull. If persecution is a dominant motif in your mythology, you will tend to enter relationships and to make choices that bring it your way. If you know you are a creative artist and therefore should be exempt from practical concerns, your checkbook may resemble more a work of art than a record of transactions. Your mythology inevitably highlights certain potentials and inhibits others.

Much of the psychological suffering people experience is entangled in personal myths that are not attuned to their actual needs, potentials, and circumstances. Attempting to follow a personal myth that is not in harmony with who you are or with the world in which you live is painful. And a mythology that is unable to serve as a bridge to deeper meanings and greater inspiration than you can find in the outer world is typically accompanied by a nameless anxiety. Pain and anxiety are often signals that a fundamental guiding myth needs to be changed. By cultivating a mythological perspective, you become able to work out many of your personal difficulties as dramas in your inner life instead of having to play them out on the rack of life.

A limiting personal myth may have muted a desirable quality since your childhood. A man's tender emotions are eclipsed by images of his father's machismo. A woman's mistrust of others may have been family policy when she was young. Other core myths, which once provided valid guidance, may now maintain outmoded and painful patterns of thought and behavior. A woman who gained her parents' praise and approval through high achievement destroys a marriage with unrelenting workaholism. A man whose rebelliousness kept his spirit alive amid childhood oppression is trapped in frivolous power struggles as an adult.

In each of these cases, other psychological forces are also at work that may eventually compensate for past limitations and bring greater dimension to the person's inner life. New myths push to be born, and their emergence, a natural part of psychological development, is usually gradual and largely unconscious. The following stories illustrate how people's myths shape their experiences and how it is possible to awaken to a new myth at any point in adult life.

DANA   *Dana longed for the affection of her father, whose lack of interest in his second daughter was conspicuous. Her father was unhappy in many ways, and Dana would intently observe his pain and try to find how she could help him feel better. As she did, she took pleasure in receiving a growing number of appreciative words and glances, and this relieved some of her anguish about his general apathy toward her. She did, however, still wonder if something was wrong with her, because she never received the affection she deeply craved.*

Dana continued to find ways to comfort her father, and she became adept at comforting others as well. It made her feel good to make others feel good. Dana found great solace in Sunday-school stories about the life of Jesus. Like Jesus, she thought, she would devote herself to loving others without expecting anything in return.

In adulthood, Dana's personal life became overrun with the needs of the many people who grew to depend on her. She was genuinely valued in her community and widely sought as a resource, but she was always overinvolved and overtaxed. A man who was interested in marrying Dana nearly left her, protesting that there was too little space in her life for him. He complained, "There are five hundred people in this town who think you are their best friend!" A series of events, including these confrontations with her fiancé, a health problem, and continual exhaustion, brought Dana to begin identifying the dysfunctional elements in her myth. She reported the following dream as a turning point when she began to recognize and question the myth that had been governing her relationships:

> The dream was horrendous. Spokespeople for the world come to me with a plan. They say they have a way to heal all the people in the world . . . and that if I truly love unconditionally, I will go along with it. They tell me they have an amazing formula that can make my body feed everyone. They want me to give up my life and be made into white bread that could feed the multitudes. They know how to bottle "Dana Essence," and they plan to squirt one drop into each loaf with an eye dropper. Then all the people would be healed. This, they say, is a much better plan than the present arrangement, where I am using up my essence by stretching myself too thin and trying to help too many people.
>
> I agree to let them kill me "mercifully," as they put it. The scheduled time for my killing is 10:30 A.M. But at 10:15 I know I don't want to give up my life essence. I go to this warehouse to see if I can call off the killing. I hear people talking, and I know it is too late. I feel in such danger that I hide in the warehouse, not knowing what my next move will be.
>
> I woke up at that point with my nose bleeding. I had developed an open

sore on the side of my nose that sometimes appears when I am stressed. It had become raw and blood was squirting out of it, reminding me of the stigmata. I couldn't stop the bleeding for a long time. Finally, when it did stop, my sheets were spattered with blood.

The dream left Dana with images of Jesus feeding the multitudes. She vividly recalled a scene from the musical Jesus Christ Superstar *in which Jesus screams at the crowd, "Heal yourselves!" She played the piece over and over that morning, and it was as if Jesus were speaking for her as well. The dream was a strong stimulus for committing herself to change the way she related to others. As she painstakingly traced the roots of her interpersonal style back to her relationship with her father, her accommodating responses to others became less automatic. A new personal myth gathered strength, prompting her to respond to her own needs as well as to those of others and to appreciate the paradox that people are best served when they are able to take care of themselves.*

FRED *Like many men born in the first quarter of the twentieth century, Fred was a stern, hardworking husband and father. His personal mythology, the product of a youth spent desperate for work in the rural South during the Depression, held that life is serious business. He believed that "you get what you earn and you earn what you get. It is best not to be too positive lest you set up expectations that will result in disappointment." For Fred, there was little room for emotion because "feelings keep you from what is important and make you look weak." Unlike many of his peers, he had no use for religion. He was bitter about his early church experiences, and he found no assurance in promises of an afterlife.*

At age fifty-five, Fred had a heart attack and was hospitalized. In the hospital, he had another massive coronary. His vital signs indicated that he was clinically dead, but he was revived. Fred had never heard of strange or poignant "near-death" experiences, and he was about the last person on the planet likely to invent one. Yet he reported:

First I was up near the ceiling and I could see the medical team trying to resuscitate me. I heard a doctor say, "He's had it!" I yelled back, "Whatever it is, I don't want it!" but nobody heard me. Suddenly, I was walking over a bridge with a dry wash underneath. On the other side was an open field. Walking to greet me was Bart [a childhood friend who had died in his early twenties]. I was overjoyed to see Bart. He greeted me warmly and told me to observe everything. But he said that I had to go back. "Why?" I asked. "Because you haven't learned a damned thing, Fred. You haven't learned how to love."

As Fred became aware of being back in the hospital room, he opened his eyes and met the gaze of a startled nurse. The words "I love you" came out of his mouth. He said "I love you" to each nurse and doctor in the room. One doctor, according to family legend, uncomfortably replied, "That really isn't necessary." His family was amazed. His daughter explains that Fred did not find it easy to say "I love you" to anyone. He would sometimes walk out of the room with a disgusted look on his face when a song on the radio or a program on television got "too mushy."

For the remaining sixteen years of Fred's life, he seemed to be making up for lost time— cultivating an ability to listen, taking an intense interest in the lives of others, traveling extensively to various parts of the world to try to understand people from different cultures, making amends for the past with his intimates, and enjoying the company of his grandchildren. At his memorial service, the theme most dwelt upon was the loving spirit Fred brought into his life.

MICHELLE *Growing up in an upper-middle-class family with an alcoholic father, Michelle was unhappy. By her midteens she had run away from home numerous times. After her parents discovered that she had been sleeping with her boyfriend and smoking marijuana, they had her committed, involuntarily, to a psychiatric hospital.*

Michelle could hardly believe what was happening to her. She became disruptive on the ward, screamed at the nurses, and was given medications that sedated and confused her. The experience was a nightmare, and she wondered if she were indeed going crazy. On her last day at the hospital, she overheard one of the few staff members she had come to trust tell someone, "People who have been in mental hospitals always return to them."

Michelle was released from the hospital after three weeks. There was no evidence that her behavior had been a sign of mental illness. But the statement, "People who have been in mental hospitals always return to them," stayed with her. She recalled it whenever she heard of the relapse of anyone who had at one time undergone psychiatric treatment. She remembered the words whenever she read newspaper accounts of former mental patients who had committed acts of violence, and she was plagued by fears that she would have a bizarre psychotic break in which she lost control of her behavior. Anytime she felt depressed, her distress was complicated by her fear that she was about to plunge into insanity. When she pulled out of her depression, she told herself it was probably only a temporary reprieve. What the hospital staff member said had become a personal myth for Michelle.

Her belief that she was mentally unstable was causing Michelle increasingly to behave as if she were. After ten years of contending with these fears, she consulted a psychologist. She was given a battery of psychological tests, which revealed that she had a high capacity for imagination and superior intelligence, but no signs of a serious mental disorder. As Michelle acknowledged that the preponderance of evidence from her life showed a basic emotional stability, she learned to diminish the worries that for a decade had kept her anxious and limited her development.

You can see the role early experiences played in fashioning Dana's, Fred's, and Michelle's mythologies, and how these mythologies shaped their subsequent development. Dana's resourceful approach for winning her father's attention initially focused on his emotional pain, but it grew into a compulsion to respond to the distress of anyone around her. Fred emphasized the value of hard work but, until his heart attack, systematically neglected opportunities for loving contact. Michelle's self-limiting myth, formed on the basis of a comment overheard in an impressionable moment, maintained her long-standing belief that she was on the edge of insanity. It made her choose her challenges gingerly, as if she were indeed dangerously unstable.

The mythologies Dana, Fred, and Michelle were living seemed natural to them, given their experiences. But important aspects of who they were and what they might become were being hindered. As their mythologies evolved—as Dana questioned her "compulsion to help," as Fred grew to learn about love, and as Michelle acknowledged her emotional sturdiness—their lives followed suit.

YOUR GUIDING MYTHOLOGY

Our fundamental conviction in writing this book is that a basic balance is shifting worldwide so that *consciousness* is beginning to outweigh *events* in influencing the unfolding of history. Early human history was shaped primarily by inherited and conditioned responses to events. Over the vast expanse of humanity's existence, self-reflection had relatively little impact on people's choices. The power of consciously examining one's beliefs and motivations before acting on them has, however, been gaining momentum since classical times, extended exponentially now by electronic communications media. Myth-making has become a progressively intentional process, and this powerful, hopeful, unprecedented development stands in counterpoint to the advancing threats to human survival as the signature of the new millennium. Propelled by the media, the growing weight of consciousness has reached a critical mass that touches all that is unfolding.

This book exercises your capacity to bring this new genre of consciousness and intention to your inner world, your relationships, and your actions. Through it, you will be exploring the ways your mythology spontaneously evolves and the

Renew the Dream That Quickens Your Spirit

ways you can mindfully participate in its evolution. To be conscious of your guiding mythology is to seek wisdom from your psychological and spiritual depths, as well as to receive inspiration from the wisest people and images around you. It is to nurture a ripening appreciation of your cultural and ancestral roots. It is to reach into the core of your being, contacting the hopes and dreams that vitalize you, as well as the demons and dark places that frighten you. It is also to cultivate an ever-deepening relationship with the universe and its great mysteries, opening you to a story that transcends your day-to-day concerns. The following pages present a systematic program for pursuing these challenges.

How Mythology Got Personal. A profound difference between your myths and those of your early forebears is that yours have *relative* autonomy from the established myths of your society. The myths and rituals guiding an individual's maturation are no longer cultural strongholds that have for generations remained stable. Because of a convergence of developments—including the speed of social change, the breakdown of community, the ascendance of the individual in Western society, and electronic media that portray the culture's diverse and rapidly shifting mythic imagery—myth-making has become an intimate matter, the domain and responsibility of each person.

Myths that have stabilized societies for centuries are exploding with self-contradiction as they attempt to accommodate unprecedented circumstances. You may be shocked by socially sanctioned behaviors that unwittingly decimate natural resources, promote violent crime, or support licentious conduct. You may be baffled as you try to bring up your children to resist temptations involving dangerous drugs, perilous sexual encounters, and brain-numbing video addictions. You may puzzle aloud about the purpose of your life as a mountain of trivial demands sucks the juice from your days. You may wonder if your struggle with such matters means you are psychologically unfit or emotionally inadequate. Perhaps, if the world looks this crazy to you, it is you who is crazy? Probably not. No one has a map that makes the excursion through today's world an easy or placid journey.

Myth-making had to become a personal venture as social change outpaced the intrinsic capacities of cultural myths to evolve. In the past, cultural myths developed slowly and often prevailed for centuries. Societies faced with changes too radical for their myths to manage tended to flounder. Today the rate of social change is meteoric, and it is accompanied by a dizzying array of competing mythic images, values, and perceptions. The meanings of "man" and "woman," "work" and "play," "success" and "failure" have all been radically challenged within recent memory. The culture's new mythology is being hammered out on the anvil of individual lives. At the same time, communications media can link you with virtually every mythic outlook ever recorded and with new mythic developments at the moment they are first expressed anywhere on the planet. Ours is to pick and choose rather than to ingest whole a unified and coherent cultural mythology. Ours is also to reflect on our guiding myths and revise them according to our experiences in the world.

Your personal myths help you find order in a universe far too immense to grasp fully (a quip from some theology circles is that for us to try to comprehend God is like an amoeba's peering up through the microscope to study the scientist). Yet within this unfathomable cosmos, your myths establish your identity, direction, notion of progress, and sense of worth. Your mythology evolves as you mature. When life becomes unsettling, when you find yourself longing for change, when you feel empty, when self-destructive patterns cannot be ignored, your personal mythology is often begging to be transformed. A myth that has become outdated may have for many years served to protect, orient, and motivate you. If you resist allowing it to evolve, you may be newly baptized in swelling tides of tumult and adversity. And the psyche does tend to conserve what has worked in the past, as when a man attempts to use the boyish charm that gained him attention as an adolescent to obtain advancement in the business world. The resulting turmoil tills the soil for mythic change. Your personal myths are being negotiated and renegotiated throughout your life.

Can you identify one of your own personal myths? Some myths are basic: "The world is (or is not) safe." "There is (or is not) enough to go around." "People are (or are not) trustworthy." "I am (or am not) a deserving, worthy human being." Others are more situation-specific: "My children will be famous." "I will never have a happy marriage." "I'm not an outdoors person." "I am meant to be a musician." "My logical abilities are so strong that I can solve any problem that comes my way." "I must work harder." "My career is too important to allow me to spend much time with my family." Each of these statements might emerge from a much more complex mythology, but they give you an idea of how some myths may decisively serve a person, how others are destructive, and how many are mixed.

Rituals That Transform. This book presents principles and structured activities for examining and modifying your guiding mythology. We speak of these structured activities as "personal rituals" to emphasize their sacred, transformative potential. Rituals are symbolic acts that bring a person or a group into contact with deeper aspects of reality than the ordinary. They accompany human beings through all the great themes of life: birth, maturation, bonding, decline, and death. Earlier cultures used elegant rituals to shape the beliefs and behaviors of their members, but only remnants of these powerful practices appear in modern life—often in ceremonies such as graduations, weddings, and funerals. In calling upon the ancient and sophisticated art of ritual to evoke inner wisdom, the procedures in this book offer a potent way for you to manifest creative responses to old dilemmas and new challenges.

The personal rituals in this program have been designed to guide you in reevaluating outdated myths and generating fresh visions. If you commit yourself to carrying out the program, you will be establishing the self-fulfilling goal that the relationship between your inner life and your experiences in the world become more intentional. By providing a structure within which spontaneous insight can occur, the rituals will help you become more adept with the inner symbolism your psyche is continually generating. They will lead you through a systematic exploration of your guiding mythology, and in the process are likely to open wider the door to your innate wisdom.

People who have completed the program typically report an expanded understanding of themselves, experience breakthroughs in their ability to interrupt destructive patterns of thought and behavior, and find deeper clarity about their own direction. We know that this is a demanding program, and we pause here in our writing to set more strongly our intention that yours may be a rich and fulfilling journey into the depths of your personal mythology.

KEY CONCEPTS

To summarize the essential ideas around which our program is oriented:

1. *It is through the spontaneous construction of reality, the creation of the myths that provide understanding and direction, that human beings, individually and collectively, come to terms with the critical challenges that determine survival, success, and wellbeing.*
2. *Men and women in contemporary cultures who are exposed to diverse belief systems and ways of life are more capable of carving out highly personal mythologies and of reflecting on their guiding myths than people in any previous period of history.*
3. *The need to become conscious of these lived mythologies is more urgent than ever before because the fate of the world unequivocally depends on the political, economic, technological, and spiritual decisions that grow out of them.*

4. *As you come to understand the principles that shape your guiding myths, you become less bound by the mythologies of your childhood and of your culture, and more able to influence patterns in your life that once seemed predetermined and went unquestioned.*

In teaching people how to examine and recast the deep-seated myths that govern their lives, we have repeatedly observed the practical benefits of simply becoming able to articulate one's guiding myths. Through the methods presented here, we believe it is possible for you to *identify* outmoded or otherwise unproductive personal myths that have been operating largely outside of your awareness; to *cultivate* alternative, more constructive inner guidance; and to *integrate* this renewed mythic vision into your life. In addition, by coming to understand your own mythology, you become better equipped to adapt to the mythology of your culture and to participate more effectively in its transformation.

A Program for Cultivating a New Mythology

The periodic crises of faith, courage, and identity that punctuate life may be treated as calls for renewal in your mythology. We invite you to enter boldly into your interior, assess your guiding mythology, transform it where it is hurting you, and strive toward attaining harmony with its wisdom. This book presents a twelve-week program that will lead you through a process that corresponds with the way personal myths naturally evolve. This process involves five essential tasks:

1. Identifying underlying conflict between a prevailing myth and an emerging myth (Weeks 1, 2, and 3)
2. Understanding both sides of the conflict (Weeks 4 and 5)
3. Conceiving a new mythic vision that integrates the most vital aspects of the old myth and the emerging myth (Weeks 6 and 7)
4. Refining your mythic vision and making a conscious commitment to live from it (Weeks 8 and 9)
5. Living from your new mythology (Weeks 10, 11, and 12)

Within each week, three sessions of about an hour each are suggested, along with optional journal writing and dream work. If this time frame is not right for you, the program can be adjusted to your preferences. It can be completed over a longer period with less frequent sessions, over an intensive four-day personal retreat, or in two weekends spaced perhaps a month apart. The book also can be completed in conjunction with psychotherapy or a self-help group, be read straight through without performing the personal rituals, or otherwise tailored to your own needs and pace. If you are currently in psychotherapy or have reason to believe you should be, we request that you use the program presented in this book in consultation with a therapist. Psychotherapy and this self-directed process for examining your personal mythology are, in fact, generally quite complementary.

Each ritual builds on those before it, so they will yield the greatest value if carried out in the order given. We begin here with some preliminary points:

Using a Personal Journal. We suggest you use a journal to record your experiences with each of the personal rituals, as well as your reflections on them. Most program participants have used an ordinary spiral binder or a more aesthetically pleasing notebook, and increasing numbers do the work on a personal computer. Describing your thoughts and feelings in a journal will help to fix your insights in your memory and foster the unfolding of unconscious processes in your awareness. Allowing journal work to take you into a deep, contemplative state that expands your consciousness is an art and, like all arts, benefits from regular practice. While your journal will provide a record of your discoveries and growth during the program, it also can be a vehicle for deepening and expanding them. In your journal, give voice to your imagination, spontaneously describing the associations you have to the memories, emotions, and ideas brought up in the program. By allowing your journal work to become a process unto itself, you will begin to uncover deeper feelings and contact earlier memories. Sense where your writing wants to lead you, and follow it.

Guided Imagery Instructions. Many of the personal rituals take you on "guided imagery" journeys. Some preparation is necessary for these experiences. We highly recommend that you obtain the audiotapes with the instructions for these imagery journeys, accompanied by powerful inspirational and shamanistic music (see the information at the beginning of the book). Feedback from readers of the previous edition of this book attests to the value of being able to turn on a tape and proceed with the ritual, and the music on the tape has been specially composed to deepen your experience. Alternatives include reading the instructions into a tape recorder and letting the tape guide you through the experience, having another person read the instructions to you, or thoroughly familiarizing yourself with the instructions and allowing your memory to lead you through the ritual. These guided imagery rituals are at the heart of the program. Be prepared to stop the tape or delay the person who is reading so you have all the time you need for each of the personal rituals. People often have to hear the instructions, or parts of the instructions, more than once in order to complete a given guided imagery ritual. Taking all the time you need to carry out an instruction or having an instruction repeated as often as you wish will only enhance the program.

If You Can't See Inner Images. You may or may not be able to register visual images in your imagination. Imagery can actually be patterned after any of the senses. Auditory, kinesthetic, olfactory, and gustatory images are all ways of coding the world. It is not necessary to look at inner pictures to imagine an experience. In fact, many people "visualize" inner images exclusively through other modes than seeing. Some are aware of hearing or subvocally sensing their thoughts; for others, it is just "a knowing." When we use words such as "image" and "visualize," we are using them in the most general sense to refer to whatever ways you experience feelings, thoughts, and fantasies.

Working with Your Dreams. Working with your dreams is a supplementary track throughout the program that can substantially enhance your experience. You are encouraged to record your dreams in your journal. We have found that the dreams people spontaneously recall as they go through the program often parallel questions the program is evoking. You will find "dream focus" instructions throughout the text, each suggesting that you request a dream to clarify or shed light on a specific question, a process called "dream incubation." You may also, at these points, review your journal to find recent dreams that relate to the theme being raised. These are optional instructions, and the book is arranged so the personal rituals can stand alone, even if no special attention is given to your dream life.

The Support Guides. The three support guides toward the end of the volume may be consulted at any time in your work. Support Guide 1: "Deepening Your Experience" offers specific suggestions for enhancing your efforts by creating an inspirational work space, taking spiritual retreats, engaging friends and loved ones, confronting personal resistances that may emerge, intensifying the personal rituals through the use of deep relaxation, and building habit patterns that bolster your intention to live from a more empowering mythology. Support Guide 2: "Working with Your Dreams" provides a primer for remembering and deciphering dreams. It offers an overview of some of the most useful approaches we have found for understanding dreams and the personal myths they reflect. Support Guide 3: "If the Program Becomes Unsettling" provides suggestions for you in the event that the program arouses painful or troubling emotions. Skim these support guides before starting the program so you will know what they contain and can consult them when they would be most useful for you.

This edition of the book incorporates new techniques and areas of emphasis that will better support your intent to understand and perhaps transform your guiding mythology. The twelve-week workbook format is more user-friendly than the previous edition. Numerous therapists and group leaders who adapted the original edition in their own settings, as well as other readers, offered invaluable suggestions from which this volume has benefited. Another change readers will welcome is that we have learned to express some of the more complex ideas presented in the original edition more simply, clearly, and concretely. Significant developments in psychological research and clinical practice since the first edition are also incorporated into these pages.

While drawing from the plethora of effective techniques and perspectives spawned by contemporary psychotherapy, the book frames the mythic confusion inevitably experienced by you and those around you as a fact of modern life rather than as an innate personal deficiency. It is attuned to the mayhem in the culture's guiding mythology and to each person's trailblazing responsibilities in living within the resulting disorder. When you constructively alter your guiding myths, empowering changes follow in how you see the world, feel about it, and function within it. We believe, in fact, that cultivating a well-articulated, carefully examined mythology is one of the most effective steps you can take for countering the disorienting grip of a world in turmoil.

PERSONAL STATEMENT BY STANLEY KRIPPNER

As I read this "invitation" for the last time before David and I send it to our publisher, I am sitting in a grove of pine trees. Although my setting is tranquil, the act of reading our words arouses me. I recall that some fifty thousand copies of the first edition of the book were sold, and I reflect on the feedback we've received. One woman approached me after a lecture expressing her thanks because, she said, "the book that you and Dr. Feinstein wrote changed my life." A couple told me that they had undertaken the thirty-one personal rituals together, keeping separate notebooks, and that the procedure had saved their marriage. One man rather hesitantly told me he had read our book six times—once each year—in an attempt to uncover as many dysfunctional myths as possible, and, he said, "the net effect was to keep me sober."

At the same time, I have spoken with several people who have become bogged down, who found our five-stage program too demanding, or who told me they could not find time in their busy lives to keep a journal or record their dreams. I have expressed my understanding, often remarking that "no single process serves everyone." But I am also aware that many people's lives are cramped by personal myths that limit them, stretched thin by personal myths that extend them beyond their capacities, or spun out of control because of a personal mythology riddled with contradictions. I think to myself that a deeper understanding of their guiding myths might assist them in changing the patterns that lead to their overwhelm, emptiness, or suffering.

I am also well aware that far too many people live on the margins of society, needing a place to sleep and a nourishing meal more acutely than they need a self-help book. This leads me to reflect on the myths of our culture that have become so badly deranged—myths that once promised family solidarity, success as a reward for hard work, and liberty and justice for all. Many vital matters today are expressed in the form of bitter social conflicts that point to divisive cultural myths:

1. The *globalists* (the "one world" advocates, who will settle for nothing less than planetary government) versus the *vigilantes* (those who will fight and die for any dab of land that favors their ethnic or religious sentiments).

2. The *multipliers* (those unconcerned by population growth) versus the *slashers* (those who would slash population growth, particularly in undeveloped countries, by punitive means).

3. The *prickles* (those who draw impermeable boundaries around their logic, their faith, or their species) versus the *goos* (those who ooze indiscriminate love and compassion for every conceivable belief system and all observable forms of life).

Echoes of such mythic conflict reverberate in our being, and they shake the foundations of our culture. Hearing the birds chirping in the trees overhead, I am reminded that the number of songbirds in our world diminishes each year because of personal, corporate, and governmental myths that sanction the exploitation of the environment. Other pervasive cultural myths have led to the trivialization of the arts, the fragmentation of families, and the dehumanization of work, play, love, and worship. I know that David passionately shares these concerns and that, for both of us, intelligently revisioned mythologies can reveal the pathways that lead beyond torn cultures and shattered lives.

PERSONAL STATEMENT BY DAVID FEINSTEIN

You were born into a world where life feeds on life. You were born into a body that is destined to experience its own death, and you may have to bear indescribable physical or emotional anguish somewhere along the way. You were born into *the* species that, after rising to the top of the food chain and gaining control of nature's resources, has the prerogative about which forms of life will suffer at its expense, but not the prerogative that none will suffer. Your own pain and joy are to a substantial extent the consequences of the choices you make, yet until you learn through trial and error, you are largely in the dark about which choices lead to which ends. Within this seemingly harebrained scheme, you possess an inborn thirst for life, an inherent capacity for sublime pleasure, and an innate passion to create beauty, pursue truth, find meaning, touch wonder, and share love. You also have an aptitude to reach within and encounter profound sources of mythic wisdom and guidance. Coming to a personal mythology that leads you through these bizarre realities in a manner that results in a fulfilling, potential-actualizing, spiritually attuned life is the most vital of the challenges facing you, and it is the topic of this book.

As the time approaches for you to decide whether to accept our invitation to work through the personal rituals presented in this program, I would like to tell you about a few outcomes I have personally witnessed. I have seen it tearfully dawn, as if for the first time, on a gruff and irritable man that he is lovable. I have seen it ecstatically dawn on a young woman, lost and bewildered, how she can take charge of her life. I have seen it dawn on a depressed and defeated man that he has tremendous untapped strength, and I have watched him subsequently use that strength so effectively it was difficult to realize he was the same person. Such dawnings sometimes flood in deliciously, infusing enough light that a person is forever changed. More often, it is many smaller dawnings that make a difference. In either case, I like these moments of dawning and discovery. They sustain the twinkle in my professional eye.

For our part of the bargain in encouraging you to take on the demanding program presented in this book, Stan and I have applied our full effort, for more than two decades, to invent or steal procedures that result in such breakthroughs. The harvest of those efforts is presented here. We know it requires a great deal of determination to chase after your dawnings rather than to just let them come to you. After all, the sun does rise by itself every day, and you have new insights about your life all of the time. This program, on the other hand, attempts to bring about insights that *systematically* revitalize your spirit, your motivation, and your sense of purpose. Our aim is to catalyze fresh perceptions that give you new and better choices than you were able to conceive.

The book guides you through an intensive workshop that Stan and I have long been teaching individually, and occasionally as a team, in clinical, educational, and community settings. We have presented the program in more than a dozen countries. We know of men's groups, women's groups, couples' groups, recovery groups, college classes, therapy groups, and co-workers meeting over breakfast who were happy enough about their use of the book to let us hear about it. This edition, written nearly a decade after the first, incorporates what we have learned while conducting some one hundred additional workshops attended by several thousand people, as well as while continuing to work privately and intensively in individual settings.

Still, it is almost too bold to ask you to trust us, who do not know you, as we offer, from out of a book, procedures that may affect you quite deeply. It is a funny world today that allows such an impersonal way of being very intimate. We are more comfortable and confident with this arrangement now, after feeling the impact of the book's earlier edition. As Stan mentioned in his comments above, the feedback has often been poignant and gratifying. We hope this volume will serve you well, and we wish for you those mythic dawnings that would arouse your inner wisdom, goodness, and joy.

FIRST STAGE

Identifying Underlying Mythic Conflict

———————— ❦ ————————

Into Your Mythic Depths

❧

The discovery of the reality of the psyche corresponds to the freeing of the captive and the unearthing of the treasure.

—Erich Neumann[1]

The family is the institution charged with creating a person-sized mythology for each of its young. It is the crucible in which the imperatives of genetics and the mythology of a civilization are amalgamated into the unique mythic framework that accompanies each person's development. Laden with the hopes and the disappointments of prior generations, your family's myths are your legacy from the past and a source of inspiration and direction for the future. The development of your personal mythology can be seen in its full texture and its continuity only when viewed against the backdrop of your family's mythology.[2]

Your ancestors formed conclusions about the world and about what was required to survive and thrive in it. These beliefs and values, as they have evolved through the generations, have been passed along for you to embrace, modify, or disregard. How your parents and grandparents perceived themselves, how they understood their circumstances, and what they trusted and valued are questions of mythic proportion, questions whose answers are at the core of your own mythology as well. If your father was a farmer, the relationship to nature embedded in your mythology differs from what that relationship would be if he had been a banker. If you are the great-granddaughter of a countess whose beauty was the toast of Europe, your identity as a woman has been influenced by her experiences. If your parents found little opportunity to expand their horizons, the way they related to these limitations will have an impact on the degree to which your own mythology tells you that you must accept your circumstances and the degree to which you believe you can change them.

SESSION 1:
Remembering the Myths of Generations Past[3]

PURPOSE: *To explore influences on your mythology that trace to your parents, grandparents, and beyond*

In this opening ritual, you will bring your imagination into the bodies and the identities of your parents and grandparents. You will be considering challenges they confronted and examining the myths that guided them in their attempts to flourish in the face of those challenges. Because their mythology resonates within your own cellular structure, psyche, and current family, you may be surprised by how vividly you are able to establish an empathic connection with your parents and grandparents, even where your factual knowledge is limited. The person you have become is, to a degree, an echo of the myths they fashioned and lived by. After completing this ritual, you will be able to understand better how your forebears, and the mythology they bequeathed to you, provide a context as subsequent discoveries about your own mythology unfold.

PREPARATION: *Read the instructions into a tape (or obtain the prerecorded tape—see the beginning of the book for information on ordering the audiotape of the guided imagery instructions), have someone else read the instructions to you, or familiarize yourself with them well enough that you can perform the ritual from memory with only glances at the book.*

Stand where you can move several feet in any direction. Find a comfortable posture and close your eyes. In a moment, you will take a step backward, imagining you are stepping into the body and the being of your father if you are a man, or of your mother if you are a woman. If your biological parent did not raise you, make a choice between your biological parent, an adoptive parent, or another parental figure for this experience. You may repeat the procedure later, if you wish, to focus on a different person. Step back now, imagining yourself becoming your parent.

Physically assume a posture that represents the life your parent led or is leading. Take a few moments to get a sense of what it must have felt like to have been in this body and this personality. With your posture, facial expressions, and movement, create a living sculpture. Move your body until your posture symbolizes for you the life this parent lived or is living. You will be reflecting on this parent's perceptions of self, situation, and destiny.

Even though you may not have access to the facts that would allow you to know with certainty your parent's answers to all of the following questions, the answers your parent lived are at some level echoing in your own psyche. So answer the questions "as if" you know the answer, and trust whatever your imagination and intuition provide. Even if not factually precise, the answers you come to may still carry the spirit of your heritage.

Attune yourself once more to the posture and the energy of this parent. Consider the following questions from your parent's vantage point, and allow your imagination to fill in the blanks:

1. What are your primary sources of satisfaction?
2. How do you understand your position within your society—its limitations, privileges, and responsibilities?
3. What is important for you to accomplish before you die?
4. If you look to a nonhuman source to explain human destiny, what is its nature?

Move out of this posture now, releasing its energy with each exhalation, perhaps physically shaking it out of your body. Come back to your own center. Consider how this parent's posture and stance in life, this parent's mythology, affected your own development.

In a moment, you will be taking another step backward, imagining you are stepping into the body and being of your parent's parent, your grandmother or grandfather (choose either gender); or you may choose a step-grandparent or grandparent figure instead. Step back now, imagining yourself becoming your grandparent. Take a few moments to get a sense of what it must have felt like to have been in this body and this personality.

Physically assume a posture that represents your grandparent's life. Dramatize this posture until it begins to symbolize what you know and imagine about the life lived by this grandparent. You will be reflecting on this person's perceptions of self, situation, and destiny.

Even though it is unlikely that you have access to all the facts that would allow you to answer the following questions with certainty, trust your imagination and intuition. Attune yourself once more to the posture and the energy of this grandparent. Consider the following questions from your grandparent's vantage point, and allow your imagination to fill in the blanks:

1. What are your primary sources of satisfaction?
2. How do you understand your position within your society—its limitations, privileges, and responsibilities?
3. What is important for you to accomplish before you die?
4. If you look to a nonhuman source to explain human destiny, what is its nature?

Move out of this posture now, releasing its energy with each exhalation, perhaps physically shaking it out of your body. Come back to your own center. Consider how this grandparent's posture and stance in life, this grandparent's mythology, affected your own development.

In a moment, you will be taking a step to the left, imagining you are stepping into the body and being of a different grandparent, of either gender, the parent of either of your parents. Again you may choose a step-grandparent or grandparent figure instead. Step to the left now, imagining yourself becoming this grandparent. Take a few moments to get a sense of what it must have felt like to have been in this body and this personality.

Physically assume a posture that represents your grandparent's life. Dramatize this posture until it begins to symbolize what you know and imagine about the life lived by this grandparent. You will be reflecting on your grandparent's perceptions of self, situation, and destiny.

As you settle into the posture and the energy of this grandparent, consider these same questions from your grandparent's vantage point:

1. What are your primary sources of satisfaction?
2. How do you understand your position within your society—its limitations, privileges, and responsibilities?
3. What is important for you to accomplish before you die?
4. If you look to a nonhuman source to explain human destiny, what is its nature?

Move out of this posture now, releasing its energy with each exhalation, perhaps physically shaking it out of your body. Come back to your own center. Consider how this grandparent's posture and stance in life, this grandparent's mythology, affected your own development.

In a moment, you will be taking a step forward, imagining you are stepping into the body and being of your mother if you are a man or your father if you are a woman. Again, choose your biological parent, adoptive parent, or a parental figure, as appropriate. Step forward now, imagining yourself becoming your parent. Take a few moments to get a sense of what it must have felt like to have been in this body and this personality.

Physically assume a posture that represents your parent's life. Dramatize this posture until it begins to symbolize what you know and imagine about the life your parent lived or is living. Consider the questions as if you were this parent:

1. What are your primary sources of satisfaction?
2. How do you understand your position within your society—its limitations, privileges, and responsibilities?
3. What is important for you to accomplish before you die?
4. If you look to a nonhuman source to explain human destiny, what is its nature?

Move out of this posture now, releasing its energy with each exhalation, perhaps physically shaking it out of your body. Come back to your own center. Consider how this parent's posture and stance in life, this parent's mythology, affected your own development.

Finally, step forward into an image of your own body and being. Find a posture that represents the statement your life is making. As you sense into this posture, formulate the core statement your life seems to be making as an actual phrase or sentence. Allow the statement to bubble up from deep within. Formulate it clearly. Say it aloud.

Let your posture become animated as you repeat your statement. Explore and experiment with the posture, the movement, and the statement. Reflect on the meaning of this statement, posture, and movement. Find any ways you might like them to change or expand. If you need a larger statement, stretch your posture to fit it. As you move into this new statement, posture, and movement, sense their meaning. When you are finished exploring them, come to a resting point.

By speculating on how your parents and grandparents might have related to the various questions, and by experimenting with physical postures representing their lived myths, you were inviting new insight into your own mythology. Reflect in your journal, or with a partner, on your encounters with the mythologies of your parents and grandparents and the intuitions about your heritage these encounters may have opened for you.

Our colleague and dear friend Ann Mortifee, after serving as a participant when we tested the program in its current format, agreed to allow us to use excerpts of her journal entries to illustrate the personal rituals. Ann wrote:

> There is sadness in the women who have come before me. Their dreams were put away, their artistry lost. They lived their lives in service of others, ashamed to express the deep longing and hunger that lived at the pit of them. Different personalities all. One highly strung and creative, one quiet and unassuming, one loving and eccentric, but each had been led to believe that her life was of less value than the lives of her husband, her children, her community. They tried desperately to be at peace with their destinies, but still they felt trapped, held down, unable to pursue the dream, the potential, the possibility of their own nature. They surrendered their own desires to the service of the family. And their sacrifice went virtually unheeded.
>
> The struggle to be free of this silent resignation has been the overriding motivation of my life. As I took the posture that expressed my own life, my arms lifted and opened and I could feel a deep determination as I said: "There is a beauty and purpose in every person's life. No matter what the cost, I will not let anyone rob me of my beauty and purpose." As I continued to stretch the posture, I suddenly saw that underneath my strength of purpose, I have a fear that my dreams are selfish, my needs indulgent. I fear there is something unhealthy about my desire to be myself and to live my full potential, that I might have to pay a terrible price for these desires, a price that might cost me the love of the ones closest to me, or even my sanity. I suddenly saw that I am not free of the sense of futility that clung to my mothers, but I am, in fact, as much a victim of the hopelessness as they themselves had been.

SESSION 2: Meeting Your Inner Shaman

PURPOSE: *To contact a source of deep mythic wisdom, personified as an inner wise person*

In your visit to your parents and grandparents, you investigated the influence of your mythic inheritance on the mythology you live each day. In the modern world, however, the family cannot draw on the support of stable or coherent cultural myths in establishing the mythology with which it will endow its young. No generation has, in fact, seen its parents' guiding myths become so rapidly obsolete as today's. In the West, where individual autonomy has ascended and community deteriorated, mythology is becoming an increasingly personal affair, the property and the responsibility of each individual. Few are well prepared for this critical challenge. Nor do we collectively know how to embrace the diversity of our guiding myths or defuse the explosiveness of mythic power struggles, as is evidenced in its extreme by the political and military violence within and between nations.

Rollo May observed that "the old myths and symbols by which we oriented ourselves are gone, anxiety is rampant. . . . The individual is forced to turn inward."[4] How do you turn inward in a manner that reliably accesses your deepest wisdom? One procedure is to personify it, thinking of it as existing, for instance, as an "Inner Wise Man" or "Inner Wise Woman." By conceiving of your most profound wisdom in a concrete image, you can use concrete procedures to beckon it. Some people do this spontaneously, having internalized a cherished grandparent or teacher or pastor or coach who provides guidance during imaginary discussions. Others dialogue with a religious figure or deity; recall Tevye's conversations with God in *Fiddler on the Roof.* In our workshops, we have adopted the image of the native shaman to help people gain access to their primal wisdom.

Shamans—the spiritual leaders, healers, and "technicians of the sacred"[5] in tribal cultures—provide a model for guiding the Western mind back to its estranged primal roots. The shaman's powers and ecstatic visions offered guidance and explanation to tribal people for natural events that were otherwise unfathomable. The shaman was the steward of the culture's guiding mythology, adept at guarding, transmitting, and transforming it. As myth-making has become more highly personalized, modern individuals are called on to assume these shamanistic responsibilities personally. You are beckoned to become skilled in tending to and, as necessary, transforming your guiding mythology. To cultivate your Inner Shaman[6] is to develop within yourself the skills for becoming a mindful agent of your own evolving reality. Your Inner Shaman can be a guide to the hidden and unutterably rich landscape of your inner depths. The Inner Shaman has three essential responsibilities in relationship to your unfolding mythology:

1. to infuse your guiding mythology with deep wisdom through sacred journeys;
2. to apply your mythology creatively to new challenges;
3. to revise and advance your mythology on the basis of new experience.

The first responsibility involves maintaining a conduit between ordinary reality and the hidden realities that may be accessed through nonordinary states of consciousness. Just as tribal shamans regularly entered these hidden realities through their dreams, vision quests, and sacred ceremonies, emerging with new images and direction for their people, your Inner Shaman can guide you as you take periodic inward journeys that infuse your personal mythology with renewed spirit. The ability to take such journeys can be developed, and a central feature of this program is to invoke the nonordinary states of consciousness that can be attained through deep relaxation, guided visualization, and focused concentration.

The second responsibility is to infuse your choices in the world with the spirit of your guiding mythology. The Inner Shaman taps into mythic wisdom and astutely applies it to the changing contours of your life. Traditional shamans turned to their intuitive powers when attempting to influence physical and social events toward desirable outcomes. The Inner Shaman directs your efforts, aligning them with your inner mythic wisdom, as you meet life's demands and opportunities. A theme, particularly in the later part of the program, will involve developing the capacity to direct your energies, through the use of focused intention and imagination, with a clarity and potency fueled by your Inner Shaman's wise and inventive ways.

Third, your Inner Shaman fosters the evolution of your existing mythology. The tribal shaman had to find a balance between established customs and cultural innovation, guarding tradition while also introducing new mythic visions to the society. New myths were required periodically, when existing guidance and understanding could not adapt to new circumstances—as at times of prolonged drought or threats from other clans. The shaman's journeys often resulted in a new and inspiring vision that refined or replaced an existing myth. But reveries and fresh glimpses into the nature of the unknowable encountered in nonordinary states do not necessarily constitute sound mythic guidance. The Inner Shaman is also challenged to bring seasoned judgment and discernment to visions from the edge.

It is possible, it is desirable, and it is a goal of this program that you cultivate all three of these shamanistic abilities. At any point in the program and after, you may call on your Inner Shaman for assistance in maintaining a passageway between your waking consciousness and your inner depths, for creatively drawing on mythic wisdom in meeting new challenges, and for enlarging and refining your guiding mythology.

Do not feel limited to the image we have presented of a tribal shaman. While we use that image to evoke a primordial sense of spiritual wisdom, your Inner Shaman may appear in a different form. Through this ritual, people have told us of encountering Jesus, the Buddha, Athena, an unknown Master, a beloved grandparent, a legendary ancestor, an ancient druid, a youthful priestess. Be receptive to the image your psyche offers you, and let our use of the term *Inner Shaman* evoke that image. When the figure does emerge into your awareness, it may be a significant moment in your life.

While your Inner Shaman will probably seem like a manifestation of your imagination, be open to the possibility that he or she also connects you with larger forces. A sense of the profound may accompany this first meeting. Your Inner Shaman's appearance may suggest a spiritual connection, perhaps by being in a ceremonial setting or around ritualistic objects, being surrounded in light, or in some other way being markedly different from the mundane.

PREPARATION: *Again, the instructions are arranged so you may have someone read them to you, use a tape, or become familiar enough with them that you can lead yourself through the ritual from memory. Feel free to modify the instructions in any way that makes them more fitting or comfortable for you. Begin by finding a setting in which you can become deeply relaxed. Sitting or reclining, close your eyes and take several deep breaths.*

As you settle into this safe, secure spot, notice your breath. With each inhalation, breathe in the fullness of life. With each exhalation, release, relaxing more completely. Breathe in. Release. Allow your belly to soften. As you relax, imagine that your heart is gently opening.

You will, in your imagination, be finding a path that takes you to the dwelling place of your Inner Shaman. While you may be able to see this path in your mind's eye, remember that it is not necessary to be able to "see" inner pictures to take an imaginary journey. The imagination has many channels besides vision. You may imagine your path through intuitive feelings, descriptive words, or a wordless knowing. Affirm to yourself your desire to go within and meet your Inner Shaman. Your efforts here will earn the right to gain access to deep wisdom.

The path to your Inner Shaman begins at a hole in the ground at the base of a mountain. As you look in, you realize there is a long tunnel. Your tunnel may head down into the earth or up into the mountain. With resolve, step into the passageway. You enter a timeless and dreamlike reality. You are not troubled by the ordinary laws of physics regarding your size, speed, gravity, or the presence of light. You move forward for a long time. You are starkly alone, lacking landmarks, acutely aware of your vulnerability, need, and hope. Without knowing how, you find you have come to a stone tablet inscribed with those beliefs you rarely have challenged. Read them, and recognize that these have been your commandments. Take time to consider them.

Gather your courage, for you must enter ever more deeply into mysterious places of your being. The challenges make you worthy of the guidance you desire. The Inner Shaman is most pleased to meet the prepared and serious seeker. Moving beyond the tablet, you eventually find yourself on a stone prominence overlooking the Valley of Your Youth. Your sight and hearing are strong, and you feel compassion as you survey the emotional world of your childhood. Without faltering, consider the terrors, deprivations, confusions, and blessings of your early years. Do not flinch or condemn, for your task is to affirm your stamina in having survived.

Continue to move one slow step at a time, ever onward, until you discover yourself in the Graveyard of Lost Illusions. Scattered about are symbolic reminders of the painful lessons that have come to you during your life's journey. On your right is a broken balance scale, an emblem of your naive belief that life is fair. There are other symbols representing lost relationships, opportunities, status, and dreams. Breathe deeply, registering all you have overcome. You have prevailed.

Leaving the Graveyard of Lost Illusions, you can now enter more fully into the hidden places of your being. The challenges have proven you worthy of the guidance you desire. Soon you can see a light at the end of the tunnel. As you approach the light, you know you are coming closer to the sacred dwelling of your Inner Shaman. You notice that the tunnel opens into a clearing. In the clearing is a path that takes you into an extraordinary ancient forest. You walk onto the path and begin to explore the trees, the sky, the undergrowth. A river runs nearby. Take a breath. You can be fully present. As you begin to walk, you may ease into the beauty and wonder of the lush green foliage.

Ahead of you, the branches of two large trees touch and form an archway. You know that on the other side of that archway is the home of your Inner Shaman. Mustering your determination, you prepare yourself for the important moment when the two of you will meet. Moving forward, you step through the archway. Behold. In front of you is your Inner Shaman.

Respectfully greet this wise and compassionate being. Use your senses to discover what you can of the appearance and temperament of this mysterious individual. Take in the physical statement made by your Inner Shaman's body, skin, size, and age. Sense deeply into the nature of this inner friend who is always there yet rarely visible.

Thank your Inner Shaman for having met you. Use words, gestures, or silent intuitive communication. Recognize your Inner Shaman's bottomless affection for you and belief in your worthiness. Your Inner Shaman acknowledges your life's journey and the courage it has required. Your survival has qualified you for the wisdom to come.

You realize that you have a question to ask of your Inner Shaman, one that will help you identify an area of your personal mythology that is calling for your attention. As you formulate this question, prepare to ask it with reverence, knowing that if an answer exists, you are likely to receive it soon.

In a moment you will respectfully ask the following question: "What beliefs, hopes, or habits are hurting me or causing problems in my life?" Ask this question now. Prepare to receive your Inner Shaman's response. You may hear it in words or in silent intuitive communication. Receive the answer now. Respond to your Inner Shaman with an acknowledgment or further inquiry. When the discussion is completed, stand with your Inner Shaman in silent, reverent contemplation.

You will soon be taking leave of your Inner Shaman, for now. Before you do, your Shaman will give you a ritual of return, a procedure you can follow so you can visit again at will. This return ritual will be described to you in the way in which you learn best, perhaps through words, movement, or images. Remember that the laws of ordinary physics do not apply here. You may be told to find your way back by again visualizing the route you used for this visit, or a different route, by using the sound of a gong, a ritualized movement, or the repetition of a few chosen words. Receive now the procedure that will bring you back to your Inner Shaman.

It is almost time to return to your ordinary awareness. Be mindful in your leavetaking. With a gesture of parting, convey your good-bye. Walk through the archway and back into the ancient forest. You realize that the forest, the lush green plants, the river, the dwelling place of your Shaman, the entire scene exists within you. Savor its spirit before you return. Now bring your attention to the opening from which you entered the path, and return through that spot, naturally and comfortably bringing your awareness back to your body.

Prepare to return to your ordinary waking consciousness. You will be able to remember all you need of this experience. Very gently, begin to rouse yourself. Move your fingers and toes, your hands and feet. Feel your circulation. Stretch your shoulders, your arms and legs, your neck and face muscles. Take a deep breath. Bring your attention back into the room. Open your eyes, refreshed, as if waking from a wonderful nap, alert and fully competent to creatively meet the requirements of your day.

Each of your first several journeys to your Inner Shaman will probably be easier than those before it. A learning process is involved in guided imagery experiences. Do not be discouraged if you were unable to stay attuned to all of the instructions. Some people have to repeat the journey three or four times before finding the Inner Shaman. Most people who are unable to have such a meeting the first time out, however, make a connection on the second visit. If you did encounter your Inner Shaman, describe the visit in your journal. If not, we suggest you proceed with the program while making an agreement with yourself to take, within the next week or so, another journey to meet your Inner Shaman. Ann wrote about each of the destinations on the path to her Inner Shaman:

Beliefs Written on My Stone Tablet: It is always better to be kind. You can't trust anyone but yourself, and even that's shaky. You are alone in the world. No one loves you as much as you love them. Most friendships end up in betrayal.

Valley of My Youth: I saw myself speaking with adults and not being sure what they are saying back to me; I saw myself loving my time alone in nature; and I saw myself poking holes in mosquito netting because the sound was so delicious, and being spanked for it.

Graveyard of Lost Illusions: The symbols were a cross, representing my basic belief in an understandable God; a friendship ring for the many friends and lovers who have passed; a lock of brown hair, symbolizing my youth; and a white dress, depicting my lost innocence.

As I moved through the sights in the tunnel, I finally came to a land much like the African savannah, with vast stretches of grass. But rather than being dry, the land was lush and green with a lake at which animals were drinking.

I moved between the arched trees and found myself in a cave with a beautifully fit and powerful old black woman. She exuded an almost detached strength. It was clear to me that we had met before and that she was deeply committed to my growth. As we looked intensely at one another, everything changed. I was no longer in the cave, but in a room with a stained-glass window. A gentle woman, radiating the most profound waves of love, was looking into my eyes. She had the compassion of the Madonna and I knew that she too had been watching over me. Suddenly she was gone and the black woman was in her place. These two images kept oscillating back and forth until I realized that they were two aspects of the same being. A woman as wild as a lioness and as gentle as a dove.

I asked her, "What is trying to emerge in my life?" She answered, "Peace, acceptance, joy, freedom from compulsion, and from the need to prove that you are good." I asked, "How will I receive those?" She answered, "By listening to your body's desires. By doing only what you truly want to do. By letting pleasure be your teacher." I asked, "Where should I go now? What should I be doing?" She shook her head with great affection, as if she could not believe that I would ask such an obvious question. "Give up the search," she answered. "You are already doing what you have been asked to do. And you have already arrived at the place you seek. You have only to realize it." But not realizing it, I found this a very frustrating answer.

PURPOSE: *To explore basic concepts about your personal mythology*

In very different ways, your visits to your ancestors and to your Inner Shaman each brought your awareness into the realm of your personal mythology. You will be exploring and working within that realm for the remainder of the program. Like this opening chapter, each of the next ten chapters is divided into three sessions and closes with "dream focus" instructions. Each of those sessions, except this one, is organized around a personal ritual. This session presents, instead, a conceptual framework about your personal mythology. It is part of a discussion about how your personal myths evolve that runs throughout the book.

RECOGNIZING YOUR PERSONAL MYTHS

How can you recognize a personal myth? Would you see it in images? Would it come through as thoughts that tell you what to do? Would your heart race if it were challenged? Does it unfold like a story? We want to take you into the inner world of a single individual, a boy, to demonstrate how personal myths develop and may come to be expressed in each of these ways.

The boy is a bundle of impulses, aptitudes, uncertainties, ideas, memories, needs, fears, and longings. He depends on models from the outer world to help him order this highly charged interior and give him direction. The cultural heroes who touch him emotionally are powerful influences in helping him organize his inner life. The boy will consciously and unconsciously mimic the heroes to whom he is most strongly drawn.

What makes one hero more attractive to him than another? Those idolized by his peers and venerated by the culture have powerful appeal. If he has internalized the cultural message that men are to appear brave and strong, a figure like Rambo might reach a vaulted place in his imagination, with the Rambo image becoming a model in his attempts to manifest the ideals of courage and strength. Closer to home, perhaps the boy resents an ineffectual father and has desperately been looking for someone he can admire who is as different as possible from his father. As he makes the model his own, it guides his activities, and he measures himself against it.

He subliminally compares the image portrayed by Rambo with his own life. He will find or create opportunities for behaving according to the image. When he acts tough, brave, or independent, he feels affirmed for having lived up to his ideal. The qualities and behaviors he associates with Rambo provide reference points as he maps his personal world.

Once he has incorporated that image, however, he is also controlled by it. Consider him in a situation that he finds threatening, such as encountering the class bully. He may feel fear and uncertainty, but the image so strongly prohibits such feelings that he represses or denies them. He may even become ruthlessly aggressive in an impulsive attempt to defeat fears that would not trouble his hero. Punished for having injured the other boy with a rock, he defiantly responds, "Nobody's going to beat me up!" He is not consciously *trying* to live up to the image, he is *compelled* toward these behaviors with little thought. While people are generally unaware of the personal myths that configure their every experience, unnamed myths nonetheless continually influence them.

You do not simply adopt, full-blown, the myths of your culture. And even those myths that you do adopt evolve with time. The young boy's mythology is further shaped by what happens to him when he acts in accordance with the Rambo image. Some parts of it will be supported and others will not. Perhaps his persona of toughness gets him into fights. If he wins the fights, he may adopt the image with even greater fervor. If he loses, he may stop acting so tough, but also experience an inner crisis as he is forced to reconcile the discrepancies between how he feels he is supposed to be and who he is. We all face many such crises during our lives.

You can see how uniquely *personal* myths can become. The image at the core of a personal myth is also generally more complex than in the Rambo example.

Rarely in our diverse culture, with its daily onslaught of media figures, is a personal myth organized primarily around a single image. And what of a boy whose temperament favors more tender sensibilities? Perhaps he is repelled by pretense and bravado. The Rambo image may have little emotional appeal for him. He will flounder until he is able to find or invent other models. Ideally, his culture will be bountiful in providing constructive alternatives. For many boys and girls today, the culture's supply of viable heroic images is impoverished, transient, and ultimately disempowering.

STAGES IN THE DEVELOPMENT OF YOUR PERSONAL MYTHOLOGY

As people develop emotionally, mentally, and spiritually, they spontaneously move through five fundamental stages in the evolution of their personal myths, more or less consciously, again and again throughout their lives. The following case history illustrates these stages as they were experienced by a woman who was a participant in a group that met weekly to work with its members' personal myths.

Adele[7] was content with her responsibilities as a mother and homemaker while her children were still young. When her daughter and two sons reached adolescence, she returned to college, where she earned a master's degree in journalism. Her amiable marriage had been more dutiful than impassioned, and once the children had left home, the marriage dissolved with surprisingly little attempt by either partner to salvage it.

Adele had taken a job with a midsized newspaper to write feature articles. While she had looked forward to the freedoms she could enjoy when her responsibilities as a parent ended, she found herself obsessed with her work, spending every waking moment thinking about and researching stories. She wasn't particularly ambitious for her career, and turned down invitations to write for two larger papers; yet she was driven, at the expense of most of the pleasures now available to her, and an ill-defined sense of emptiness would sometimes engulf her. Her endless activity shielded her from this feeling, but the busier she became, the more intense and frightening was the feeling when it did break through.

By the time Adele sought psychotherapy, she was fifteen pounds below her normal weight, was having difficulty sleeping, and was secretly questioning the validity of everything she was doing. After three months of treatment, her depression had lifted, she was eating and sleeping better, but she was still feeling trapped and alone in the face of her public role. Her columns were widely applauded but ceaselessly expected. She was referred to an intensive weekly group that focused on its participants' guiding myths.

The group provided a haven where she could begin to explore the feelings of emptiness that so frightened her. These feelings were readily traced to her childhood. Her father had died when she was seven, and since she was the eldest of three children, much of her childhood died with him. Bringing herself back into the experience, she was able through her adult eyes to name the myth that had guided her through her childhood years, through college, and through successfully rearing her own children, but which was now breaking down: "There is a job to do and I will do it well, even if it kills me." A tremendous amount of grief broke through with this realization. While she had mourned the loss of her father, she had not mourned the loss of her childhood. She also came to understand how her guiding myth had led her into a pallid, dutiful marriage, and how living according to the myth was now squeezing the passion out of her career. During this process, as the dysfunction of her old myth was becoming clear to her, no comforting alternative myth appeared, no better way of orienting herself.

Adele recorded six dreams, over four months, in which she was caring for an injured animal. In the first dream, the animal was a black bunny; in the fifth and sixth dreams, it was a she-wolf. The animals grew healthier and stronger in each dream, until, in the final dream, the wolf accompanied her to her home at the edge of a forest. The wolf looked longingly into the woods, stared at her, again glanced at the forest, turned to her, licked her cheek, and trotted off. Adele hid her sadness as she watched the wolf disappear into the wild. The dream helped her recognize how she had long ago separated from a primal, wild part of herself while smiling and hiding her sadness. She thought it a positive sign that the animals were growing stronger in the dreams.

After these dreams, Adele became aware of impulses she had not previously registered, including a romantic attraction to a longtime collaborator and an interest in friends' invitations to go river rafting that she had routinely turned down. She had not dated during the three years between the dissolution of her marriage and the start of her therapy group, telling herself she had already "paid her dues." Her colleague responded to her subtle signs of interest, but as they became romantically involved, he complained that she had no time to cultivate a relationship. Similarly, after expressing interest in rafting to her friends and having had them help her buy some gear, she canceled what was to be her first trip because of work. We see here the expression of conflict between a prevailing myth and an emerging myth. The old myth had locked itself onto her job: her columns had to be superb, even if it did kill her. But another myth was beginning to arise, which she first glimpsed in the wild yet self-assured passion she associated with the wolf and in her mercurial interest in romance and white water.

In a guided imagery sequence led by the group facilitator, two images appeared spon-

taneously, which Adele later interpreted as symbols representing two faces of her passion. The first was of her head bulging with a dense purple energy. Working later with this image, she realized that her major problem was not that her life lacked passion, but that all of her passion was narrowly channeled into her work. To accomplish this efficiency, she continually filtered and regulated her passion through her mind, and the dense purple energy clogging her head symbolized the arrangement quite well. The second image depicted the purple energy, now more fluid than dense, dancing throughout her entire body, leaving her with feelings of freedom and rapture. She began to refer to her old myth, which seemed focused, controlled, and serious, as "The Passion of the Mind," and to the emerging one, which seemed spontaneous, playful, and joyful, as "The Passion of the Body."

In dialogues between the part of her that identified with the old myth and the part that identified with the emerging myth, each character was severely critical of the other. "The Passion of the Mind" claimed the high road, with its focused productivity and ability to succeed against difficult odds. But Adele also realized this guiding myth was yielding diminishing returns. It had been an immensely effective strategy when she was seven and forced to care for her two younger siblings. It was an adequate strategy for the rich and rewarding job of bringing up her children. But now, with no intimates, and no interests outside her job, "The Passion of the Mind" was taking her down an ever-narrowing path.

"The Passion of the Body," however, was unpredictable and impossible to control. When she would, in the group sessions, attune herself to it, she would first hear the harsh judgments of her mind, telling her she was wasting her time with this useless activity, and that she should take control of herself. Once the group leader had Adele "breathe into" the purple energy that was compacted in her head, and to her amazement, her sense of constriction and emptiness began to transform. She started to feel warm sensations move throughout her body. She realized that when "The Passion of the Mind" was activated, which was most of the time, she simply didn't feel her body, was not aware of it unless something was wrong. It was not a source of pleasure. But when she "breathed into" the purple energy, she felt an aliveness in her body that dissolved her sense of emptiness. This was "The Passion of the Body" at a level she had rarely experienced.

The group helped Adele design a ritual she could use to evoke "The Passion of the Body" between sessions. She set aside Friday and Tuesday evenings for the ritual: Fridays to usher her away from her work week and into "The Passion of the Body" for the weekend, and Tuesdays to bring "The Passion of the Body" into her work week. She prepared for her ritual by turning off the phone and lighting candles in her bedroom and bathroom. She began with a long relaxing bubble bath in the candlelight. After the bath, she did a brief yoga routine designed specifically for uplifting one's energy. Then, lying on her bed, she listened to classical music, allowing the music to move through her body, selecting pieces that would evoke *a potent psychological process.[8] These sessions became like meditations, and rich imagery danced in and out of the music for her.*

In response to an assignment given her during a group session, Adele made up a fairy tale about the two faces of her passion. She selected a middle-aged female librarian to represent "The Passion of the Mind" (exaggerating old stereotypes about librarians) and a beautiful girl to represent "The Passion of the Body." The girl, however, was emaciated from having been locked away in a cave for many years. In the story, the librarian is at first disdainful of the girl but eventually helps her back to health and is herself revitalized in the process. Personifying the two sides of herself in this manner allowed Adele to create a forum to explore her inner conflict and try out possible solutions within the safety of her imagination. The parable of the healthy girl in passionate rapport with the librarian became the symbol of Adele's new myth, which she called the "The Passion of the Dance."

Adele made choices differently when she was living with "The Passion of the Dance." As a journalist, she saw firsthand much that was disturbing. She had mobilized "The Passion of the Mind" to bring her stories to the public in a way that stirred people, and she had been effective. But when Adele looked at the world through "The Passion of the Dance," she gained new insight into the people she was investigating. Her writing changed. It had been on the evangelical side. Now she was writing simple, poignant stories about human suffering, injustice, courage, compassion, and triumph. People liked this shift, and she heard more frequently that stories she had written had inspired constructive action by readers.

In the meantime, Adele focused on only one writing assignment at a time, rested when she needed to rest, and with a neighbor did aerobic dancing for about twenty minutes a day before dinner. She cultivated a new and deeply nourishing love relationship. As she felt success in translating her new myth into her life, after two years of weekly meetings that had been supplemented by periodic psychotherapy sessions, she left the group. She continued to devise new rituals that supported "The Passion of the Dance," and she kept a journal for working with her dreams and reflecting on her evolving mythology.

The mythology that dominated the first half of Adele's life organized it into a series of endless tasks and instructed her to complete them all, flawlessly, no matter the personal cost. Her mythology was like a special lens that made these tasks jump out at her, luring her to submit to unrelenting pressures. Other possible ways of organizing her life passed unnoticed. Adele's shift to a new guiding myth illustrates the five-stage process you will explore in this program. Each is organized around a specific task:

1. *Identifying Underlying Mythic Conflict in a Personal Problem, Pattern, or Concern.* Adele knew she was unhappy but didn't know why or how to make herself feel better. She came to recognize two opposing forces at play within her, which she named "The Passion of the Mind" and "The Passion of the Body." Each had its own mythology, its own way of telling her about where to focus her attention, what to value, and how to behave. "The Passion of the Mind" dominated her life, its expanding influence throwing her severely out of balance. This imbalance was at the root of her unhappiness. Like Adele, when you are able to conceptualize a personal problem in terms of its underlying mythic conflict, you are able to seek a solution from a deeper level of understanding.

2. Understanding Both Sides of the Conflict. Adele was overcome with compassion for herself as a little girl when she recognized the determination and stamina she had to muster to care for her younger brother and sister. This gave her respect for the myth she called "The Passion of the Mind," even as she was beginning to renounce it. At the same time, she looked on, and not without discomfort, as another myth was emerging to challenge "The Passion of the Mind," one that was more attuned to her physical body and her personal needs and desires. You will find that as you name the discord in your underlying mythology, opposing and often confusing parts of yourself can be understood, and you will have greater opportunity to bring them toward new levels of resolution.

3. Conceiving a New Mythic Vision That Integrates the Most Vital Aspects of the Old Myth and the Emerging Myth. Adele came to view the areas of distress in her life as arenas for working through her deeper mythic conflict. The conflict between the two myths expressed itself in the tension between working and river rafting, working and dating, working and everything else. It was also reflected in her two different styles of writing her columns—one more evangelical, the other placing greater confidence in the reader's visceral ability to form conclusions based on facts rather than to have to be persuaded. Adele found a new image that surpassed both "The Passion of the Mind" and "The Passion of the Body": the radiant girl working in joyful harmony with the librarian. "The Passion of the Dance" retained the most vital aspects of each side of the conflict, yet added, with the element of teamwork, a quality that transcended either side.

4. Refining Your Mythic Vision and Making a Conscious Commitment to Live from It. Adele realized that "The Passion of the Dance" held the potential of helping her resolve vital external and internal conflicts. As she refined and contemplated this image, her commitment to it deepened. When you have sufficiently understood the merit in both sides of a mythic conflict, and worked toward their resolution, the path is paved for a new mythic vision. Such visions inspire commitment to change.

5. *Living from Your New Mythology.* Adele did not automatically begin to live according to "The Passion of the Dance." Her rituals were structured activities that strengthened this new mythology and anchored it into her life. Her resolutions to get enough rest, to accept no more assignments than she could handle with equanimity, and to exercise regularly were other ways of supporting this new mythic vision. Once you have committed yourself to a carefully formulated new mythology, such steps take on symbolic as well as practical meaning. They not only transform your activities and relationships, they shift your awareness to the larger perspective evoked by your new mythology.

Your Personal Mythology in Its Cultural Context

Everything you do and think bears the distinctive shape and signature of the society in which you were raised. Infants are genetically programmed to learn the language of their caregivers, and partially because language carries myth, they are also predisposed to assimilate the myths of their family and culture. School, religious institutions, television, movies, newspapers, advertising, and other cultural imprinters leave indelible images on the child's developing mythology.

Even activities that might seem spontaneous, natural, or universal are dictated by the basic assumptions and underlying images in the culture. What you eat and the way you eat it, what you wear and how you wear it, whether your thinking is oriented toward the present or the future, whether your experience of the moment accents thoughts or feelings, how you greet strangers and receive friends, and how you acquire, accumulate, and display material possessions are all fashioned, in important ways, by the mythology of your culture. Yet, like tinted contact lenses, cultural myths are difficult to examine while you are wearing them.

Customs that seem strange to an outsider are accepted without question within a culture. They carry meanings that render them perfectly sensible in the logic of the local mythology. Before the Chinese revolution deposed the emperor, daughters of the noble classes had their feet bound; this arrested the foot's development and ultimately left the women unable to walk. The practice bestowed status because it accentuated the ownership of servants who could carry the women where they wanted to go. Of course, it also ensured that the women were unable to roam. In the United States, high heels and tuxedos are required for many occasions in which one expects to be served, and an endless series of fads from hula hoops to pet rocks became, in a brief moment of celebrity, compelling purchases for countless people. As a graffiti poet wrote in a Mendocino, California, washroom: "Culture is ubiquitous, that's why people act ridiculous."

The guiding myths within contemporary culture are often twisted, fractionated, and confusing, and they appear in less distinguished guises than the elaborate stories and exotic rituals of tribal and ancient peoples. The spirits and deities whose authority was unrivaled in those cultures have faded for the most part into antiquity. Now we find an abundance of mortal heroes and heroines, both real and imaginary, in novels, comics, and drama. The shimmer of an alluring television character may temporarily color a child's identity. While these images are less than venerable—rather than reach back through the generations, they appear suddenly and fade ever more abruptly—they are still disseminated through powerful media and leave strong impressions.

Myths permeate all areas of modern life. They are reflected in and transmitted through stage, screen, and song; education, religion, and politics; literature, art, and architecture; advertising, fashion, and design. They are intertwined with our child-rearing practices, sexual norms, and social systems. They are maintained by the slant of our history books and news stories, and exposed by the salary differential between a good schoolteacher and a baseball star. The myths operating in modern societies tend to support material progress and the control of nature, rather than the attunement and participation with natural cycles that characterize traditional mythologies. As the bumper sticker satirizes, "He who dies with the most toys wins."

Tanya, an African-American teenager, grew up in a comfortable racially mixed neighborhood. Her father was an accountant and her mother worked as a bank teller. In many subtle and not-so-subtle ways, they let their daughter know that they would never have been able to succeed in their careers had they not accommodated to the white power structure. Tanya grew up associating with many white peers, sharing their interests, and engaging in conversations that rarely mentioned her ethnic heritage.

Upon entering junior high school, she found her mythology challenged by a new peer group, one that ridiculed her for "thinking and acting white." They criticized her hard work, her good grades, her way of dressing and grooming. Tanya spent many sleepless nights crying, split between powerful opposing mythologies. She found herself continually negotiating between a desire for upward mobility as modeled by her parents and a need for acceptance within her peer group.

As a high school sophomore, Tanya was befriended by an African-American English teacher who assigned novels, essays, and poems written by black authors. Sensing Tanya's hunger for role models and her interest in the arts, she loaned her videos of black actors and actresses performing Shakespeare and other dramatic works. Tanya became profoundly inspired by these creative individuals. They certainly did not "think and act white," yet they expressed their opinions and described their life experiences in ways that bridged their ethnic identities with the wider culture. Such writers as Alice Walker, Toni Morrison, and Maya Angelou became exemplars for Tanya, and she eventually majored in English literature in college. However, reconciling the myths of her parents' and her peers' subcultures would be an ongoing challenge.

A primary role of myth has been to carry the past into the present. Through this binding of time, a culture's accumulated knowledge and wisdom are brought to each new generation. Today, though, the surge of new situations for which our mythologies must provide guidance is unprecedented. Jean Houston has estimated that each of us processes eight times as much emotionally significant information as our great-grandparents.

The guiding values and cherished convictions of previous generations are often all but useless in dealing with contemporary issues. Long-enduring myths, such as the parents' right to bring into the world as many children as desired, have been cracking under the strain of abrupt shifts in the foundations of social organization, such as overpopulation. The myth of continual upward mobility collides with a spiral of diminishing resources. The myth that the future will take care of itself is contradicted by the obvious jeopardy that ecological deterioration bequeaths to future generations. Cultural images that glorified the compliant female defined her as an appendage to the male. The belligerent foreign policies that were traditionally thought to convey a nation's strength created a Damocles' sword of mutual destruction that reverberates in the nightmares of our children. Cultural myths have been drifting toward obsolescence more swiftly since World War II than in any previous period of history.

The diversity of the mythic images we encounter through electronic and other media can also be overwhelming. For most of civilization, the myths held by the individuals in a society were relatively uniform, allowing for little question or variation. To challenge the culture's prevailing mythology was to risk censure and even death. Ancient mythologies were bound by tradition or, occasionally, altered by a shaman's sacred vision. But in today's complex civilizations, no single unifying force is powerful enough to preserve cohesion in the multitude of contrasting mythologies people regularly encounter. Guiding myths that were exalted in recent memory are becoming outmoded at a disorienting pace. The same U.S. president who called the Soviet Union "the evil empire" was negotiating a few years later as an ally with that nation's leader. The half-life of a viable myth has never been briefer—no generation has seen the parents' guiding myths become so rapidly obsolete as today's—and the need to unshackle ourselves from dying myths is ever more pressing. As history has advanced more rapidly, so has the need to become more facile in revising the myths that instruct and support us.

It is likely that your attitudes and values differ from those of your neighbors in ways that could not have been imagined in tribal cultures. Never have so many troubling as well as auspicious visions competed for popular attention, nor have there ever been media so capable of parading those visions in front of you. Growing up is no longer a matter of following in the well-trod footsteps of ancestors who may for generations have been in the same trade, held similar religious convictions, and considered the tradition-bound roles of men and women part of the natural order. Rather than be compelled to follow early beliefs, family codes, or antiquated cultural images, we are called on to participate in selecting, realigning, and updating the myths we follow. And in our disillusion with the spellbinding cultural images of the past, combined with the capacity of our imaginations to soar beyond the real and the present, we can each envision a daunting range of future possibilities.

CHANGING YOUR PERSONAL MYTHOLOGY

One quality of a vital personal mythology is its capacity for change. But change does not occur in a vacuum. No one's mythology or behavior exists in isolation from its social, economic, and political context. It would of course be naive to suggest that transforming your personal mythology can overcome all of the circumstances that imprison the human spirit, but changing your mythology *can* reveal freedoms that previously were not evident. Freedom has been defined as the "state of mind you enjoy when you are aware of a choice and have the power to choose."[9] Both your awareness of choice and your power to choose can be enhanced if you recognize undesirable patterns in your life that are being supported by habitual, insidious guiding myths.

Your mythology is regularly challenged to incorporate information that contradicts its premises, to adapt to new circumstances, and to expand as you accumulate experience and as you mature. You can consciously participate in and cultivate its evolution. Some people, however, spend a lifetime attempting to live according to cultural images that never quite fit them. Joseph Campbell describes the dilemma: "Whenever a knight of the Grail tried to follow a path made by someone else, he went altogether astray. Where there is a way or path, it is someone else's footsteps. Each of us has to find [our] own way. . . . Nobody can give you a mythology." [10]

The goal of this program is to teach you to participate more effectively in the evolution of your mythology, both in your inward life and in its expression in the outer world. We are not suggesting that you can control or even fully understand your mythology. Jung succinctly summarized the stalemate that is inevitably met by such efforts: "The totality of the psyche can never be grasped by the intellect alone." [11] A central aim of Jung's depth psychology was, however, to bring everyday awareness into greater accord with the deeper forces that undergird it. By reaching imaginatively and persistently toward your innermost depths, you open a door to a more profound view of your daily concerns, broaden the horizons of your self-knowledge, and tap into a power that can transform you.

Still, attempts to revise one's mythology are fraught with dilemmas. When the conquering Spaniards laid waste to Mexico in the early sixteenth century, the Aztecs felt that they had failed to honor their gods, and they increased the number of victims they sacrificed. Analogously, when people enter psychotherapy, their presenting problem is often formulated according to the premises of the old myth. Rather than speculating that the old myth may be failing them, they often assume they are not adhering to it closely enough.

A woman's prevailing mythology might instruct her to maintain a friendly, cheerful disposition at all times—to submerge her legitimate frustrations and resentments, her minor irritations about life, her responses to injustice, and generally to create a doll-like caricature of who she really is. If people do not treat her with respect, she may conclude that she is not following the old myth closely enough. Her self-criticisms and her motivation for "self-improvement" may be directed toward perfecting herself in its image. She may become even more agreeable, more passive, more falsely cheerful, regardless of the personal costs.

Like the Aztecs before her, she remains oblivious to the collapse of the old myth and scurries back to whatever psychological security it and the sacrifices it calls for can offer.

Personal myths are often in conflict. When beliefs do not match behavior, the underlying conflict becomes particularly evident. Many people think of themselves as lazy, even though they regularly push themselves beyond the point of exhaustion. Their self-talk may echo the words of a parent who long ago was frustrated with them for not working harder in school or at home. The enormous suggestive power of a father's or mother's emotionally charged remarks leaves indelible images. Perhaps, because of his father's goading, a boy works diligently and as an adult accomplishes more than might be expected of him, although always with the whip of his father's admonitions, now internalized, echoing at his back. His image of himself as lazy may be countered by another image outside his awareness. That image may have its roots in his past productivity. Even though it does not occur to him to articulate it and he continues to think of himself simply as lazy, the unconscious image may be running the show, causing him to accept and successfully meet with monumental responsibilities. The personal myths with which we consciously identify are not the only influences at work.

REFLECTING ON PERSONAL MYTHS THAT HAVE ALREADY CHANGED

By understanding how your personal mythology developed, you can more easily recognize outmoded myths and accept that their season has passed. Appreciating the relationship between early experiences and patterns in your adult life allows you to recognize and transform such patterns, instead of automatically repeating them. Many women are identifying how an unfulfilled longing for their father's love leaves them vulnerable to men who are emotionally unavailable. Many men are recognizing that the restricting models provided by the culture caused them to reject and repress vulnerable feelings. Many survivors of child abuse are finding ways to control their own abusive impulses. Many adult children of alcoholics are articulating common themes, such as an unreasoned need to please a remote or abusive partner. Unlike approaches that translate such patterns into the coin of the classical myths, this program is designed to help you identify and work with inner processes in the imagery of your own psyche. It is no less mythic because of this personalized focus, and you may discover striking parallels between your own spontaneous visions and the classical motifs.

Take a moment here to reflect on areas where your personal mythology has changed since your childhood. Can you recall being in the second grade and imagining what it would feel like to be an adult? Have the inner myths that tell you what it means to be a man or a woman, a husband or a wife, shifted? Does your work hold a different place in your life from what you once thought it would? Have the myths that show you how to balance a career and a family changed? Have you become more driven or less driven in the past decade? Do you have creative and hope-inspiring visions of yourself in old age? Where are your current myths being challenged?

Place a heading in your journal, "My Shifting Mythology." Under it, describe areas where your guiding myths have changed. These may include myths you are now questioning as well as myths where the changes are already well established. Identify as many personal issues as you can in which your mythology has shifted since your childhood. Ann wrote:

I no longer feel I serve others when I take their life responsibilities on myself.

I now recognize that needing to "save" another person is an act of superiority.

I no longer feel it is more blessed to give than to receive.

I no longer feel I serve my son by giving him everything he wants—but rather that to discipline him and hold my own boundaries teaches him more of what he needs to know about the world.

I've realized that being a woman is neither to fight for who I am or to collapse into giving my partner what he needs, but to find a central core from which I act, regardless of the response I receive.

An early emphasis of the program involves identifying trouble spots in your guiding mythology. Once such problematic areas have been identified, you will be shown, in a step-by-step manner, how to work with a single core mythological conflict. As you review and renew this area of your mythology, you also will be gaining a basic understanding of how your mythology operates and how to continue to involve yourself constructively in its evolution.

PURPOSE: *To learn how to use self-suggestion to focus your dreams on a specific concern*

In each chapter, after the personal rituals, you will be invited to experiment during the subsequent week with a procedure called "dream incubation." This is a method for evoking a dream that addresses a specific concern or clarifies a specific question. Your ability to recall your dreams will be stronger if you keep your journal and a pen or a tape recorder next to your bed and record your dreams as soon as you are awake. If you do not have or do not remember a dream, be receptive to your early-morning thoughts and feelings, and record them in your journal. An important goal here and in all the dream incubation instructions that follow is for you to invite new understanding from the deeper realms of your psyche. Remain alert for what comes through in any form— fantasies, sudden insights, early-morning thoughts and feelings, nighttime dreams.

To incubate a dream that furthers your work in the program, write in your journal, slowly and mindfully: "I will sleep soundly and peacefully tonight while dreaming about my Inner Shaman's answer to my question about beliefs, hopes, or habits that are causing problems in my life. When I awake, I will recall my dream." Then repeat, with intentionality, several times before falling asleep, "I will have a meaningful dream, and I will remember it."

If you do not recall a dream the first morning, repeat the procedure. A practice effect can be established. Do not be concerned if the relationship between a dream you recall and the question you asked is not readily apparent. Often, you will find as you examine the dream that it did touch on your question in ways that were not obvious at first. Structured dream interpretation techniques, such as those presented in Support Guide 2: "Working with Your Dreams," may bring you to a deeper understanding of the dream's meaning. In addition, incubating a dream using the same focus on several consecutive nights can bring progressively deeper insights about an area of personal concern. Ann reported the following dream:

It was almost not like a dream at all. I had a sense of people coming and going. I was watching them with almost no emotion, merely curious to see who they were and if they would stay or leave. It was like the sea that flows up the beach and then retreats. Waves of people, moving like the tide. Perhaps this dream, like my shaman, is trying to show me to accept the ebb and flow of life. I have wanted life to be consistent and dependable and understandable. This dream of people coming and going like the tides is somehow telling me that what I have to accept in life is that this is life. There is never going to be a stable consistency to it. It is always going to be like the tide, rising and falling, people coming and going.

The dream incubation instructions are an optional track in the program, but one whose benefits can be substantial. We encourage you to experiment with the procedure and to look over Support Guide 2 if you have not yet done so.

The Presence of Your Past

✧

Like Icarus I soared toward the sun with my wings of wine, not realizing that by flying so high I would fall as deeply into the sea as Icarus and my alcoholic father before me.

—Linda Schierse Leonard[1]

Whether or not you think much about it, the past continually winds its way into your present. In your visit back to your parents and grandparents, you explored how the choices of earlier generations live on in you. Not only can threads from your ancestors' myths be found in the fabric of your own guiding mythology; your mythology is woven also from your unique life experiences.

If your mythology is to remain relevant to your circumstances and level of psychological and spiritual development, you must periodically reorganize your view of the past. We first become "self-conscious mythmakers,"[2] according to psychologist Dan McAdams, in late adolescence when we confront the problem of identity and begin to develop a stable psychological foundation. Later, the fanciful stories we created as adolescents to celebrate our unique origin and destiny are replaced by attempts in young adulthood to formulate a somewhat more realistic sense of identity. These new formulations reconstruct the past in a manner that more astutely depicts its connection to the present. The *formation* and *reformation* of personal identity is the central psychological task of the adult years.[3]

In this chapter, you will create a Personal Shield. Its symbols will represent passages from your younger years, along with past hopes, expectations, disappointments, and ambitions. After you have created your Shield, you will analyze its symbolism. Just as societies tell stories about creation and about their own origins, you are continually elaborating upon an inner story—consciously and unconsciously—to interpret your past, organize your present, and lead you into the future. Portraying your past on your Personal Shield—from a new, inquisitive, and spirited vantage point—allows you to begin to rewrite your life story in a manner that, while realistically accounting for all you find to be challenging, beckons to higher possibilities.

SESSION 1:
Creating Your Personal Shield

PURPOSE: *To create a ceremonial object that symbolizes your unique mythology and its origins*

Many themes from classical mythology, such as Odysseus' heroic journey, Persephone's descent to the Underworld, the quest for the Holy Grail, the tale of Psyche and Eros, and the dialogues of Krishna and Arjuna, speak to concerns that are still germane to the modern psyche. While the twenty-first century cries for new myths, any of these venerable stories still provides a structure that could be meaningful to most readers for examining their own lives.[4] Throughout most of this program, you will be uncovering your inner story in the metaphors provided by your own psyche. But your Personal Shield will be organized according to the Creation story that has been a cornerstone in the development of Western culture. We turn here to the sequence of events in the biblical account of Genesis—with its motifs of "Paradise," "Paradise Lost," and "Paradise Regained"—to place a mythological frame around your life story as you depict it on your Personal Shield.[5]

The Eden myth recalls the fabled time in humanity's development before individual consciousness had progressed out of a supposedly idyllic identification with nature and the life of the body—*Paradise*. With the Fall from innocence came an awakening of *self*-consciousness, paid for, however, with an anxious sense of separation from the natural order—*Paradise Lost*. Growing up has many parallels.[6]

An increasing awareness of estrangement between oneself and the environment is a part of growing up that has been mythologically likened to "the time when each child reenacts the 'fall' of Adam."[7] The human embryo typically develops in an environment that meets its needs for warmth, safety, and nourishment. Infancy and childhood can provide long stretches blessed by innocence and wonder. Even in social and economic circumstances where childhood is hardly a carefree idyll, boys and girls often enter into fantasy worlds that provide a measure of security, hope, and dignity, fueled by the potent images found in stories, television, and movies. Progressively, though, a disquieting separation from childhood fantasies and innocence is inevitable. While these separations from Paradise are sometimes experienced as the achievement of independence, bringing joy and satisfaction, the severance is also often a source of anxiety and grief.[8] Psychologically, the Genesis story depicts the child's gradual "fall" from innocence, Paradise Lost.

Paradise Lost is often recalled in terms of disappointments, betrayals, and traumas. Some people bemoan their early misfortunes, often justifiably. But adversity is also a critical ingredient in developing a mature response to life. Therapy clients who grew up as privileged, overindulged children, whose parents managed to protect them from adversity, tend to exhibit a pattern of character flaws that might be termed "the psychopathology of affluence," among them cynicism, selfishness, boredom, and a sense of meaninglessness.[9] Although these parents lovingly indulged their children, and gave them much of what they wanted and needed, they failed to provide the challenges that would promote self-discipline and mature coping skills. Parenthood is full of such "damned if you do, damned if you don't" dilemmas. Paradise Lost, ironically, often carries the seeds of future wisdom.

And stories of Paradise Lost are accompanied by visions of *Paradise Regained.* Most of us, in our heart of hearts, hold a vision of how we want our life to unfold. The vision may be vivid or vague, but it raises a sail and catches the wind, moving us in a specific direction. This guiding vision is worth articulating, examining, and perhaps reenvisioning. It was often formed as a response to suffering and threat, to the experience of Paradise Lost, and its fervor is often sustained by an unconscious wish to recover the inner tranquillity of a dimly recalled Paradise. Such visions of Paradise Regained are likely to lead to a *Quest* that ushers you to an unexpected and not always welcomed destination. By creating your Personal Shield, you will be exploring your mythic biography, organized according to your unique rendition of Paradise, Paradise Lost, the vision you formulated of Paradise Regained, and the Quest that vision has led you to pursue.

When you took the imaginary excursion back to the lives of your parents and grandparents, you were reconstructing history according to available facts and considerable conjecture. In this ritual, you will be returning in your memory and imagination to significant events from your past, again reconstructing history according to available facts and inevitable conjecture.

PREPARATION: *In creating the Personal Shield, most people who have gone through our program have simply used the back of a paper plate or cut a white piece of construction paper into a circle. Your Personal Shield should be round, at least ten inches in diameter, and you should be able to draw or paint on it. A more elaborate way of making the Personal Shield is to stretch white muslin in an embroidery hoop and use textile paints. Occasionally, a program participant has built a frame for an animal skin. In addition to the material that you will use for your Personal Shield, you will need crayons, colored pens, or a paint palette.*

Once you have gathered the materials, divide your Personal Shield into five equal sections (drawing five spokes out from the center) and, on the outer rim, label the sections with the words "Paradise," "Paradise Lost," "Paradise Regained Vision," "My Quest," and "A Renewed Vision."

The following instructions will evoke the imagery you will draw on your Personal Shield. As will be the case with the majority of the guided imagery sessions from this point on, the instructions will ritualistically establish a sacred time and space by invoking the presence, love, and wisdom of your Inner Shaman.

Again, arrange to have someone read the instructions to you, use a tape, or familiarize yourself with the instructions well enough that you can lead yourself through the exercise unassisted. Find a setting in which you can become deeply relaxed, keeping your journal, your Personal Shield, and the drawing implements nearby. Sitting or reclining, take a deep breath, and close your eyes.

Settling into this safe, secure spot, focus on your breathing. In this and the subsequent inner journeys, you will be using a meditation for opening your heart and inviting the support of your Inner Shaman. You will also use a physical gesture to support your heart's opening.

Place your closed hands over your chest. The meditation goes like this: Notice breath. Soften belly. Open heart.[10] As you sense or imagine your heart opening, extend your arms outward, unfolding your hands like flowers blooming, until they come to rest comfortably at your sides. Notice breath. Soften belly. Open heart. With each inhalation, breathe in the fullness of life. With each exhalation, release your tension, relaxing more completely. Breathe in.

Release. Your heart is gently opening. Focus inward and call to your Inner Shaman, your inner wisdom: "My heart is open to you. Be with me on this journey."

Go back now in your memory to a happy scene from your childhood. Recall how you once viewed the world from the height of a child and with the curious eyes and inquiring ears of a child. Sniff unashamedly the good odors around you. Move, skip, dance, or roll with the unfettered abandon of childhood. Explore your world, unconscious of threat. Tuning in to this happy memory from long ago, sense how right it feels to be alive. Sense who is with you and what is occurring. Re-create the scene vividly, filling in the details with your imagination.

If no memories have come to you, allow your imagination to present you with the way your life might have at one time included a sense of safety or wonder or joy. If still no memories or images come to you, continue to breathe peacefully. A scene may yet appear.

If you have come to a scene from your past, focus on the most pleasant, peaceful feelings in your body as you continue to imagine the scene. Direct your breathing into these feelings, allowing them to intensify and fill your body. Allow every cell to come to life as the feelings invigorate you. The feelings can become deliciously vivid as they continue to build.

Focus on the part of your body in which the pleasant sensations are most intense. Notice the color of these sensations. Trace with your fingertips or in your mind the shape of this part of your body. Explore its interesting texture. In a moment, you will recognize a symbol emerging out of these colors and shapes and textures.

Watch as a symbol appears that represents this happy time for you. You may actually see the symbol take form, or you may sense it in another way—through feeling, inner word descriptions, or an intuitive knowing. The symbol will further evolve over the next few moments. Relax as it becomes increasingly clear.

In a moment, you will begin to draw your symbol. You may find that it is changing even as you are creating it, or that you have more than one image to draw. Or an additional image may occur to you while you are drawing. Draw whatever comes to you. Perhaps after listening to these instructions, you still have no sense of having had even moments of happiness in your childhood. If that is the case, leaving the Paradise portion of your Personal Shield blank can be a powerful statement in itself. Also, do not be concerned about what may be "aesthetic" or "correct." As long as the drawing is meaningful to you, it will serve its purpose.

Open your eyes and draw your symbol on the Paradise portion of your Personal Shield. (If you are reading these instructions into a tape, add: "Now turn off the tape until you have finished drawing your symbol.")

After you have drawn your Paradise symbol or symbols, look at the Paradise Lost portion of your Personal Shield. Again, close your eyes and relax more fully with each breath. Move forward to a time when the happiness represented by the Paradise portion of your Personal Shield was interrupted. This may have involved a change in your circumstances, a betrayal, a personal tragedy, a memorable failure, or something much more subtle. Allow the scene to emerge. Sense who is with you and what is occurring. Feel your body's response to this event.

Attend to your feelings and sensations as you think about this loss. Notice the color of these sensations. Focus on the part of your body where these feelings are strongest. Trace with your fingertips or in your mind the shape of this part of your body. Explore its texture. In a moment, you will recognize a symbol emerging out of these colors and shapes and textures.

Watch as a symbol appears that represents this difficult event or circumstance. You may actually see the symbol take form, or you may sense it in another way. It will further evolve over the next few moments. Relax as it becomes increasingly clear.

Once you have come upon a symbol that represents this part of your life, open your eyes and draw it on the Paradise Lost section of your Personal Shield. If you did not see a vivid image, create the symbol as you complete this second portion of your Personal Shield. (If you are reading these instructions into a tape, add: "Now turn off the tape until you have finished drawing your symbol.")

Now that you have drawn a Paradise Lost symbol on your Personal Shield, allow yourself consciously to breathe out any unpleasant bodily sensations. Again, close your eyes and relax more fully with each breath.

After adjusting to a disappointment of the kind depicted on the Paradise Lost section of the Personal Shield, people gradually formulate ideals and fantasies for restoring their happiness and contentment, for returning to a better time. Recall the section of your Personal Shield labeled "Paradise Regained Vision." Reflect on the ideals or images you formed about the way you wanted your life to become. As you begin to identify the ideals or images you formed at that time, recall also the feelings these ideals and images brought to you. Experience these feelings.

Attend to your feelings and sensations as you think about the hopes and aspirations of your youth. Notice the color of these sensations. Focus on the part of your body where these feelings are strongest. Trace with your fingertips or in your mind the shape of this part of your body. Explore its texture. In a moment, you will recognize a symbol emerging out of these colors and shapes and textures.

Watch as a symbol appears that represents these early hopes and aspirations. You may actually see the symbol take form, or you may sense it in another way. It will further evolve over the next few moments. Relax as it becomes increasingly clear.

Once you have come upon a symbol or a set of symbols that represents the hopes and aspirations you came upon early in your life, open your eyes and complete the Paradise Regained Vision portion of your Personal Shield. (If you are reading these instructions into a tape, add: "Now turn off the tape until you have finished drawing your symbol.")

Look at the progression of symbols on the Paradise, Paradise Lost, and Paradise Regained Vision sections of your Personal Shield. Look at the portion of your Personal Shield labeled "My Quest." Close your eyes and relax more fully with each breath. Move forward in time from your early pain and consider the journey you have taken toward your vision of Paradise Regained. Think about what you have done to attempt to make your life better—activities you have carried out, personal qualities you have cultivated, accomplishments you have attained. Reflect on the dilemmas you were facing, what you attempted to do about them, and the outcome of those actions.

Attend to your feelings and sensations as you think about your life's quest to bring yourself toward an image of Paradise Regained. Notice the color of these sensations. Focus on the part of your body where these feelings are strongest. Trace with your fingertips or in your mind the shape of this part of your body. Explore its texture. In a moment, you will recognize a symbol emerging out of these colors and shapes and textures.

Watch as a symbol appears that represents your Quest in the world. You may actually see the symbol take form, or you may sense it in another way. It will further evolve over the next few moments. Relax as it becomes increasingly clear.

Once you have come upon a symbol or a set of symbols that represents your Quest, open your eyes and draw this on the section of your Personal Shield labeled "My Quest." This drawing of your personal Quest is the last drawing for now.

In your journal, under the heading "Personal Shield," briefly reflect on the process of creating it. Where were your feelings strongest? Were there any surprises? Describe your most important insights. Ann described and reflected on each of the symbols from her Personal Shield:

> Paradise Symbol: I drew a circle with wavy lines flowing in and out of it. The circle represents me as a young girl, believing in the trustworthiness of those around me. The lines are the free, trusting, unobstructed movement of my senses, giving and receiving wonder.
>
> Paradise Lost: I drew a circle (myself) separated from another circle (my sister) by a dark line (distrust). Jagged disconnected lines go in every direction. The lines represent all the words, senses, and feelings that are no longer fluid or trustworthy.
>
> Paradise Regained Vision: I drew an upper circle (me) with several other circles (everyone else) around it. Wavy lines flow from the top circle. They are all the words and deeds that flow from me toward others in endless acts of giving, but there are no waves that can bring the flow from others back to me.
>
> My Quest: I drew five circles in a larger circle with wavy lines flowing between them and toward a central ball in the middle of them. The circles represent humanity, myself included, connected through a shared vision.

SESSION 2:
Your Personal Shield as Autobiography

PURPOSE: *To explore how the symbols on your Shield represent significant passages in the development of your personal mythology*

You may be wondering, as you dredge up these memories from your childhood, "How do I know this actually happened?" The debate over "recovered" memories is complex, socially charged, and has caused psychotherapists to take a hard look at the way memory works.[11] Memory was once believed to operate like a computer: everything experienced was somewhere recorded. Current research indicates that memory is more like a river, more fluid than computerlike. The flow of memory does not follow a linear course but rather winds in and out of events, fears, and wishes, cascades through emotional peaks and valleys, ebbs and flows through hidden recesses of the mind. Memories can be fragmented, remolded, distorted, deconstructed, reconstructed, or recombined, as well as accurately retrieved.

Sometimes a person will recall a long-forgotten experience from childhood or adolescence, and it will match an account in a letter, diary, newspaper clipping, or the memory of another person who was present at the time the event is believed to have occurred. The memory is verified. At other times, an intensely vivid image of an event from earlier years may break through, thoroughly convincing, but another family member provides a markedly differing account. Finally, an old diary verifies that the event could not have occurred as recalled. Perhaps several reliable people concur that "Uncle Joe wasn't even with us at the summer cottage that year." The contradictory evidence indicates that what seemed to be a "lost" memory was actually a "false" memory.

Memories may have their origins not in actual events but in a dream, a fantasy, something overheard in a conversation, read about in a novel, or seen on television or in a movie, unconsciously elaborated over the years into an entirely persuasive recollection.[12] The psychological reasons for such distortions are often as complicated as they are compelling, perhaps lending support to a stabilizing guiding myth that relies on fabrication to account for indiscriminate personal misfortune.

Actual events may also be repressed or concealed under "screen memories." Freud spoke of screen memories as a series of images of actual events that *screen* related events that may be too painful to recall. For instance, a woman who as an adult is provided with compelling evidence from her older sister that she was abused by Uncle Joe in the summer cabin has for decades remembered being with him in the cabin, but only with the whole family present, which according to her sister also occurred. The woman's recollection of the innocent events served as a screen memory.

If a newly "remembered" event involves an instance of alleged abuse on the part of a family member, the potential complications are legion. While such memories may certainly be accurate,[13] a healthy skepticism about them is appropriate, particularly if the recall was evoked by hypnosis, guided imagery, or an overly zealous book, support group, or counselor.

Some of the memories people experience in the personal mythology program can be neither verified nor disconfirmed. The memory may be portraying the event accurately, or it may be a reconstruction laced with fantasy, a "screen memory," or a combination of actual life events and a scene imprinted in childhood from a storybook, movie, or television program. Verifiable or not, however, newly recovered memories tell you something about your inner life and may provide significant information that puts certain puzzles about your personal mythology into a new perspective.

We suggest that for the purposes of the program, you treat the memories that emerge, including memories in which you know you filled in certain gaps with your imagination, as good historical novels, as best guesses about what actually happened. At a minimum, they are metaphors that in some way symbolize your deepest wounds, fears, or desires. It is not possible to make up something that doesn't reflect your inner being, and whether you assume that the memories the program elicits are based on actual events or are dreamlike metaphors, these memories will somehow symbolize emotional struggles from earlier in your life and can provide new insight for overcoming current difficulties.

Having created your Personal Shield, you will now be telling your life story, using the four symbols as the cardinal points for organizing your personal history. In the process, you will be creating a mythic autobiography. If you are working with a partner or with a group, we suggest that you describe the significant events of your psychological development as they are associated with the symbols on your Personal Shield. If you have been working alone, it may still be useful to share this experience with someone who cares about you. A great deal can be encapsulated in as little as ten minutes. Have a tape recorder going as you tell your story, and later, make yourself very comfortable and listen to the tape. Alternatively, you might simply tell your story to the tape recorder, unwitnessed, or write it in your journal. After orally sharing the thoughts and events related to the symbolism on her Personal Shield, Ann summarized the story in her journal:

Paradise: It was early morning on the farm in Zululand [Ann was born in South Africa, where she grew up until age ten, when her family moved to Canada]. The sun was rising, the birds singing, the smell of earth and cows and warm sun filling the air. I hear milk hitting the side of a metal pail, see the pink of the cow's swollen teat against the brown hide as the golden sun spills across the coral. I recall laughter as the farm boy squirts milk into the smiling faces of my sister and me. Everything so alive and familiar. Joy, simple and sensual and true. I believe I was an ecstatic child, given to great joys and great sorrows. I felt profoundly connected in bodily sensations of pleasure and pain. My feelings were trustworthy and clear. I had no reason to doubt my senses.

Paradise Lost: I am hiding in the compost pile at the bottom of the garden. I have been waiting for my sister and our friends for so long that I have finally realized that the game of hide-and-seek is over. They have run away and are somewhere laughing at me. I cannot believe it. Never could I have imagined that they would do such a cruel thing. What possibly did they think was funny? I become deeply confused. I no longer know who to be in the world if I have to second-guess everything. How can I ever trust someone again? How can I ever play with my friends after this? A cold wind sweeps through me and I say to myself, "I am alone. I'm not the same as other people. I must never be unkind to anyone like they have been unkind to me. I must never become like them." From that point in my life I decided that to want love from others would only lead to disappointment. I kept the flow of energy moving outward in a steady stream so that nothing painful could get into me. What I didn't realize was that nothing nurturing could find its way in either. My lack of trust has played itself out in many different scenarios: abusive situations, non-nurturing relationships, and a deep-rooted mistrust of intimacy.

Paradise Regained Vision: So that I would not have to feel the full weight of my sadness, I constructed a reality based on giving. I tried to become a safe place where people who are sad or afraid can lay their head. Knowing that I could expect nothing for myself, I tried to find joy and fulfillment without the need of return. Even when others were generous with me, I was too primed for giving to be able to receive their gestures. And so in the end, I became the very thing I least wanted to be, someone who rejects the spontaneous openness of others.

My Quest: My quest has been to create a world where all are welcome, where healing is a gift we all share, and where beauty and kindness flourish. To that end I have been involved with many organizations that work with hunger, poverty, health, and human rights. My art has been aimed at showing the possibility of harmony and love. What I did not realize through all of this work was that it was I who was hungry and searching for healing. That it was I who was lonely and in need of love.

PURPOSE: *To learn a technique that deepens your understanding of the symbols on your Personal Shield, and that you can also use with other symbolism*

SESSION 3: Exploring the Symbolism of Your Personal Shield

Having drawn your Personal Shield and considered how its symbols may represent milestones in your inner life, you will be examining your Personal Shield's symbolism in one additional way. You will be using a technique called "creative projection." [14] In this technique, you imagine "becoming" the symbol and giving it a voice. You pretend you *are* the symbol. You would say, "I am . . ." and then describe yourself as the symbol, staying in the first person, present tense, active voice. If, for instance, you had drawn a small blue rowboat on your Personal Shield, you might begin by stating "I am a small rowboat. I am blue." You might then elaborate from your imagination, "I am on a stormy sea," and continue to talk about yourself from the identity of the rowboat. The technique can be used with dream symbols, artistic creations, or imaginative fantasies. It may be particularly illuminating with symbols that evoke discomfort, sadness, anger, or confusion.

As you identify with the symbol, let your words flow spontaneously and unrehearsed, giving full license to your imagination. If you are working alone, you may want to keep a record by talking into a tape recorder or writing your thoughts directly into your journal. If you are working with a partner, your partner's job is simply to listen, gently remind you if you wander away from the first-person present tense as you identify with the symbol, and prod you to go beyond what you might have rehearsed. Refrain from discussing the process until after you have gone as far as you can in the voice of your symbol.

Begin with several deep breaths and choose one of the symbols from your Personal Shield, examining it, and beginning to speak *as if you are* that symbol. As you finish examining each symbol from your Personal Shield, summarize in your journal the way you identified with it and elaborate on the meaning the symbol seems to hold for you. Ann wrote:

> Paradise Symbol: I am a center through which life flows unobstructed. I trust the world in which I live and the people around me. I am content and delighted by existence.
>
> Paradise Lost Symbol: I am a circle separated from all others by walls of doubt. I cannot trust the information that my senses bring to me. I am alone and full of sorrow.
>
> Paradise Regained Symbol: Although I am separated from all others, I choose to bring forth love into the world. I can only give, I cannot receive. I am strong in my commitment, and alone.
>
> Quest Symbol: I am a circle seeking to create a world of harmony. I am in shock.

We will also draw from the journal entries of other program participants to provide more variety in our illustrations of the personal rituals. Frank, an investment counselor who was thirty-five when he went through the program, examined a fist he had drawn on his Personal Shield:

> The symbol in the Paradise Lost portion of my Shield is a picture of a fist striking an innocent belly—specifically my belly, when I was four and a half. Okay, I am a fist. I am clenched. I am moving very rapidly. I have anger in

me. I have incredible anger in me. That anger just wants to express itself. Wants to hit out. That anger is strong. And there is this kid playing with my toys. I have an excuse to put my anger right into his stomach. And that's what I'm doing. Wham! That felt good. I feel my power—instead of my usual helplessness. I feel contact instead of isolation. I feel dominance instead of feeling dominated.

Frank reflected further:

Going from the warmth and safety of a loving, nurturing, and I guess overly protective home into kindergarten was totally overwhelming. I never seemed to know what was going on or what was expected of me or how to relate to the other kids. One day, one of the tougher boys was playing with a wooden train set. He went away and I started to play with it. Now, I wasn't certain he was through with it, but he had left it, so with a shade of trepidation I went over and played with it. But he returned, saw me playing with the trains, and without a word belted me in the stomach. I don't think I ever knew anything could hurt that much. All my breath was jerked out of me, and I found out what it means when they say someone "sees stars."

It never occurred to me that it was wrong for him to have hit me—I always assumed he was justified because I <u>should</u> have known he was coming back and <u>shouldn't</u> have been messing with the toys he was using. For me, that fist represented an irrational authority that has always kept me in my place. I couldn't comprehend what was going on when I got hit, so I just took on a sort of unquestioned sense of being oppressed around strength or authority. I never really thought about what was on the other side of the fist.

"Becoming" the fist really humanized it for me. I believe that my associations to the fist may have been very similar to what was going on for that kid. While I don't remember thinking of his fist for decades, it represents a sense that I must be overly careful, a kind of self-oppression that I carry with me to this day. Somehow I believed I was bad because I was playing with those toys. So I accepted moral restrictions: I shouldn't ever break any rules; I must even abide by unwritten, imperceptible, and invisible rules. So now I put a lot of energy into second-guessing what might offend someone, what might cause someone to be angry with me, and I wind up stifling my spontaneity, and then I'm very uneasy around other people.

I tried real hard to never make the teacher or the principal or my classmates mad at me, and I still try not to make others, even strangers, uneasy around me or to give them any reason to judge me as doing something wrong. What a burden! What's striking is how I gave the kid who hit me so much authority to judge me. This gives me greater understanding of the oppressive powers that seem to surround me in social situations, and the fist is a symbol that lends me some objectivity about them.

You can see how Frank's elaboration on this single symbol from his Personal Shield revealed a persistent, self-limiting aspect of his personal mythology. Use the creative projection technique to explore each of the symbols on your Personal Shield.

USING YOUR PERSONAL SHIELD FOR EMOTIONAL PROTECTION

Sometimes when you request a dream, initiate a fantasy, or attempt some other way of contacting your deeper self, you will experience unsettling feelings. In addition to the suggestions offered for taking care of yourself in Support Guide 3: "If the Program Becomes Unsettling," we recommend the method described here, which will show you a way of using your Personal Shield for emotional protection.

During the Paradise Lost imagery instructions for the Personal Shield, a woman in one of our workshops recalled a repressed childhood incident involving sexual molestation. Because this event led to a disturbing court appearance when she was twelve, its sudden reemergence was vivid and extremely upsetting for her. She was not at all prepared to address it in the group. Alerted to her situation, one of us worked with her privately while the group proceeded.

She was able to respond to instructions for relaxing deeply. She was asked to imagine her Personal Shield as a powerful container capable of accommodating whatever she needed to have it hold. She was helped to find a symbol that could represent her molestation memory, and she drew it on the Paradise Lost portion of her Personal Shield. She was able to visualize the intense emotions she was experiencing being sent directly into the symbol. She used her imagination, breath, and intention to transfer the emotions from her body into her Personal Shield.

By "depositing" her feelings for safekeeping until she would be ready to work with them, she was neither denying the experience nor forcing herself to process it before she was prepared, and she was able to participate meaningfully in the remainder of the workshop.

You may use your Personal Shield in a similar manner whenever a dream or one of the rituals triggers an upsetting memory or feeling you do not wish to focus on. While it will sometimes be necessary to draw a new symbol, a symbol that is already on the Personal Shield will often be suitable, and the feeling can be channeled directly into that symbol. First draw or select the symbol in which you will store the unpleasant feeling until you are ready to work with it more directly. Then vividly imagine the energy of the feeling transferring from your body into your Personal Shield. You can accomplish this through your gaze, by exhaling directly into the symbol, and by expressing the feeling as a sound whose vibration enters the symbol. Continue until you feel cleansed. You might want to shake out any unwanted emotional residue with strong exhalations and rapid free movements of your hands and body. Conclude with several deep and relaxing breaths.

After setting aside your Personal Shield, reflect in your journal. You might also consider a journey to your Inner Shaman to discuss the experience. If the feeling persists and is overbearing, turn to Support Guide 3: "If the Program Becomes Unsettling," and use one or two of the procedures suggested there.

During your work in the remainder of the program, we suggest you keep your Personal Shield nearby to provide emotional protection and spiritual support. You can also *imagine* bringing it with you on any of the guided imagery rituals.

PURPOSE: *To enlist your dreams in identifying issues for your focus in the program*

With a tape recorder or a journal and pen next to your bed, prepare to incubate another dream tonight. Write in your journal, slowly and mindfully: "I will sleep soundly and peacefully tonight while dreaming about an area of my mythology that is inviting my attention. When I awake, I will recall my dream." Then, with deliberation, repeat several times before falling asleep, "I will have a meaningful dream, and I will remember it." If you don't recall a dream the first night, repeat the self-suggestions until you do. When you have remembered a dream, consider using Support Guide 2: "Working with Your Dreams" to go more deeply into the dream's meaning. Ann reported the following dream:

DREAM FOCUS:
An Area of Your Personal Mythology That Is Inviting Your Attention

I was climbing with a family up a hill somewhere in the Middle East. It was biblical times. As we hurriedly climbed the pathway, the sound of a tempest wind is heard moving behind us. The patriarch of the family admonished us not to look back, but the wife is not able to resist. She turns and is immediately petrified, turned into a pillar of salt. I know it is Lot and his family.

The scene changes to disclose a large dusty courtyard with streets running into it. About a hundred people are there. I hear the sound of the tempest wind again, but this time it has the added sound of fire. Suddenly, from out of the sky, tongues of flames lick the air. Each time the fire touches the top of someone's head, the person reacts violently. I sense that some of the people are strong enough to bear the fire but that most are damaged by its intensity. I know this to be Pentecost.

The scene changes again and I find myself standing alone on an open plain, although I sense that there are others somewhere about. I hear the sound of the tempest nearby. It has a subtler tone than before. It is moving slowly toward me, a wall of intense vibrational sound. I feel afraid as it begins to enter my body. As soon as the wall finds an area in my body that is not able to hold its power, it pulls back far enough for me to work with the area of resistance. I put my hand into my body and pull out something dark and shadowy. Once the thing is removed, the wall of sound begins to move deeper into me once more. This sequence happens several times. I suddenly know that just as the human being has been building a vessel that is strong enough to hold the fire of Spirit, so the spirit has been learning how to temper its power to be able to marry the body without destroying it.

Ann used the creative projection technique to explore this dream further. Consider using it with your own dream. The symbols Ann worked with included Lot's wife as a pillar of salt, the worshipers at Pentecost who became agitated with excitement, the substance that she was taking out of her body, and the wall of vibration.

Lot's Wife: I am Lot's wife. I am a pillar of salt. Punished for my curiosity, my risk, my courage. My spirit was willing but my flesh too weak. I should have obeyed my husband's demands. Men are always right. I have been put back into my rightful place, a pillar of salt, useful only as a seasoning for the food of the family.

The Worshipers: I am a worshiper at the time of Pentecost. And I have gone crazy. Drunk with power, off balance from seeing too much too soon, unable to contain the power, I am made useless to myself and to others. I am unprepared to take the next step.

The Substances I Take out of My Body: I am the dark sludge, the resistance, the unconscious parts that do not want to be healed. It is my job to keep the melodramas of life going, to hide and sabotage the evolving spirit of humanity. I would rather you go crazy, or die, than let go of the past. I am the fear that holds you captive.

The Wall of Vibration: I am the wall of sound, the <u>aum</u>, the "In the beginning was the word." I want to merge with you; to know the exquisite poignancy of the human dilemma; to find myself through your experience. I have been courting you all these many eons. Is it time?

As I reflected on what this dream is telling me about where the myth that governs my life requires attention, I realized that I need to change my relationship to my fear of having to pay a terrible price for consciousness, for freedom. I need to be willing to leave my thoughts of madness and punishment behind me, let go of the pains of those who have tried and failed, and allow myself to be overwhelmed by an energy that is beyond me.

Recognizing When a Guiding Myth

Is No Longer an Ally

❦

Error is just as important a condition of life's progress as truth.
—Carl Jung[1]

Among the most significant findings of psychology since the 1960s, according to Martin Seligman, is that "individuals can choose the way they think."[2] That you can transform your personal mythology is the fundamental assumption of this book, and to change your guiding myths is to change the way you think. In the process, the emotional residue of experiences that are at the root of self-defeating ways of thinking can also be recognized, healed, and released. The personal rituals in this chapter will help you identify dysfunction in your personal mythology, trace its roots to events in your past, and invite a healing process to begin.

A conflict or failing in a personal myth may point to the growth edge of your psychological and spiritual development. As you reach new stages in your own maturation, and as your circumstances change, myths that once offered effective guidance often become unworkable and even destructive. Inevitably, some of these guiding myths—and the habits of thought and behavior they maintain—will restrict you, burden you, or repeatedly place you in situations that hurt you.

Difficulties making a decision, self-contradictions, puzzling dreams, persistent fear or anxiety, nagging confusion, tenacious ambivalence, and physical disruption may signal internal mythic conflict and provide clues for its resolution.

Nancy was nineteen when she participated in an intensive weekend therapy group. After an adolescence filled with sexual confusion, she had the year before participating in the group fallen in love and entered a satisfying relationship with another woman. By the time of the group, she was comfortable with her identity as a lesbian, although she wished to work on underlying feelings of turmoil and anger in regard to her family's adamant rejection of her lifestyle. Her overriding concerns at the time of the group, however, focused on severe pain in the area of her right ovary and fear of surgery because a medical examination a few days earlier had revealed a growth at that site.

Nancy asked for help with the terror she felt around the physical disruption. Initially, the group leader had no intention of exploring any emotional basis of her tumor, hoping, rather, to assist her in relieving some of the fear that seemed to be aggravating the pain. The presenting problem involved somatic complaints, and a body-based therapeutic approach was used. The events of the subsequent two and a half hours spontaneously revealed the possible involvement of a mythic conflict in the development of her tumor and apparently marked its reversal.

She was asked to lie down on a mat, breathe deeply, and visualize each inhalation traveling to the site of the pain while, with each exhalation, the therapist's hand exerted pressure on her diaphragm. This is a fairly common procedure in body-oriented psychotherapy, which establishes the support of physical contact and sometimes induces a spontaneous release of chronic tension and a flooding of feelings. She was encouraged to make a sound with each exhalation, which was the beginning of an intensive emotional release, resembling at various times an exorcism, death wails, and childbirth.

Nancy reached a crescendo of deep, convulsive wails, which were accompanied by a long series of spasmodic movements originating in her abdomen. As these began to subside after a substantial expenditure of energy, her face spontaneously distorted, and she raised her head, neck, and upper back. Then, in a loud, haunting voice, she began repeating the words "You will have your baby! You will have your baby!" Her physical expressions became reminiscent of those of the possessed adolescent portrayed in the movie The Exorcist. *This sort of "possession" by a repressed aspect of the personality is actually not unusual in intensive therapeutic settings. It had the effect of forcing into Nancy's awareness a deep conflict that she did not know how to resolve. While she had pushed the conflict outside her awareness, it was apparently smoldering in her reproductive organs. Now, as the raging voice continued to assert itself, its theme never varied. This forceful outpouring seemed to build to the maximum Nancy's body could tolerate, finally culminating with an explosive emotional release.*

This was followed by deep sobbing that gradually led to a buildup of sensation in her legs and pelvis. As Nancy's feet pushed down into the mat, her body took the posture of a woman giving birth. She struggled with this for some time, until there was a cathartic release and she triumphantly lifted an imaginary baby over her head. She was asked to talk with the image and give the image a voice so a dialogue could be established. As she began, she appeared to be increasingly identified with the baby, finally letting her hands down and "becoming" the baby, assuming the fetal position, gurgling, and urinating. After some time, an aura of peacefulness surrounded Nancy as she gradually came back to her adult self.

She was asked to speak to her tumor and then to give the tumor a voice and carry on a conversation with it. This became a lengthy and moving process in which Nancy came to view her tumor as an expression of an inner desire toward becoming a mother, a wish she had been suppressing in the service of her lesbian identity. She attributed such statements as "I have to be born!" and "You are my mother!" to the tumor. She reached a point where the rage she had been feeling toward the tumor transformed into an acceptance and even an appreciation of the information it was providing about her deeper longings. She then felt equipped to deal with the conflict at a conscious level.[3]

The pain had subsided markedly by the end of the session and did not return. Interestingly, a sonogram administered a few days after the session revealed a three- to four-centimeter growth on the site of the ovary, which her physician insisted was an ectopic pregnancy until she convinced him this was not possible. Within a few weeks the growth had completely disappeared. A five-year follow-up showed no recurrence.

Nancy believed she could not have a baby because she was not sexually interested in men. A deeper part of her, however, subscribed to a different personal myth, which held that having babies is a vital part of being a woman. When the myth you consciously hold is incompatible with another driving myth, the conflict may lead to a wide variety of contradictory behaviors, it may inhibit you from taking actions that would obviously benefit you, or it may manifest in a physical symptom, as was apparently the case with Nancy.

The Jungian analyst Marion Woodman points to the danger of remaining "in the grip of a mythology that may . . . succeed in destroying us for what we still consider the highest and noblest end."[4] Recognizing when a guiding myth has become dysfunctional or when two inner myths are incompatible quickens you toward becoming a more conscious participant in shaping the way your life unfolds. With Nancy, you saw the potent forces that can be unleashed when a primordial impulse, such as a woman's drive to bear children, is systematically suppressed by her mythology.

Your Personal Shield and its symbolism provide a broad overview of the events that shaped your guiding mythology. Here the program shifts to concentrate on personal myths that are no longer serving as allies in your development. As you mature and as your circumstances change, your myths are continually challenged, and you are spurred to recognize when an old way is no longer "the path with heart."[5] Jerome Bruner notes how difficult this can be: "When the myths no longer fit the internal plights of those who require them, the transition to newly created myths may take the form of a chaotic voyage into the interior, the certitudes of externalization replaced by the anguish of the internal voyage."[6] This program assists you in building within yourself a psychological container for tending to that anguish, and it offers guidance on the voyage. By the end of this chapter you will have identified at least one area of your personal mythology that is causing difficulty for you and that you might productively focus on in the remainder of the program.

SESSION 1:
Assessing Your Mythic Conflicts

PURPOSE: *To create a broad overview of the points of conflict in your life and of their mythic dimensions*

Psychologists have used the word *complex* to describe various constellations of thoughts, feelings, and behavior that are organized around core guiding themes and that tend to cause problems in people's lives. Alfred Adler coined the term *inferiority complex,* for example, to describe people's overreactions to their perceived shortcomings. The core theme of a complex often corresponds to a classical myth, and many a psychological complex has been named after a myth.

Freud held that the Oedipus complex, based on the son's competition with the father for the mother's erotic love, must be resolved if the son, as an adult, is to develop healthy relationships with women and with other men. Henry Murray identified the Icarus complex.[7] In the Greek myth, Icarus, son of Daedalus, had an inflated estimate of his capacities and went so close to the sun that the wax on his artificial wings melted, plunging him to his death. The Icarus complex leads people to reach too far and expect too much, until they fall and become psychologically disabled with fear or apathy. The Jonah complex, in contrast, was described by Abraham Maslow as portraying the "fear of attaining one's full potential."[8] Just as Jonah, in the biblical account, rejected his call from God and ended up in the belly of a whale, many individuals evade their inner calling and find that their lives also become entrapped in a limiting structure. Carl Jung, who introduced the term *complex* to psychoanalysis, believed that each person's psyche is the repository of several complexes, often emerging from conflicts in negotiating archetypal, or universal, themes.

The areas of your mythology that are the most primed for change are likely to be marked by personal conflict. Self-defeating behavior patterns, irrational fears, disturbing dreams, or inconsistencies between word and deed may bring your attention to personal myths that are limiting you and are ripe for transformation. Occasionally a person in one of our workshops reports being unaware of any personal conflicts, despite the opening rituals designed to uncover inner discord. Even these people, whether particularly blessed or in denial, can identify troubling conflict or disharmony between their own personal myths and the myths of the family in which they were reared or the myths of the society in which they live, and a focus on one of those conflicts can also be your focus in the program.

Write the words "Conflict Survey" at the top of a fresh page in your journal and divide the page into three columns (if you are working on a word processor that does not easily do columns, simply make three lists). Label them:

1. Self-Defeating Behaviors Tied to Mythic Conflict
2. Irrational Feelings Emerging from Mythic Conflict
3. Symptoms, Symbols, and Metaphors of Mythic Conflict

Look at the first column of your survey and consider patterns of behavior that hurt you or fail to bring you what you need. Identify limiting habits you seem unable to change, mistakes you seem destined to repeat, kinds of choices on which you seem to stumble. Describe these self defeating behavior patterns.

Ann was in her midforties when she went through the program. She had been enormously successful as a composer, playwright, and performer—known particularly for works that raise consciousness—and she was the mother of a six-year-old son, Devon. She had recently been awarded the Order of Canada "for her outstanding contribution to her community and country in the areas of the performing and healing arts." She had by that time written and produced two musicals, seven albums, three ballets, and an opera score, performed for royalty, closed the 1994 Commonwealth Games with one of her songs, "Healing Journey"—heard by half a billion people worldwide—and was receiving reviews asserting that her songs induced "a depth of intimacy that many people don't reach with their spouses." When we asked her for permission to use her journal as one of our case examples, we told her that we hoped she would not require us to disguise her identity although, anonymously or not, we definitely wanted to use the material. We also emphasized that we could readily understand, since she is a public figure, if she did not want to advertise her private blemishes. Her response expresses the spirit she brings to sharing her story with you:

> One of the dangers for people who have powerful personas in the world is that they create the illusion in those who watch them that they don't have issues to work with. Part of my journey is to allow myself to be seen in the paradox of my nature—its power and its insecurity, its strength and its weakness—and to show that in the end it is our duality that gives us our humanity. It is not a matter of "I am better (or worse) than you." It is that "I am different from you" and "I am just like you."

In working with her conflict survey, Ann identified numerous self-defeating behaviors that she could see were tied to her mythic conflict:

> I allow people into my inner circle who don't support me or my work or who have repeatedly abused my trust.

> I don't place my own needs for exercise, creativity, or leisure close to the top of my list of priorities.

> I back away from conflicts that might cause the other person discomfort.

> I walk on eggshells in my own home, as if I might hurt my loved ones if I allowed myself to be expressed fully.

> I allow people to believe I feel closer to them than I really do.

Go to the second column of your Conflict Survey and think about emotional patterns that are difficult for you, such as unrealistic fears, inexplicable anxiety, unwarranted dissatisfaction, or unrelenting ambivalence. Perhaps you have carried these feelings so long that you have put them far in the background because you believe you can do nothing about them. Perhaps you no longer even notice them. If you are willing to focus on these feelings and patterns, you give yourself an opportunity to work with them, heal them, and free the energies they command. Describe these difficult feelings in this column.

The feelings Ann identified as emerging from her mythic conflict included:

I feel uncomfortable when I am with someone who is expressing deep friendship when I don't feel as they do.

I dislike it when someone is defining how I feel. I would rather terminate the conversation than insist on them hearing me.

When someone close to me is unhappy, I feel anxious, as if it were my fault.

Whenever I do well at something, I feel uncomfortable if it is noticed by my loved ones, almost as if I were somehow robbing them of what is rightfully theirs by my success.

I have a deep fear that I take up too much space and harm others by my presence in their lives.

I sometimes feel that the lack of peace in my life is a reflection of the saying "There's no peace for the wicked."

In the third column of your survey, describe or draw any images from your dreams, fantasies, or artistic creations, such as the figures on your Personal Shield, that seem to represent conflict in your personal mythology. Ann identified the uneasily connected circles from the Paradise Lost section of her Personal Shield and a lyric from one of her songs, "I won't stay silent any longer!"

Sometimes an inner conflict expresses itself in a physical symptom that can be thought of as a natural symbol of the conflict, as we saw with Nancy. Neck and shoulder pain may be the uninvited consequence of a mythology that guides you, in one way or another, to take on the burdens of the world. The pain, in this context, is an organic symbol of the conflict between the dictates of your myth and the dictates of your body. Digestive problems may correspond with the consequences of a long-standing myth that are "difficult to stomach." Ulcers, headaches, and hypertension are sometimes reflections of psychological stress and underlying mythic conflicts, and evidence has been mounting that psychological factors also play a role in a broad range of illnesses not usually thought of as "psychosomatic" in nature.[9] Reflecting on her recurrent headaches, Ann noted:

Often when I want to take time for myself but also feel that others need me, the only way I can give myself permission to say no is to have a headache.

The headaches are always in the right part of my skull. It is like the rational left side of my brain is trying to take over my intuitive nature.

Just as a body condition may be a metaphor of an internal mythic-level conflict, so may the circumstances in your life. A woman may be torn between a suitor who is kind and a suitor who is inconsiderate or abusive. How could this possibly be a difficult choice? Her guiding mythology may have her continually seeking a symbolic substitute for a father who was withdrawn, absent, or worse. When a suitor appears who meets the criteria dictated by the myth, the suitor is cast in the symbolic role, and the curtain rises on a mythic-level drama. Can she win from this symbolic father the love she never received from her actual father? Unless she can unmask him with an awareness of his role in her mythic drama, she is compelled to reenact her early dilemma, and with a high emotional charge.

Ann identified the following circumstance as an outer representation of an inner conflict:

> A therapist friend came to visit and stay with me and my partner. She is deeply interested in the body's knowledge, and her view of the world deals with the psyche and the body. She is very concrete and makes quick judgments. My partner is more interested in the spiritual, larger perspective. He takes the long view and forms his opinions very deliberately. In the tense interactions between the two of them, I was able to observe these two aspects of myself finding it difficult to come into a harmonious acceptance of one another.

In addition to symbols from your Personal Shield or other expressive works, scan your body and your circumstances for natural symptoms, symbols, and metaphors that point to inner conflict that you might want to focus on in this program, and describe or draw them in the third column of your survey. Be speculative. Reflect deeply. Whenever you recognize an area of underlying conflict, you are taking a step toward participating more consciously in its resolution.

Keep your journal with you for a few days and add new items to your Conflict Survey as they occur to you. Most people can readily identify several areas of conflict or concern. If you are having difficulty finding even a single area that might be valuable to explore, you might incubate a dream, requesting that a fertile conflict be brought to your attention. Even if you do not recall a dream, begin to write in your journal about possible conflicts as soon as you are awake. When you have completed your list of conflicts, put a star next to the items you consider particularly problematic. By the end of this chapter, with the assistance of the following personal rituals, you will have chosen a single area for special attention.

PURPOSE: *To discover a core conflict in your guiding mythology*

Your Conflict Survey portrays behaviors, feelings, and symbols that correspond with conflicts within you and between you and elements of your world. Here you will journey to your Inner Shaman to be shown how these may point toward a core conflict that could be a valuable focus for you in the program. If you are already fairly certain about the conflict on which you wish to concentrate, this journey to your Inner Shaman will help you confirm that choice and add to your understanding about it. If you have not yet settled on a conflict, it will enlist your inner wisdom to help you choose.

Some people feel, at this point in the program, an inner pressure to identify just the "right" focal conflict. If you find yourself straining, we assure you that there is no "wrong" way to do this. We have found that as people go along in the program, the mythic issues they need to face and are ready to face turn out to be peculiarly embedded in whatever concerns they select here.

We refer to this phenomenon, where many aspects of your mythology are contained in a single symbol or issue, as the "holographic principle" of personal mythology. Each part of a hologram contains information from every other part. In a similar manner, the mythic conflict you select here will embody, in a fundamental way, your entire mythic system. Working through one area will have an impact on your entire mythology. Therefore, it is far less important that you *rationally* decide on the "right" conflict than that you select an area for which you have some emotional charge. Your work with that conflict will lead you where you need to go.

PREPARATION: *This ritual will take you on another journey to your Inner Shaman. Select a setting where you can become deeply relaxed. Remember that even if you have had difficulty contacting your Inner Shaman in previous guided journeys, a practice effect will assist you in each attempt; we advise that you find within yourself a relaxed, optimistic attitude as you begin. Also keep in mind that even if you do not make vivid contact with your Inner Shaman, you may still come back from the journey with new insights. Sitting or reclining, take a deep breath, and close your eyes.*

Settling into this safe, secure spot, focus on your breathing. Place your closed hands over your chest. Notice breath. Soften belly. Open heart. As you sense or imagine your heart opening, extend your arms outward, unfolding your hands, like flowers blooming, until they come to rest comfortably at your sides. Notice breath. Soften belly. Open heart. With each inhalation, breathe in the fullness of life. With each exhalation, release any tension, relaxing more completely. Breathe in. Release. Focus inward and call to your Inner Shaman, your inner wisdom: "My heart is open to you. Be with me on this journey."

Sense yourself moving closer to your Inner Shaman. Feel your anticipation. You are very close now. You can sense your Inner Shaman's presence. When your Inner Shaman appears, take a deep breath. Make a gesture of greeting. Savor the presence of this wise inner friend. Your Inner Shaman is aware of all of your self-defeating beliefs and behavior patterns. At their core is a central issue that would be particularly valuable to focus on in the program. Listen as your Inner Shaman identifies for you an area you might want to spotlight for special attention. Take a few moments now to discuss this area of focus with your Inner Shaman. It is time now to bid your Inner Shaman good-bye. With a gesture of farewell, begin to return to your ordinary waking consciousness.

You will be able to remember all you need of this experience. Very gently, begin to rouse yourself. Move your fingers and toes, your hands and feet. Feel your circulation. Stretch your shoulders, your arms and legs, your neck and face muscles. Take a deep breath. Bring your attention back into the room. Open your eyes, refreshed, as if waking from a wonderful nap, alert and fully competent to creatively meet the requirements of your day.

In your journal, describe this journey to your Inner Shaman and specify the area or areas of conflict that were discussed. Ann wrote:

At first I couldn't focus on any one thing. It seemed like a swimming of energies that imploded on one another. I asked my Inner Shaman to help me focus. Finally I was given the words that at the heart of my conflict is an inability to stay steady with what is right for me. I asked: "What is the central issue keeping me from staying steady?" She answered, "It is a question of self-worth. You relate your self-worth to the responses and well-being of others. When they are happy, you feel worthy. When they are unhappy, you feel unworthy. All of your energy therefore is focused on their feelings rather than your own. Energetically, you have to pull back and keep your own life force in your own body so you can act on what you know to be right for you."

Whether or not this visit to your Inner Shaman was successful in helping you identify a core area of conflict, you will be approaching the issue from a different angle with this next ritual. You will be guided back in time to an early experience that is related to current difficulties in your life. By connecting present feelings to past experiences, not only will you be further identifying areas of conflict in your mythology, you will also be examining possible sources of that conflict.

PURPOSE: *To discover the relationship between the mythic conflict you have been examining and events from your childhood*

Old myths that are in conflict with your needs, with your potentials, or with more effective guiding myths often have their roots in early attempts to compensate for traumatic, humiliating, or other painful childhood events. People often follow the guidance of an old and dysfunctional myth, even though it limits and hurts them, in order to uphold an unconscious covenant that the myth will protect them from feeling the pain of early emotional wounds. "If I push myself hard enough, then I will be seen as worthy." Exploring the emotional roots of inner conflict is a step toward resolving the conflict and the conflicting myths that maintain it.

PREPARATION: *With this ritual, you will immerse yourself in your feelings around a current area of conflict and then move back in time to an experience from earlier in your life. Begin by finding a setting in which you can become deeply relaxed. You are likely to come to an early loss, deep disappointment, or other trauma whose scars have not been entirely healed. Keep your Personal Shield nearby for support and protection. Sitting or reclining, take a deep breath, and close your eyes.*

Settling into this safe, secure spot, focus on your breathing. Place your closed hands over your chest. Notice breath. Soften belly. Open heart. As you sense or imagine your heart opening, extend your arms outward, unfolding your hands, like flowers blooming, until they come to rest comfortably at your sides. Notice breath. Soften belly. Open heart. With each inhalation, breathe in the fullness of life. With each exhalation, release any tension, relaxing more completely. Breathe in. Release. Focus inward and call to your Inner Shaman, your inner wisdom: "My heart is open to you. Be with me on this journey."

You will be focusing now on a single area of inner conflict. Perhaps your Inner Shaman identified it for you in the previous ritual. Perhaps it is one of the conflicts you listed in your Conflict Survey or one revealed when you requested a dream that shows you an area of your personal mythology that is inviting your attention. If none of these has yielded a conflict that seems appropriate for your focus, simply reflect now on aspects of your life that are not working well for you: self-defeating behaviors, areas of irrational feelings, persistent confusion or frustration. With your next several breaths, allow a single focus, a single area of conflict—internal or external—to emerge and become clear to you.

As you think about this conflict, notice the feelings the conflict evokes in your body. Identify the part of your body in which you experience the feeling most fully. If the feeling is vague, imagine yourself breathing into it and intensifying it. If the feeling is so strong that it is distracting, imagine that your next few exhalations are breathing out some of the excess intensity. Trace with your fingertips or in your mind's eye the area of your body activated most strongly by this feeling.

As this feeling absorbs your attention, further observe the way your body reacts to it. Experience the feeling through your breathing, muscle tension, and temperature. Find a word that describes the feeling.

You will be using this feeling to lead you back to an earlier period of your life, to one of the first times you had this feeling or one like it. Notice the flow of sensations that make up the feeling. Imagine that these sensations form a bridge that can carry you back into your past. As you step onto this bridge, the passageway to your childhood is clear, and you can follow the feeling back to an early memory. You are safe and comfortable as you move over the bridge. Crossing the bridge back in time, you come to a scene from your childhood. The scene becomes more clear and vivid with each of your next three breaths.

If you have not yet come upon a scene, relax. Take another deep breath as you allow the scene to emerge. It may reveal itself in pictures, word descriptions, or simply a "knowing." If a scene doesn't spontaneously come to you in the next few moments, make one up in your imagination.

In this scene, you are seeing out of the young eyes and hearing through the young ears of a child. As the scene becomes more vivid, sense your age. Notice who, if anyone, is with you. Where your memory does not offer answers, allow your imagination to fill in the gaps. Picture or sense what you look like at this age. Notice the setting. Recall what you are wearing. Focus now on the events that brought about the feeling. Recall or imagine as many details—sights, sounds, tastes, smells—of this earlier time as you can.

Reflect on some of the decisions you might have made as a result of this experience and others like it. What conclusions did you come to about yourself? What rules or codes of conduct did you adopt? What attitudes toward other people began to emerge? What views of the world? What philosophy of life? Summarize this philosophy of life as a single statement, such as "If I do what I am told, I will be safe" or "No matter what I do, I am in danger and must protect myself."

Imagine now that you, at your current age, have gone back in time to visit this younger version of yourself. As an adult, you enter the scene. Approach the child and sensitively make contact. Provide the comfort or affection you needed back then, when you were so young and uncertain. In addition to comfort and affection, you have some advice and information about the path that lies ahead. Allow a conversation to develop between your current self and this younger self.

Now gently place your adult hands on the child and lovingly send peaceful, healing energy and support to the small body. A healing of old emotional wounds left over from this period can begin to occur. Savor it.

It is time to say good-bye to this younger self for now. You will be visiting your inner child of the past in subsequent personal rituals. For now, allow a spontaneous embrace. Take a few last moments together and then say good-bye. It is nearly time to return to ordinary waking consciousness. Begin by coming back now across the bridge, toward the present moment.

Prepare to return to your ordinary waking consciousness. You will be able to remember all you need of this experience. Very gently, begin to rouse yourself. Move your fingers and your toes, your hands and your feet. Feel your circulation. Stretch your shoulders, your arms and legs, your neck and face muscles. Take a deep breath. Bring your attention back into the room. Open your eyes, refreshed, as if waking from a wonderful nap, alert and fully competent to creatively meet the requirements of your day.

We have found this journey to your past (adapted from a hypnosis technique called the *affect bridge*[10]) an effective way for connecting current difficulties with early experiences. From these connections, you can focus on the decisions that shaped a guiding myth. People quite reliably go back to a time when they were forming attitudes, values, and codes of conduct that are now causing conflict. The memory that emerges in this ritual usually played an actual role in creating a myth that has become outdated, or at least symbolizes a set of experiences that were involved in the formation of that myth.

If this was not the case for you, we invite you to repeat the procedure. Regardless of how often you use it, the affect bridge can continue to be a potent tool for uncovering the mythic roots of psychological conflict. Again, keep in mind that if the experience brought up issues you are not ready to work with, you can use your Personal Shield to contain those issues until you are ready to work with them, or you can draw from other strategies as discussed in Support Guide 3. After her journey back in time, Ann wrote:

> The feeling I started with is a panic that someone will die if I don't give them what they need. I went back to the farm in Africa. I feel the discomfort of driving by in the truck, with the black men and women having to walk. I know that our house is so big compared to the huts of the farm workers. I can feel that just by being born white I receive privileges that I have not earned through merit. I feel anxious and somehow endangered. I feel bad about my good fortune. I feel ashamed and unworthy of the gift. The way things are does not seem to bother others. This makes me very nervous.
>
> I'm with my mother in the bedroom. I must be six or seven. Thinking my mother will protect me and get rid of the governess, I've finally gotten the courage to tell her that the governess has been beating me and stuffing my head in the toilet. But she says, "Nonsense, darling, you must be imagining it. Just go and apologize to her and everything will be fine." I feel totally unprotected and shattered. I don't know who to trust.

Once you have described your journey back in time, identify the decisions you made, the conclusions you came to about yourself and your world, and the attitudes, codes of conduct, rules of behavior, and beliefs you adopted as a result of this experience. Ann wrote:

> Decisions (made as a result of my mother's not believing me): The truth doesn't pay off, because no one will listen to it anyway. Telling the truth about something that is difficult or hurtful is not worth the pain of not being heard.
>
> Conclusions: There is no one in the world I can trust. Other people are too self-concerned to care for me. No one and nothing is safe in the world. I must not be worth protecting.

Attitudes: Keeping things pleasant is more important to people around me than facing the truth.

Codes of Conduct: Don't worry about myself, worry about keeping difficult truths from others so they don't get upset or uncomfortable. Suffer my own difficulties alone.

Rules of Behavior: I must try to equalize unfairness. I must not enjoy the fruits of my gifts. I must serve others first, because I have too much.

Beliefs: My gifts have placed me in a position that is higher than others. I should be ashamed of this conceived position of superiority. I must pay penance for my position and my superior thoughts about it.

Then describe the dialogue you carried out between yourself as a child in the scene and your adult self, Ann wrote:

Young Me: But it isn't fair: if I didn't have so much, there would be more to go around.

Older Me: That may be true, but guilt will neither make life more fair nor bring you the wisdom you seek.

Younger Me: I know how to make them feel better about themselves. I must never show that I have more material success, happiness, insight, or opportunities than they do. And with my life I will try to convey to them that they too can somehow have all that I have.

Older Me: You are who you are, and you have been given what you have been given. I will be patient as I watch you over the years painfully learn the flaws in your thinking.

Another participant, Meg, a freelance writer, was fifty-five when she went through the program. Starting with a hypodermic syringe she had drawn on the Paradise Lost section of her Personal Shield, she went back to the following scene and reflections:

I feel very young when I think of the syringe. I remember my mother vomiting and crying out to my poor father for an injection, "Please, Ben, just one shot." She was in withdrawal from morphine that had been medically prescribed. The cycle seemed endless. She would choke herself to unconsciousness with her asthma, be revived with adrenaline, become hyperactive, be brought down with morphine, and instantly become addicted.

I have plenty of feelings for the little kid, cowering in bed, uncomforted, who heard this every month for years. I have even more empathy for the kid who learned to give an injection at age nine. The crowning horror of my childhood was the time I came home from third grade and found my mother, at 3:30 in the afternoon, sprawled across the kitchen table, with her fingers in a cup of cold coffee. I did as I had been instructed, filling the syringe with adrenaline to the 5 cc mark, pressing the plunger carefully to release any air bubbles, and then dealing with her as well as I could remember. That was the hardest part. She was unconscious, and while she was not a large woman, I was only nine.

I pushed her back in the chair and opened her robe. I had never seen my mother's breasts before. When I was instructed on what do in an emergency, they showed me on my own bony chest, demonstrated how to count the ribs and how to find the place beside the sternum to push the needle. They had me practice on a lemon. I found that pushing the needle into her body was infinitely harder than into the lemon—at one point I was afraid that the needle would bend or break. But I did as I had been told. Within a few minutes she revived enough to lie on the couch. Within an hour or so Dad was there, and he called the doctor, who came over to help my mother the best he could.

Later, Dad told me that I had been a "brave little soldier" and had done well. I don't think I ever cried about this incident until I was an adult. I've tried, most of my life, to be a "brave little soldier," not to cry but to take care of business. I also have had an unspoken, nearly unconscious, contempt for people who are chronically ill, seeing them as exploitative and treacherous. I'm basically a squeamish person. I've been able to take care of my kids when they were sick, and able to handle emergencies and birthing situations, but I'm secretly sickened by illness. I've <u>hated</u> myself when I've been ill, associating illness with my mother and her wretched helplessness that (unintentionally, of course) distorted my childhood and my father's life with her constant need for nursing, until she died the month I turned twelve.

I learned that I have to be cool, maintain myself, do that which is repugnant to me in order to justify my existence. I have to perform far beyond what is reasonable to expect from one equipped as I am. But I learned that adopting this behavior could earn genuine heartfelt praise from the most important person on earth—my dad—for my being a "brave little soldier." I didn't know what to do with my panic, but I decided to hide it since it didn't fit the program of being a "brave little soldier."

I have learned that performance justifies existence, and I have reached the conclusion that my own performance is always suspect at best, and hypocritical at worst. I let people think I'm brave, while underneath there is really a scared, inadequate little kid ashamed to admit that she's mad as hell at being put in this position by her parents, by the doctor, and/or by God. It doesn't seem fair, but she can't admit her fears without giving up the pleasure of being seen as a "brave little soldier."

Some part of me believes that everyone can look right in my eye and see that my façade of competence is constructed of words and gestures, not of substance. Another part of me vehemently disagrees because I am, authentically, a capable, goodhearted, decent woman. I see my quest in life as seeking to nurture, but God help anyone who doesn't appreciate and acknowledge my "selfless" giving. If people don't respond to me as a "brave little soldier," I deny them closeness and intimacy.

Meg's "brave little soldier" theme kept her attention on how she was performing in the world at the expense of tenderness and intimacy with those who might recognize her vulnerabilities and lend support. Just as she had helped her mother, she felt compelled to nurture those in need. But inside of her was still an "angry little girl" who wanted to be nurtured and, at the same time, seen as a "brave little soldier."

By identifying an area of your mythology that is no longer serving as an ally and exploring its roots in your personal history, you have reached a landmark in the program. Some people, however, feel discouraged at this point, believing that the negative behavior patterns they have identified are almost impossible to change. If you are feeling that way, remember that you have been giving yourself instructions that *invite* areas of conflict and difficulty to reveal themselves. It is never easy to delve into your own dark side, yet the instructions have been formulated to elicit aspects of your personal mythology that you are ready to deal with productively. The program will support your forward movement. In the process, you are taking an active and courageous step away from a mythology that is suppressing your spirit and toward one that will nourish your inner radiance.

In the next part of the program, you will further crystallize in your awareness the prevailing though outdated myth, the emerging myth that is challenging it, and the conflict that simmers between them. Review your recent dreams for insights they may shed in any of these areas. The following dream incubation suggestion will further prepare you for the work to come.

New Light on Your Mythic Conflict

PURPOSE: *To deepen your understanding of competing mythic forces within you*

Use the same technique as earlier to incubate a dream. With a tape recorder or a journal and pen next to your bed, write in your journal, slowly and mindfully: "I will sleep soundly and peacefully tonight while having a dream that sheds new light on my mythic conflict. When I awake, I will recall my dream." Then, with deliberation, repeat several times before falling asleep, "I will have a meaningful dream, and I will remember it." If you don't recall a dream the first night, repeat the process each night until you do. After recalling a dream, consider using Support Guide 2 to go more deeply into the dream's meaning. Ann reported and reflected on the following dream:

I am in a large house trying to contact a very dear friend of mine. He will not notice me. The rejection is so familiar. The frustration grows until it is almost unbearable. I keep flying over the place where he is, hoping to understand what he needs so that I can give it to him. He continues to spurn my attempts at contact. I am aware that someone is watching me and wanting me to leave. A new person approaches me, sent by two psychiatrists I know. They have suggested that I will probably support their cause. He is selling, for $12.50, a bag of fish food that will be thrown into the ocean to feed the world's fish. He is very excited by the amazing vision of his organization. I think how futile the cause, but it is of such importance to him that I buy a bag.

I prepare to leave the house, when I see my friend. A grief hits me. There must be something I can do to make contact. I swoop down. There is a sense that everything is going on without me. Nobody cares whether I'm there or not. I fly out the window. There is a sense that a chorus of people are watching and cheering me on. I go a short distance and then turn back. I must have overlooked something. I have to try again. Maybe this time I will find the right way to approach him. The dream ends.

The basic dilemma I would like to shed light on is why I so often don't speak from my own center. I am always trying to find the center of the other and to unobtrusively give them not who I am, but what they want. The unspoken contract of some of my most important relationships is, in the extreme, that I do all the reaching while they ignore my need for contact. The person with the fish food seems to be much like me, wanting to feed an impossible number of fish. My giving him money for the fish also reminds me of the way I support causes I know are futile. This dream emphasizes the stupidity and vanity of my desire to save the world. By being so focused on the other's needs, I never allow myself to pursue my own dream.

Second Stage

Understanding Both Sides

of the Conflict

Bringing the Roots

of Mythic Conflict into Focus

The psychological quest for wholeness ends in the union of opposites.

—Jean Shinoda Bolen[1]

A nation's history is subject to continual revision, not only to incorporate newly discovered facts but also to advance new myths. Even the Creation story at the heart of a culture's identity—portraying the beginnings of time and the relationship of the group to the natural world and the cosmos—needs to be revised, sometimes to accommodate the designs of those in power, sometimes to accommodate advances in consciousness.

Many cultural myths are expressed in stories that offer people guidance through spellbinding imagery, moral example, and spiritual truths. Biblical parables, Sufi stories, and other wisdom literature are traditional bearers of mythological insight. An old Hasidic proverb observes: "Give people a fact or an idea and you enlighten their minds; give them a story and you touch their souls."[2]

Discussing how modern men and women have developed the capacity to form identities separate from those prescribed by the tribe or nation, Anthea Francine notes that we must now seek "in the story of our own lives" the spiritual guidance "once found revealed only in the form of myth and fairy tale."[3] Given the diverse roles and elaborate identities that are compulsory in today's complex societies, weaving your memories into a meaningful story about your past is a viable way of discerning the larger story playing itself out in your individual saga. In this chapter you will create the first of a three-part Fairy Tale that will serve as a personal parable for exploring the mythic dimensions of your own history and provide you with cogent guidance into the future.

Richard Gardner, a psychiatrist, has developed an approach that applies the power of storytelling for helping troubled children.[4] He asks a child to tell him a story that has a beginning, a middle, an end, and a moral. As Gardner listens for the psychological themes that run through the story, elements of unresolved conflict are revealed. Gardner, in turn, tells the child a story that also has a beginning, a middle, an end, and a moral. His story is built around the psychological tensions that were portrayed in the child's story. In retelling the story, however, Gardner has the characters find better ways to handle the core conflicts. By speaking to the child at this mythic level, he creates an opportunity for the child to adopt a new personal myth that will be more effective than the one that has been operating.

Gardner describes a story told by Martin, a withdrawn seven-year-old, with a bitter, self-indulgent mother who, while sometimes warm and caring, at other times openly expressed her dislike for her son. Martin's story was about a bear who was trying in vain to get honey from a beehive without being stung. In his response, Gardner's story also featured a bear who craved honey. Gardner's bear knew that bees were sometimes friendly and would give him a little bit of honey, and he also knew that at times they were unfriendly and would sting him. At these times, Gardner's bear would go to another part of the forest, where he could obtain syrup from the maple trees. Gardner's story offered Martin a mythology for acquiring love from his mother without provoking her hostilities, and for discovering alternative sources of affection to compensate for her deficiencies.

Viewing yourself as the hero or heroine in your personal Fairy Tale allows you to peer into your own nature and appreciate more fully the miracle of the human journey as it is manifest in your unique story. In the following ritual, you will represent your personal history as a story. In the process you will be further identifying critical points in the development of your mythology. You will also be anticipating new directions that are emerging, and revisiting times of wounding that you can now comprehend more fully and begin to heal.

PURPOSE: *To create a parable about the early development of your guiding mythology*

You have already worked with many of the raw materials you will be weaving into your Fairy Tale. Part One will be a story about the events symbolized on your Personal Shield, including your very personal Fall from Paradise, the way you dealt with that loss, the vision you adopted of Paradise Regained, and the beginnings of a Quest governed by that vision. Part One of your Fairy Tale may also be patterned after the early rules of conduct and philosophy of life you identified in the previous personal ritual or conflicts that have appeared in your dreams. You might want to pause here and review your Personal Shield and your journal entries describing your dreams and your journey back to the roots of your mythic conflict.

The setting of your Fairy Tale can be an ancient kingdom, a futuristic city, a faraway galaxy, a primitive culture, a period of history, a land of elves and gnomes, a family of deer, chipmunks, chimpanzees, or sea otters, or any other context you choose. Label a page of your journal "Fairy Tale—Part One." Compose Part One of your Fairy Tale using one of the following approaches: Find a comfortable setting and allow the story to emerge in your imagination, tell the story to another person as you are creating it, or dictate it into a tape recorder. Then write the story in your journal. Before you begin, take time to center yourself on the aims of Part One, which are to portray metaphorically (1) an innocent and hopeful time from your childhood; (2) its loss; and (3) the philosophy, beliefs, and rules of conduct you developed in attempting to adjust to that loss. These beliefs and rules may be very similar to those you identified on your journey to the roots of mythic conflict in the previous ritual.

Start with words such as "Once upon a time" and allow the story to unfold. Begin with a main character. The main character will symbolize you, at an earlier time, in a fantasy setting. This hero or heroine is struggling with a problem or conflict similar to one you faced in your childhood. The story will include people and circumstances that contribute to this conflict in the main character's life. And it will end by portraying how this hero or heroine feels the conflict can be solved, and the philosophy, beliefs, and rules of behavior he or she adopts. It is not necessary to rehearse. Let your spontaneity take the story wherever it will go. Editing and interpretation can come later. At this point, do not judge what emerges. You may be surprised by unexpected twists in the plot or new characters who may suddenly appear. Also, be wary of comparing the literary merits of your Fairy Tale with any imagined standards, or even with the following examples. The people whose stories illustrate the personal rituals in this book were chosen in part because they are especially skillful with their use of words. Here is Part One of Ann's Fairy Tale.

In faraway days, in faraway times, there lived a lovely girl. Her eyes were the color of dark mulberries, her voice as clear as mountain streams, her heart as tender and guileless as the wild rose that blooms upon the hill. She did not know it, but before she was born, a Being of Light had visited her and placed within her heart a small round pebble of gold. No one knew it was there, of course, but all could feel its strange glow whenever they were near her.

The girl did not know that the world was different for her from what it was for others. She did not know that long after she was gone, people would remember her and the golden light that had surrounded them while they were in her presence. Because every encounter she experienced was touched with the same glow, she naturally assumed that it was so for everyone else as well. But it was not so. And because she could not imagine wanting anything but joy and fullness for others, she could not imagine that others did not feel the same way toward her. But they did not. Hidden out of sight, where she could not see, there were those who sought to shame her for the light she carried.

One morning, while she was in her garden, tending to her flowers, friends from the village passed by. The girl waved and the pebble in her chest began to glow brightly. But instead of returning her greeting, the villagers pointed and jeered and laughed at her. One of them picked up a stone and threw it, striking her on the cheek. Then the villagers turned and walked away, leaving the girl to stare after them, her mulberry eyes filling with tears, a tiny drop of red blood finding its way down her cheek. For a long time she stood there, not knowing what to do, not knowing what to feel. She stood there all through the afternoon. She stood there as the golden sun went down. She stood there as the night grew dark and the pebble in her chest grew dim.

And so it came to be, as the years went by, that the girl grew more and more unsure of herself. She feared there was something wrong with her that she could not see, but that others could. And so she tried to change herself. But it did not help. She grew more and more ashamed. She grew afraid, and very, very sad. There was something wrong with her. She could feel it. She could feel the weight of it, like a stone inside her chest.

Part One of Ann's Fairy Tale, as you see, is closely related to both her journey back in time and her Personal Shield. It begins in a paradisiacal setting, portrays Paradise Lost in a single incident, and reveals the code of conduct that governed an unsuccessful Quest toward Paradise Regained. Part One of your Fairy Tale will inevitably depict a trauma, betrayal, or other disappointment that darkens the life of the main character, and it will reflect some of the decisions you made to cope with these difficult conditions. Meg reviewed her journey back in time and her Personal Shield before creating this story:

Once upon a time there was an island separated from a continent by a wild strait, impassable by boat or swim stroke. A little girl, Juanita Margaret, lived upon the island. She was busy from dawn to dark with her tasks. Two times a day she went to watch the tides change below the cliffs. She checked the quails' nests for eggs and new chicks. She monitored the polliwogs as they magically became frogs, and she gasped in wonder as the butterfly emerged from the cocoon and unfolded its wings. She spent time gathering sour-grass bouquets and driftwood dragons. She ate loquats and mulberries that grew on the trees, and she gathered seaweed and mussels from the rocks by the sea.

She kept an orphaned ground squirrel, a lame coyote, and a nest of swallows in her cave. The squirrel taught her about seeds, thrift, industry, foresight, and planting. The coyote showed her the value of patience, stealth, and suppleness. From the swallows she learned of delight, nesting, and freedom. At night she slept in a hollow she'd made in the notch of a cliff, facing the sunset, at the edge of the sea. The moon and the storms were her nighttime companions.

Juanita Margaret did not know that she was in exile, a creature to be pitied, remarkable, in an embarrassing way, to the people on the mainland. They were busy, too, in hurrying from this place to that place, talking about property and assets, arranging their clothes and their expressions, actively meeting one another in a continuing process of confrontation, seduction, deception, denial, torment, and illusion. Her wholesomeness offended them.

No one remembered exactly who had put Juanita Margaret on the island, but the truth was that they had been glad to get rid of her. They were uncomfortable when they saw that she would rather climb the cypress tree than try on a new dress. They became upset when they saw that she was loud, demanding, curious, and unhampered. They were annoyed with her coarse, naturalistic behavior. They kept sending her outside to play so that they could read their newspapers and magazines in peace. One morning she climbed into an old boat to play; a storm came up, carried her away, and she was washed ashore on the island. When she never came back, everyone seemed relieved.

One day, a man on the mainland took a telescope and looked at Juanita Margaret's island. He saw how many wonderful fruit trees grew on the island, and how clear the water was on the narrow beaches below the cliffs. He thought, "I could put a resort there and make a million dollars." Before long, engineers studied the strait between the mainland and the island. They put in a bridge and a highway. They took out the loquat and mulberry trees to build the Orchard Motel. They put a single loquat and a lonely mulberry tree into pots in the lobby. They cut stairs into the cliffs and made them as permanent as possible with concrete and steel handrails. The trashcans overflowed.

Some men came and saw Juanita Margaret sitting behind the bushes in the parking lot, eating scrap food from bags thrown out of cars. She didn't go with them willingly at first, but they offered her warm socks and cinnamon rolls, and in the end, she agreed to return to the mainland.

Juanita Margaret went to school, leaving her squirrel, coyote, and swallow friends to save themselves if they could, because she didn't know what else to do. She was just a little girl. Inside, she was furious at the changes that had come into her life, and at the people bossing her around without asking her opinion. Now she had to sleep in a bed, wash in a tub rather than the ocean, speak softly, be respectful, make everyone proud, and live up to her potential. She was told that "some things aren't nice to talk about" and "your temper will be the death of you." The worst insult for a bungled job or sloppy workmanship was to call it "womanish." She was learning the ways of becoming a proper young lady.

Once you have written Part One of your Fairy Tale in your journal (or spoken it and later entered it), reread it. Then reflect on the meanings it holds for you, treating it as a dream and using the creative projection technique or a method called *focusing*[5] to reflect on your most vivid reactions to your story. The essence of focusing is to direct your attention to your bodily reactions about an experience and then begin to obtain a "felt sense" about their meaning. Ask yourself what name you would give to the bodily reaction, whether the bodily reaction reminds you of a past experience, and what you might learn from the "felt sense." You might want to repeat the procedure to be sure you obtain the same results and answers. If you feel a tension release in your body, you know that you have gleaned important information about your "felt sense." Ann used the focusing technique on her reactions to the incident in which the girl in her Fairy Tale was hit in the cheek with the stone.

> The feeling I carry in my body is "shock." Something in me has been paralyzed. Something cannot move. I am shocked. I am immobilized by the tragedy of the human dilemma, the choices we make, the cruelty and violence, the loneliness, the lost confusion that cannot find its way home. I am overwhelmed by the immensity of it. I am in a state of shock, and I have been here for a long, long time. I am afraid something is terribly wrong with me.

Meg used the focusing technique to explore her reactions to several aspects of her story. When she examined her bodily response to the way Juanita Margaret was pitied, in exile, and embarrassing to the people on the mainland, she wrote:

> My face feels flushed, exposing my sense of inadequacy. My eyes want to look defiant or challenging. I feel resentment in my mouth: tight lips, set jaw, controlled breathing. I can identify a smugness too, a sort of superiority. I sense these feelings in my upper lip, with a kind of a sneer pulling at my face.
>
> I have always resented, intensely, any hint of mockery or patronizing. I am very quick to jump to the conclusion that I am being made fun of, and I am ruthless in defending myself. I've always had a tendency to create scapegoats, to generalize, and to reject anyone or any group whom I saw as having the wherewithal to put me down. I've been absolutely unwilling to be vulnerable to such groups. I've been a dismal failure whenever circumstances have put me into positions where it would have been politic for me to ask permission, give unwarranted strokes, belittle myself, or conform to stupid bureaucratic rules, protocols, and standards.

When Meg considered the way Juanita Margaret was always being "sent outside to play" because she was loud, curious, and unhampered, she noticed:

My stomach is tense, not upset, but muscularly tight. My breathing is conscious, controlled, and slow. I feel rock hard and immovable, rigid, unyielding, and violent in my determination to hold my ground. I feel an "I won't" in my neck, jaw, and eyes.

I never learned to give in gracefully. I've fantasized murder, vandalism, and mutilations. I've collapsed. I've gone down fighting. I've slammed doors. I've nearly suicided. I have learned how to say "I'm sorry" sincerely, but not how to back down from a stand I see as one of principle. I can compromise and be a team player or partner as long as I don't feel put down or asked to yield a principle. I've been hypersensitive to insult, expecting it and soliciting it. What a distasteful realization! What a losing way of doing business!

We see from these comments, and from the first segment of her Fairy Tale, that Meg is on a highly individualistic journey. In the original vision of Paradise portrayed in her Fairy Tale, she had been alone (and she was, indeed, an only child). You will see when we get to Part Two of her Fairy Tale that her vision of returning to Paradise Regained is also an isolated journey. While she does want to nurture and love, it must be on her own terms. Her alter ego, Juanita Margaret, did quite well when she could nurse wounded animals and homeless birds. When placed in a social context, however, she scavenges food from the hotel trashcans and meanders through life without peers, playmates, or friends. Once off her island, there is a rebelliousness in Juanita Margaret that seems dissonant with the "earth child" who had befriended the creatures of nature.

When you reflect on Part One of your Fairy Tale, or on your work with any of the other personal rituals, we encourage you to begin by focusing on your strongest feelings about the experience and taking cues from your bodily responses.

SESSION 2: Healing an Ancient Wound

PURPOSE: *To tend to an emotional wound that may be keeping you entangled in a dysfunctional personal myth*

The Paradise Lost symbol on your Personal Shield, your journey back to the roots of your mythic conflict, and Part One of your Fairy Tale may each have brought emotional wounds to the surface that will now be responsive to healing. Certain dreams also provide a window on such wounds and can spontaneously initiate a healing process. Once you have recognized unresolved emotional trauma, you can direct your energies toward healing it. Although the healing process may require a substantial period of time, consciously setting the process in motion can bring an immediate sense of peace, freeing energy and creativity for transforming limiting myths borne of the wound.

Stuart, a farmer whose amateur photography had been exhibited in prestigious galleries, had lost both of his parents during his early adolescence. He unconsciously, and sometimes all too consciously, was haunted by a personal myth that he too was destined to die before his children were fully grown. The untimely deaths of his parents topped a long string of traumatic childhood experiences, and imagining his own early death somehow helped him live with death's uncertainty and his unresolved grief. If he knew he would die young, he did not have to worry about when death would come. But once he had children of his own, he bargained with God to allow him to see them reach maturity. Then he would willingly die whenever fate decreed. As his children approached the age that he had been when his parents died, however, he began to feel terrified about having made this pact. Although only in his midforties and newly remarried to a woman who wanted to have a child with him, he felt that having another child just as the term of his bargain was coming to a close would be a show of arrogance and an irrefutable invitation to death before the child was grown. He could not think himself out of this fear.

Changing a myth of this magnitude, so deeply embedded in your identity and sense of the future, can be facilitated by what therapists speak of as "working through" emotional wounds that are yet unhealed. The following ritual will help you identify an area from your past that is ready for further working through, and it will get you started in the process. Stuart, for instance, needed not only to work through the upheaval caused by his parents' deaths but also to attend to the other traumas from his childhood, which included physical and sexual abuse. Psychologically working through wounds from your past can lead to a healing that opens the way to planned as well as spontaneous transformations in your mythology. If the pattern seems intractable or the pain overwhelming, outside support is often wise. Stuart entered psychotherapy as he began to sense the raw emotional wounding on which so much of his guiding mythology was built. Announcing to his wife that he would like to have a child with her was a milestone in the transformation of that mythology.

Even without outside interventions, your psyche is continually dealing with and attempting to heal old wounds that are interfering with your current functioning. Emotional wounds that have not been worked through have an energetic pull. They tend to distort perceptions, particularly in situations that feel similar to the circumstances that caused the initial wounding. They may lead you to focus more on the dangers, to miss the opportunities, and to be weighed down by the emotional load you are carrying from the wound. Unhealed wounds also tend to inhibit you from taking further emotional risks in the areas of the wounding.

Abandoning a familiar though failing myth for an untried though promising emerging myth is almost always an emotional risk. But emotional wounds can point the way toward spiritual renewal. Jean Houston notes that while "suffering cracks the boundaries of what you thought you could bear," it also may contain the seeds of healing and transformation. This truth has long been recognized. Houston goes on to say that "in the Greek tragedies, the gods force themselves into human consciousness" when the soul has been wounded, and it is "only at this time of wounding that the protagonist grows into a larger sense of what life is all about and is able to act accordingly." The soul's development involves a recurring "wounding of the psyche by the Larger Story."[6] Because life had been organized around the old story, the wounding of the psyche by the Larger Story is a crisis of immense proportion. But if you cannot open yourself to this larger reality, you are doomed to repeat the same old story continually. As Houston affirms, the wounding "becomes *sacred* when we are willing to release our old stories and to become the vehicles through which the new story may emerge into time."[7]

In this ritual, you will identify an emotional wound from your past that is interfering with the resolution of your mythic conflict, and you will be consciously initiating a process of emotional healing. Before beginning the ritual, reflect on this question: Is there an aspect of your old myth that you believe will be difficult to change although its shortcomings are evident? Ann wrote:

> I have to own that I am one of the very blessed. I have been given ten talents. I have gifts that make my life easier and more filled with possibility than most people will ever know. I've spent my life trying to make the world more fair by making myself smaller. If I'm not willing to let this smallness go, I will never allow myself the opportunity to actually see if I could do something beautiful with the light I have within.
>
> The part of the old myth that is so hard to give up is the fear that if I

stepped into my fullness, I would find myself totally alone. What if I get trapped in snares of vanity and lose my compassion? What if my power is not true power at all but grandiose illusions and I become off balance and ungrounded? What if I get lost and cannot find my way home?

PREPARATION: *After reflecting on aspects of your old myth you believe will be difficult to change, describe your observations in your journal. The ritual will begin with a focus on circumstances in which an important wounding occurred. Don't be concerned at this point with whether the difficulties you identified seem related to your wound.*

You will need a pillow for this ritual. Once you have one, find a setting in which you can become deeply relaxed. Again, keep your Personal Shield nearby for support and protection. Sitting or reclining and holding your pillow, take a deep breath, and close your eyes.

Settling into this safe, secure spot, focus on your breathing. Place your closed hands over your chest. Notice breath. Soften belly. Open heart. As you sense or imagine your heart opening, extend your arms outward, unfolding your hands, like flowers blooming, until they come to rest comfortably at your sides. Notice breath. Soften belly. Open heart. With each inhalation, breathe in the fullness of life. With each exhalation, release any tension, relaxing more completely. Breathe in. Release. Focus inward and call to your Inner Shaman, your inner wisdom: "My heart is open to you. Be with me on this journey."

Review in your mind Part One of your Fairy Tale and the personal experiences that your Fairy Tale represents. In those experiences, you suffered a wound to your heart or to your dignity or to your sense of well-being. Breathing deeply, sense where that wound lives in your body.

Take the pillow and hold it close to you, positioning it so it is in contact with your wound. Feel the changing sensations in your wound as you give it this attention. Imagine that this pillow now becomes your younger self, the self who experienced this wounding. Hug the pillow and comfort it.

Still holding this younger self, represented by your pillow, imagine that your Inner Shaman is concerned about your suffering and has come out of the depths to help you. Your Inner Shaman makes contact with you, placing one radiant, healing hand directly on your younger self, where the pain is greatest, and the other hand on the part of your body that holds the wound. Your Inner Shaman channels the healing forces of the universe directly into the wound. Feel a soothing warmth entering your body as your Inner Shaman's breathing keeps a perfect rhythm with your own. With each inhalation, a fresh charge of healing light enters your body. With each exhalation, you release the stale, the old, the residue, as your wound begins to respond to the healing light. Remain aware of the hands over your wound as the healing process continues.

Now your Inner Shaman has some counsel for you. Listen as you are told how to protect yourself better and avoid reinjuring your wound. Once more, your Inner Shaman lays a hand over your younger self's wound, giving you both another dose of this creative healing power. If you have any questions, ask them now, and listen for your Inner Shaman's answers. When you are ready, tell your Inner Shaman good-bye.

Bring your attention to the pillow you have been holding, and give affection and courage to your younger self. Tenderly comfort this younger self with your touch and presence. Give your thoughts and kindness generously to turn hurt into useful experience. Be the adult you would have liked to have there for you.

Shower this younger version of yourself with all the love you have. You may want to hug tightly. You may find yourselves crying together. As you continue this embrace, feel your younger self merging back into you, returning into your present body and mind. Be aware of the ways healing has taken place, and also feel the gifts your younger self brought to you—innocence, enthusiasm, creativity, anticipation. You have given your younger self the best advice and love you could offer. As this younger self reintegrates into your being, feel how the healing that has taken place refreshes you.

With your next deep breath, come fully into your current age, fully into the present moment. Notice whether your sensations have changed. You may repeat this healing ritual, or any part of it, as many times as you like. Make a commitment to yourself to check in periodically on this younger part of yourself and this early wound, so that you may provide all the healing energy they need.

Prepare to return to your ordinary waking consciousness. You will be able to remember all you need of this experience. Very gently, begin to rouse yourself. Move your fingers and toes, your hands and feet. Feel your circulation. Stretch your shoulders, your arms and legs, your neck and face muscles. Take a deep breath. Bring your attention back into the room. Open your eyes, refreshed, as if waking from a wonderful nap, alert and fully competent to creatively meet the requirements of your day.

Summarize this experience in your journal, and reflect on its meaning. Ann wrote:

The place in my body carrying the deep wound that caused the loss of Paradise is the same place through which I entered the world of the Inner Shaman. As the Inner Shaman came forward, she made it clear to me that it was my wound that was leading me to my power and wisdom. As she placed her hand on my heart for healing, she split into two women. She said to me that the Madonna-like part of herself was the part that had always been openly active and available in me, but that the tenderness of unconditional love is dangerous unless it is united with the other aspect of herself, the truth of the Dark Discerner.

It became clear to me that healing was not the ability to be rid of the wound, but the ability to include it, be tempered by it, and move forward having distilled the gift it had to bring. As I held myself as a young girl, I saw that her gift to me was the gentle sweetness and compassion of the Madonna, and that the gift that I, as a woman, had been cultivating for her was the strength and power of the Dark Discerner.

You may extend this ritual in several ways. You may repeat it as often as you wish or invent variations. Sometimes the process brings other difficult memories to mind, and you may carry out these same instructions to attend to whatever wounds are associated with those events.

If, however, this experience opens old wounds that continue to plague you even after you have completed the ritual and reflected on it in your journal, refer to the section toward the end of Week 2 that describes how to use your Personal Shield to protect yourself. Use that technique or any of the other suggestions provided in Support Guide 3 to work with the emotions you have uncovered.

PURPOSE: *To initiate a bereavement process that emotionally and symbolically releases you from an outdated personal myth*

With your Personal Shield, your journey back in time, and Part One of your Fairy Tale, you explored modes of thought and rules of behavior that are no longer serving you. Nonetheless, we all have an emotional bond to the past and to our earliest dreams and ways of being—our earliest attempts to make sense of the world and solve the problems it presented. To move on creatively to new solutions and new ways of being requires a degree of separation from the emotional chains that bind you to old patterns. Through this ritual, you will sever

SESSION 3:

Saying Good-bye to an Antiquated Myth

such an emotional tie to a dysfunctional pattern rooted in your past, draining out the emotion as if from an abscess.

This ritual for separating from your old myth is patterned after a potent five-part ritual developed by Peg Elliott Mayo for working with people who are in bereavement:[8]

1. The bereavement ritual begins by having the person in mourning imagine that the person who has been lost is in a chair that faces the bereaved. The departed one is made real by conjuring the person's feel, smell, look, and sound. The bereaved person then addresses the departed one with a series of statements that begin, "I remember." For example, "Ted, I remember when you proposed to me." "Ted, I remember when the car nearly swerved off the road." "Ted, I remember when you took me ice skating."

2. The bereaved person next dredges through past angers, disappointments, and other difficult feelings. A series of statements is made, each beginning with the words "I resent." "Ted, I resent the way you were always late when we would go out." "Ted, I resent that you gave me so little credit for all I did for you."

3. The bereaved person next addresses to the departed one a series of statements that begin with the words "I appreciate." "Ted, I appreciate all the flowers you brought me when I was sick." "Ted, I appreciate how you would carry more than your weight in supporting the family financially without making me feel guilty." (Steps 2 and 3 are sometimes reversed, depending on the feelings that emerge during the first step, "I remember.")

4. The bereaved person then creates a benediction, a eulogy that identifies enduring gifts from the relationship that he or she wants to affirm and retain. "Ted, I take with me the love you gave me." "Ted, I take with me all you taught me about computers and about the habits of the birds around our house."

5. The final step is to say "good-bye"; remember that the word is a contraction from Old English, meaning "God be with ye." The bereaved person is asked, "Are you ready to release [the departed person's name]?" If so, the bereaved is told to give the departed a blessing, with an explanation that the process is an affirmation, not an abandonment. Then the bereaved is told to let the image fade.

We have adapted this bereavement ritual to help people move beyond an old myth. Even when the old myth is clearly dysfunctional, separating oneself from it often arouses feelings of loss and grief. Using this ritual treats the old myth like a living entity, which, in a way, it is. Putting the old to rest leaves room for the new to emerge. Before you go through the ritual, consider Ann's experience. Ann wrote of her old myth: "I am saying good-bye to being incapable of speaking on my own behalf and being compelled to give others whatever I sense they might need." In the ritual, she spoke directly to her old myth:

I REMEMBER feeling unheard. I remember feeling alone and unprotected. I remember having twelve cats when I only wanted one. I remember not having enough moments in a day to give myself even a bath because of caring for the needs of others. I remember when I pitched a tent in my backyard because I had so many guests there was no room for me. I remember allowing a partner to treat me as if I were absolutely inconsequential.

I REGRET how much of my life I have given away to serve others who didn't particularly appreciate it. I resent how my health and well-being have suffered by my not taking care of myself. I resent how much money I have given away to support people who had no intention of using it for their highest purpose, even though that was my understanding of the bargain. I resent how I haven't stood up for myself and have allowed people to walk over me.

I APPRECIATE the kindness and compassion you developed in me. I appreciate the independence you have strengthened in me. I appreciate the deep intuitive knowledge that came to me by being able to anticipate the needs and feelings of others. I appreciate the quality of personality that has made me accessible to others.

I TAKE WITH ME my compassion for the loneliness of others. I take with me my independence. I take with me my ability to read people's needs. I take with me my concern for others.

GOOD-BYE: I sense my attachment to the old myth as cords that connect me to many, many people, fanning out from my chest and tying me to the lives of hundreds of people. I can feel them stretching like elastic that is getting thinner and thinner as I move away from the people, so I don't have to care for them in that compulsive way. I also see several cords that are much larger, going to people who have been key in my life, also stretching, like I am drifting away and they are drifting back, leaving more space between us. I can feel that the cords are not even going to have to be cut; they will just dissolve. It feels like I am calling out my good-bye over a long distance. It feels timely and it feels right.

PREPARATION: *Survey your Personal Shield, your journey to the past, and Part One of your Fairy Tale. Be alert for a problematic pattern of beliefs or behavior, and the old myth that supports it, from which you feel a need to separate. In addition to choosing the area of your guiding mythology you will focus on in this ritual, you will need your pillow from the previous ritual. Keep in mind that some of the instructions here will ask you to personify and speak to your old myth.*

When you are ready, stand and pick up the pillow. In the previous ritual, the pillow represented you at an earlier age, a time of wounding. In that wound were the seeds of your old myth. Now the pillow comes to represent the spirit of your old myth. Hold the pillow so you can face it and speak with it. Imagine yourself transferring the energy of your old myth into the pillow. Place the feelings, the thoughts, and the patterns of behavior you associate with the old myth in the pillow. Begin a series of statements with the words "I remember." For example, "I remember when I was six and I wanted so desperately to get my father's approval, and I remember how just yesterday I was still groveling for my wife's approval." Feel each memory in your body. Let it touch you. Feel free to walk around the room as you carry out these instructions. Begin now, "I remember . . ." (If you are reading these instructions into a tape, add, "Turn off the tape and take all the time you need.")

Now begin to tune in to the resentments and regrets that have built up on the basis of experiences associated with this old myth. Your "I remembers" have probably already put you in touch with old hurts, resentments, and regrets. Form these feelings into sentences beginning with "I resent" or "I regret." For example: "I resent your humiliating hold on me." "I regret all the energy I've wasted trying to get approval." State all the resentments and regrets that come to you. Repeat those which are particularly strong, using the tone and volume of your voice to release the resentments and regrets entwined with your old myth. Begin now, "I resent . . ." or "I regret . . ." (If you are reading these instructions into a tape, add, "Turn off the tape and take all the time you need.")

Next are acknowledgments of ways your old myth strengthened you or made you wiser or provided you with experiences you value. These statements begin with "I appreciate." For example: "I appreciate all the good times I've had because you taught me how to tune in to what other people are feeling." "I appreciate that I finally did get some positive attention from Dad because of you." Deeply recognize how your old myth was an attempt to serve you, to deliver something you needed. Also appreciate your own creativity, long ago, in devising this solution to face the dilemmas of your childhood. Begin now, "I appreciate . . ." (If you are reading these instructions into a tape, add, "Turn off the tape and take all the time you need.")

Now deliver a benediction for this strategy from your past, from which you are about to disengage consciously. Emphasize what you wish to take with you even after you leave the old myth behind, beginning a series of statements with "I take with me." For example: "I take with me my ability to read other people well." "I take with me Dad's affection." Begin now, "I take with me . . ." (If you are reading these instructions into a tape, add, "Turn off the tape and take all the time you need.")

The final part of the ritual is to say good-bye and to release yourself from your old myth. You will still be able to keep the memories, learnings, and abilities it brought to you, but you are emotionally clearing the way to open yourself to new mythic guidance. Find the place in your body that you feel most strongly connected to the pillow and the old myth it represents. Visualize or sense the nature of the connection—it may be like a tube, a light, or a cord. Consider how you can best release yourself from it—cutting it, untying it, stretching it, letting it fade. You may not be ready at this point to fully release yourself from it, and you may repeat this part of the ritual another time or several more times. For now, visualize and sense the connection between yourself and your old myth diminishing as much as possible. When it has, say good-bye and mindfully release the pillow.

Take some quiet time to reflect. Use your journal. Go on a walk. Listen to music.

PURPOSE: *To invite your deep unconscious to offer a symbol or insight into a new direction in your guiding mythology*

Review and reflect on the Paradise Regained image on your Personal Shield. You will be asking for a dream that shows you how things might become. It need not be realistic; it might be only an imaginative glimpse into a more satisfying future. Using the familiar technique for incubating a dream, with a tape recorder or a journal and pen next to your bed, write in your journal, slowly and mindfully: "I will sleep soundly and peacefully tonight while having a dream that reveals a renewed image of Paradise Regained. When I awake, I will recall my dream." Then, with deliberation, repeat several times before falling asleep, "I will have a meaningful dream, and I will remember it." You may also hold in your mind the Paradise Regained symbol from your Personal Shield or another positively charged image as you are repeating the statement. If you don't recall a dream the first night, repeat the process each night. Remember, also, that morning thoughts and feelings, or daydreams, may provide insight on the issue. After recording a dream, you may want to refer to Support Guide 2 to go more deeply into the dream's meaning. Ann reported and reflected on the following dream:

> I am with my parents in South Africa and we have just moved into a summer cottage by the sea. It is very small and beautiful. I am standing on the veranda when they call for me. As I enter the house I notice dust and bits of sawdust falling from the rafters above. My mother says, "How disgusting. Rats. We must get some traps." I say to her, "There's no need to hurt them. I have a sonic instrument that gives off a frequency that you won't be able to hear, but that rats dislike. I'll place it in your cottage and they will leave peacefully."
>
> I look out through the window and notice another cottage. I realize that it is to be mine, and I am thrilled to have such a wonderful place for myself. I leave my parents' cottage and walk toward it. It is so beautiful among the grass and trees, and the view that leads down to the sea is so inviting that I think to myself, "Perhaps I don't need a cottage at all. The sky is so big, I just may sleep out of doors and under the moon all summer long."
>
> To my parents' cottage, I associate Paradise Lost. I have never wanted to see the dysfunction and abuse in my family, I didn't want to see that there were "rats" destroying the structure and stability of the "house." I said, in effect, "Let's not kill the rats, let's find a gentle (albeit ineffective) way to deal with this problem." It is interesting that I chose a sonic device because that's where I hid out, my music. The sense of not even needing shelter, of being innocent in the world, able to trust the elements, able to trust the natural way of things, even if the cottage was beautiful, is an image of Paradise Regained that excites me.

Contacting Resources for

Mythic Renewal

Psyche is moving at remarkable speeds past the limits most of us
have lived with for thousands of years into an utterly different state
of being.

—Jean Houston[1]

The Greek sea god Proteus was capable of changing shape in response to
crisis. Robert Jay Lifton, the psychiatrist who has painted chillingly realistic portraits of both human evil and courage in studies based on in-
depth interviews with Nazi doctors, Hiroshima survivors, Vietnam veterans, and
political and military prisoners who have been subjected to systematic torture
and brainwashing, uses the Proteus myth to describe human adaptability in response to crisis.[2] After a long and unflinching look into the jaws of human de-
structiveness, Lifton concludes that people possess an innate faculty, a "protean
self"—capable, like Proteus, of assuming varied shapes, forms, and purposes at
will—that is highly resilient and creative, particularly in the face of challenge
and peril.

World conditions have been calling to this capacity as never before. As Lifton
asserts, "Without quite realizing it, we have been evolving a sense of self appropriate to the restlessness and flux of our time." While all of us, as individuals,
groups, and nations, have been "schooled in the virtues of constancy and stabil-

ity," our world and our lives have become inconstant and unpredictable. As a result, we view ourselves as "unsteady, neurotic, or worse." But this assessment is in relation to an older version of personal identity, where inner stability was derived from robust traditions and a relatively intact relationship with the symbols and institutions of a culture.[3]

This older sense of identity has become antiquated in the face of three historical forces[4] that evoke our protean potential: the threat of human extinction, the mass media revolution, and the breakdown of the social arrangements that ordinarily anchor human lives, such as stable marriages and reliable career ladders. The social turmoil, the massive threats to our collective survival, and the bombardment of media images that unrelentingly reflect to us these hazards have led to a dangerous fragmentation of the self. For example, a person might conclude that "with all the pressures and problems of contemporary life, it is impossible to maintain a stable relationship, so why even try?" Or, "I am so confused that I don't know what I really believe." Ironically, such challenges can also lead to a renewed self-identity. The complexities involved in marriage, interpersonal relationships, and careers demand that we give serious attention to our values and priorities. Lifton describes the ability of the self to transform experience symbolically—to continuously receive, re-create, and extend all it encounters— as "the great human evolutionary achievement."[5]

With the development of a protean capacity in the self, ideas and systems of ideas can now be embraced, transformed, dismissed, and reembraced "with a new ease that stands in sharp contrast to the inner struggle people in the past endured with such shifts."[6] Lifton believes that this protean capacity to deal with new levels of complexity and ambiguity represents a leap forward in the evolution of the self. Your personal mythology is more protean than that of any generation past, more capable of changing its shape. Yet your mythology evolves according to a surprisingly straightforward logic. A long-standing myth is challenged by an emerging myth. Both myths pull on you simultaneously. You unconsciously and sometimes consciously attempt to resolve the conflict between them. The stakes are high. The conflict can leave you divided against yourself or lead you into greater breadth, wisdom, and compassion.

How do new mythic images arise? As always, dreams provide a glimpse into the deepest workings of the psyche. In wish-fulfillment dreams, the impulse toward pleasure and immediate gratification dominates. As a new myth emerges, it tends to appear first in a raw form that seeks immediate satisfactions, directing you to meet needs, fulfill desires, and reach toward possibilities where the old myth has been ineffective. As with wish-fulfillment dreams, however, the early guidance of a new myth is usually not well attuned to the requirements of the real world.

We refer to such emerging structures as counter-myths, since they are often based on experiences that represent a counterpoint to the existing mythology. The first flights of a fledgling counter-myth will probably be tested outside your awareness. As its struggle with the old myth intensifies in your psychological underworld, the counter-myth begins to break into consciousness, often through dreams, fantasies, unfamiliar impulses, novel ideas, or the emergence of an unfamiliar quality in your personality. A hazard of becoming aware of your counter-myth is that the counter-myth may seem so appealing that you are drawn to abandon uncritically the old myth and organize your life around it. Such leaps often meet with failure and discouragement, and when they do, they may have the paradoxical effect of strengthening the old myth. Over time, as you begin to experiment with the counter-myth's guidance, it will become tempered by reflection and real-world experience. This ability to form, test, and refine counter-myths is a measure of your protean capacity.

SESSION 1:
Finding the Roots of Mythic Renewal in Your Past

PURPOSE: *To contact a childhood experience that provides a prototype for a constructive counter-myth*

The ghosts of your old myth raise their heads in a fury when they feel their territory being threatened. Even a shift from a highly dysfunctional to a highly constructive guiding myth may be accompanied by profound anxiety, terrifying nightmares, and bewildering self-doubt. In the turmoil, you may become uncertain of changes you recently affirmed with great hope and enthusiasm. After all, the old myth did once help you adjust to losses, separations, betrayals, or other trauma.

Amid such inner conflict, certain childhood memories can give substance to more self-affirming visions. Often, even people whose childhoods were heartrending can recall a grandparent, a teacher, a pastor, a special place, a special time, a moment of triumph or achievement to serve as a source of inspiration in difficult circumstances. Such memories may provide the raw materials for forming an empowering counter-myth that points to a more auspicious future. In this personal ritual, you will be exploring an early experience you can draw on in this ongoing project of transforming your guiding mythology.

PREPARATION: *Reread in your journal, or at least bring to mind, the personal ritual where you identified the roots of mythic conflict in your past (Week 3, Session 3). You will* *begin this ritual by focusing on the* opposite *of that feeling. You will then follow that feeling back to events from your past that can serve as models as you envision promising new directions. Have the instructions read to you, read them into a tape and let the tape guide you, or familiarize yourself with them enough to be able to lead yourself through the experience. Find a setting in which you can become deeply relaxed. Again, keep your Personal Shield nearby for support. Sitting or reclining, take a deep breath, and close your eyes.*

Settling into this safe, secure spot, focus on your breathing. Place your closed hands over your chest. Notice breath. Soften belly. Open heart. As you sense or imagine your heart opening, extend your arms outward, unfolding your hands, like flowers blooming, until they come to rest comfortably at your sides. Notice breath. Soften belly. Open heart. With each inhalation, breathe in the fullness of life. With each exhalation, release any tension, relaxing more completely. Breathe in. Release. Focus inward and call to your Inner Shaman, your inner wisdom: "My heart is open to you. Be with me on this journey."

In the earlier visit back in time, when you explored the roots of a mythic conflict, you identified the conflict and noticed your dominant feeling as you thought about it. Recall that feeling. Bring to mind a word or phrase that describes the feeling. For this experience, you will be evoking the opposite of this feeling. Find a word or phrase that describes its opposite. If more than one come to you, settle on the one that strikes you as the more hopeful and constructive. The opposite of "angry" could be "calm," but it could also be "peaceful." Find the polarity of your earlier feeling. Bring that feeling into your body the way an actor can embody a feeling at will. Breathe into the feeling, expanding and intensifying it. Once you have established the feeling within yourself, experience it fully. Explore its texture in your body. Notice whether it has a shape or a color.

You will be using this feeling to lead you to an earlier period of your life, to one of the first times you had this feeling or one like it. Notice the flow of sensations that make up the feeling. Imagine that these sensations form a bridge that can carry you back into your past. When you step onto this bridge, the passageway to your childhood is clear, and you can follow the feeling to an early memory. You are safe and comfortable as you move over this bridge. Crossing this bridge back in time, you come to a scene from your childhood. The scene becomes more clear and vivid with each of your next three breaths.

If you have not yet come upon a scene, relax. Take another deep breath as you allow the scene to emerge. It may reveal itself in pictures, word descriptions, or simply a "knowing." If a scene doesn't spontaneously come to you in the next few moments, make one up in your imagination.

In this scene, you are seeing out of the young eyes and hearing through the young ears of a child. As the scene becomes more vivid, sense your age. Notice who, if anyone, is with you. Where your memory does not offer answers, allow your imagination to fill in the gaps. Picture or sense what you look like at this age. Notice the setting. Recall what you are wearing. Focus now on the events that brought about the feeling. Recall or imagine as many details— sights, sounds, tastes, smells—of this earlier time as you can.

Reflect on some of the decisions you might have made as a result of this early experience and others like it. What conclusions did you come to about yourself? What rules or codes of conduct did you adopt? What attitudes toward other people began to emerge? What views of the world? What philosophy of life? Summarize this philosophy in a single statement, such as, "When things get tough, I can use my wits to save the day," or "I care deeply for others, and as a result they instinctively trust me." Evoke your compassion as you look upon yourself as a child. Send the child the energy of your love. Whisper "Farewell."

Prepare to return to your ordinary waking consciousness. You will be able to remember all you need of this experience. Very gently, begin to rouse yourself. Move your fingers and toes, your hands and feet. Feel your circulation. Stretch your shoulders, your arms and legs, your neck and face muscles. Take a deep breath. Bring your attention back into the room. Open your eyes, refreshed, as if waking from a wonderful nap, alert and fully competent to creatively meet the requirements of your day.

Describe in your journal the feeling and the scene to which it led. Reflect on the self-concept, rules of behavior, and philosophy of life this experience tended to arouse in you. By contrasting your experience with this ritual and the earlier exploration into the roots of your mythic conflict, you can see how some events support myths that are self-limiting and how others provide a foundation for more imaginative and self-affirming myths. Ann wrote:

The opposite of my earlier feeling of panic was like a golden star in my
chest, light and bright. As I followed it back, I found myself with my family
in Cape Town. We were putting the decorations on the Christmas tree, very
carefully selecting where the candles could safely go. When they were all in
place we would light them. Each of us had an area of the tree to watch
carefully. I remember feeling excited and proud that I was being trusted with
the safety of the tree. When the candles were lit, I felt joy at the mystery
and the beauty we had created to celebrate the birth of a Child.

From this experience I learned the joy of working with others to create beauty. I learned that sharing an experience can be wonderful. I learned that taking responsibility for the safety of all makes me feel useful and proud. I learned that needing the help of others who were taller or more skilled to make the event successful was part of the fun and made it all possible.

The sense of destiny that accompanied the memory was that in that moment the creative artist had been stirred, and that it was deeply connected with the beauty of celebrating the mystery of the unseen powers. To this day I love to create beautiful things, alone or with others. I love to collaborate, enjoying where others are more gifted than I. And I love there to be a sense of spiritual mystery in what I do.

SESSION 2:
Part Two of Your Fairy Tale

PURPOSE: *To feel your way into new possibilities for your guiding mythology by extending your Fairy Tale in your creative imagination*

In Part Two of your Fairy Tale, the hero or heroine from Part One will go on a magical journey. There, the creative promise of your counter-myth will be revealed. Part Two will disclose a new direction. As with the counter-myth it is examining, Part Two is not bound by the "reality principle." This second segment of your Fairy Tale will suggest an ideal resolution to the difficulties that emerged in the first segment and will provide clues for achieving it. While Part One probably paralleled events as they actually occurred in your life, you will not be following your actual history in Part Two. Instead, you will be using your ingenuity to discover an inventive solution to the original problem. The journey back in time you just completed may have opened you to an intuitive sense of new possibilities for yourself, and the solutions represented in Part Two may extravagantly build on that vision. This is appropriate for Part Two. Unbridle your creativity as you pursue solutions to the dilemmas faced in Part One.

Part Two will have the same central character seeking to solve the problems that were introduced in Part One. In Part Two, however, the action will occur as a drama within a drama, rather than happening directly within the main character's life. He or she may have a dream, reverie, or vision; be in a play or read a story; meet a teacher; encounter the Inner Shaman; or speak with an animal, plant, or object. This device gives you maximum poetic license. Ann's Part Two, as you will see, unfolded in rhapsodic communication with a tree that glowed as her golden pebble had once glowed. Meg took a ride on a magical porpoise.

Read any sections of your journal you want to review. Recall Part One of your Fairy Tale. The main character was in quite a dilemma. What does the main character need to know that would help resolve this dilemma? Reflect on the attitudes, beliefs, and rules of behavior you identified in your first journey back in time. Could any of these inform your Fairy Tale character? If you could make the character so wise that he or she could move beyond the dilemmas of Part One, how would you do it? What perspectives or attitudes need to be gained? The answers may come to you in words, in pictures, or in another way of knowing.

As you begin to sense these answers, relax into them as they become more vivid. When you are ready, open your journal. Under a heading "Fairy Tale Part Two," describe what your character needs to learn. Ann wrote: "She needs to know that she is not alone, and that the beauty she seeks is within her."

In Part Two of your Fairy Tale, the main character will have an experience that leads to the lesson you just described in your journal. Whether in a dream, by meeting a sorcerer, by being taken on a magical journey, or by any other imaginative literary device, the main character discovers a more effective way to confront the initial dilemma portrayed in Part One of your Fairy Tale. Part Two need not be grounded in reality. In fact, *nothing* happens in Part Two that solves the original problem—Part Two ends where it began, *except* that the main character has grown wiser. In your imagination, create the device you will use to help your character learn the lessons you just identified.

Take time to center yourself on the aims of Part Two: *To reveal to the hero or heroine of your Fairy Tale a fresh solution to the dilemma that emerged in Part One, and to provide instruction on how to reach that solution.* Then compose Part Two of your Fairy Tale. Find a comfortable setting and allow the story to emerge in your imagination, tell the story to another person as you are creating it, or speak it into a tape recorder. Record or summarize the story in your journal. Ann wrote:

For years the young girl tried to find out what was wrong with her and thus reawaken the joy she had once known. She embarked on a long journey. She traveled to many lands. She crossed many oceans and climbed many mountains. She had many strange and extraordinary experiences and learned many things in her search for what she had lost. But no matter where she went or what she did, she grew no closer to that for which she yearned.

And then there came a day, as she was walking through an ancient grove of trees, that the weight in her heart grew too heavy for her to carry any longer. In exhaustion, she leaned her head against the trunk of a giant oak tree. She whispered quietly into the folds of its bark, "I am lost and sad and tired. Please, help me." No sound was heard except for the rustle of leaves close to her ear. And so she whispered again, "I am lost and sad and tired. Please, help me." But still no reply came. Slowly the girl sank to her knees at the foot of the tree. She placed her face in her hands and wept. "I am lost and sad and tired. Please, help me."

And so it came to be that the tree, having been asked three times, began to glow. The light grew brighter and brighter, pouring out from between the creases of its bark until the girl was bathed in its shimmering glow. And from the light, the softest voice began to speak. It whispered to her of pebbles and gold and lights from long ago. And the radiant glow from the tree felt strangely familiar. It spoke to her of a time when she too had shone like the morning sun. But the girl felt afraid. Was this not the very light that had caused her to be the recipient of such rejection? Was this not the light that had brought such loneliness into her life?

But the tree spoke gently to the girl and showed her that it was not the light that had hurt her so, but that she herself had caused the wound. When she turned her golden pebble into stone because of the rejection of others, she had weighed herself down and darkened her heart with despair. And the girl knew that the tree spoke true, and she felt ashamed. The light was indeed a blessing and not a curse. And though it required courage, it was her gift, and it was beautiful and good. And she felt the golden pebble begin to glow within her chest once more. And the weight in her heart grew light and the darkness lifted and she rejoiced.

As evening approached and the time for departing drew nigh, the thought of leaving the tree caused the girl to feel afraid. It was the loneliness that came with her gift that she feared the most. And she felt the weight of it grow heavy in her chest once more as her resolve weakened and the pebble began to lose its glow. But the oak tree stood firm. "Whether you hide your light or not," it said, "the pebble is there, and there it will remain. It is your choice to dampen its light and live in loneliness and sorrow, or to let it shine and to allow its brilliant solitude to teach you the ways of joy."

Here is Part Two of Meg's Fairy Tale:

Juanita Margaret was sitting on the mainland beach one day, looking across the raging strait that separated her from her ruined island. She saw the harsh bridge, made of iron and asphalt, bristling with cars like busy ants on their hill. She was wearing a lovely pink ruffled dress, but she had soiled it by playing with puppies, and there were paw marks blemishing the ruffles.

Imagine her surprise when a porpoise swam up the shallow surf and called out to her, "Juanita Margaret! I've come to rescue you! Mount my back, and I will take you on a great journey."

He was smiling at her, and his voice was as vibrant as the ruby throat of a hummingbird. She went, of course, and climbed on his gray-blue back, grasping his ribs with her legs and clinging to his dorsal fin for balance. He moved across the water in jubilant leaps, arching his back and singing joyously as he traveled. Juanita Margaret forgot that she was odd and foreign, riding a porpoise across the waters wearing her dainty pink dress.

"You are learning a great lesson, Juanita Margaret, in the way you learn best—by doing. Do not forget this lesson: Take time in your life to be spontaneous in nature, without agenda, without time constraints, and you will be wrested from your complaints. I am taking you now to visit some other teachers. Fear not that harm will come to you when I dive beneath the surface. You are equipped for survival and your faith will protect you even in an alien environment."

So saying, the porpoise arched high into the air and dove beneath the surface, Juanita Margaret safe upon his back. The world beneath the sea was shimmering with green and golden light, the white sand lay in gentle mounds, and a tall forest of kelp grew from black rocks. The porpoise swam into the forest of waving plants, each moving independently in the currents. "You see the flexibility of these stems and leaves, responsive to the moving waters? When mighty storms come through this part of the ocean, the kelp forest is whipped from side to side, scourged with driven sand, tested to its limit. Only the weary, old, or poorly rooted plants are torn loose to be cast on the shore. The plants that have gripped the stones with their roots, and that have put their growth into sturdy trunks, are secure and even invigorated by the storm. You see it is possible to be firm and still move with the currents, whether energetic or gentle." She thought she understood what he was talking about.

He took her to a submerged reef, and she saw that it was encrusted with abalone. The shells were as black as the reef, domed like oval cups and covered with volcano barnacles, hermit crabs, and sea lettuce. If she hadn't seen them long before, when she had her island to herself, she would have thought they were just bumps on the rock. The porpoise told her to speak to the largest abalone in the cluster. "Hello," she said, tentatively.

"Hello, yourself," answered the abalone in a slow and draggy voice. "What brings you here today?"

"I think you're supposed to teach me something."

"Do you have any idea what it is?" The abalone sounded puzzled and a little resentful.

"Maybe if you described yourself and your life, I might get a clue. Right now I just think you're pretty much a dull and surly fellow." Juanita Margaret had the habit of saying what she thought, without much consideration of how it might feel to the person she was talking to.

The abalone was silent, and the bubbles coming from his vent holes nearly stopped. When at last he spoke, it was with a distant air, as if he didn't much want to have anything to do with her but felt obliged to answer. "I am, as you say, dull. I have been on this spot for many years. It is a good spot because the current sweeps a lot of plankton my way and I have flourished. It is true that I am not a scintillating personality, that I am politically isolated, that I am drab and lack a rapier wit. I have captured no prizes and have never been to war. My body is muscular, my personality is a yawn, and my attitude is tenacious. I fear only the marauding starfish, who is both tenacious and mobile, able to pry me off the rock and eat me.

"I have a secret, though, Juanita Margaret. Under my drab and unprepossessing exterior, I am a great artist. I go nowhere, engage in no social activities, not even family reunions, because I am at work on the most beautiful sculpture-painting-architecture imaginable. I am preparing the inside of my shell, hidden from sight, as a permanent memorial to God. To learn from me, you must be less concerned with your everyday outer shell and must put your care into making the inside as beautiful as possible. With me, my secret beauty will be concealed until my death. With you, who knows?" With that the abalone let loose a long spout of bubbles, and Juanita Margaret knew he had said what he had to say.

As if in a trance, Juanita Margaret pondered what she had learned from the porpoise, kelp, and abalone. She promised herself she would take time from her duties to find herself in Nature, like the porpoise, to flex in the currents of life while maintaining her roots, like the kelp, and to be unbothered by the plainness of her exterior while privately, without fanfare, enriching her interior, like the abalone. The porpoise delivered her to shore, and she found she had a great deal to think about and even more to do.

When you have completed Part Two of your own Fairy Tale, review it and reflect on its meaning by reading it slowly and immersing yourself in the story. Note where your reactions are the strongest, and use the focusing technique described in Week 4, Session 1, to explore your bodily sensations at those points. Consider the meaning of these feelings and describe your reflections in your journal.

PURPOSE: *To learn more about the relationship between your old myth and your counter-myth by representing them in your body*

Part Two of your Fairy Tale is an allegory that portrays your counter-myth. It may actually introduce you to a counter-myth you have never fully articulated. Because counter-myths are formed largely in reaction to the shortcomings of prevailing myths, in *counter*point, they inevitably contain their own distortions, and it is unavoidable that conflict will exist between the old and the emerging.

In this ritual, you will be examining the conflict by representing it in your body. Mythic conflicts are expressed in people's thoughts, feelings, and behavior, and they are also often somaticized, represented by conditions or events in the body. You may feel full of zest if you have just fallen in love but may be stricken with the flu or worse after a significant loss or disappointment. In the following ritual, you will be shown how to use your bodily feelings to understand better a conflict you have already identified.

PREPARATION: *Review Part One and Part Two of your Fairy Tale. Under the heading "A Body Metaphor of Resolution," describe in your journal, in a single sentence, the old myth represented by Part One of your Fairy Tale and, in another sentence, the counter-myth implied or embedded in Part Two.*

We remind you one final time that in this and in all subsequent personal rituals that include guided imagery, you may use the prerecorded instructions or speak the instructions into a tape and let the tape lead you, or have a partner read the instructions to guide you through the exercise, or make yourself familiar enough with the instructions that you can lead yourself through the experience unassisted.

Find a setting in which you can become deeply relaxed. Again, with your Personal Shield nearby for support, sit or recline comfortably, take a deep breath, and close your eyes.

Settling into this safe, secure spot, focus on your breathing. Place your closed hands over your chest. Notice breath. Soften belly. Open heart. As you sense or imagine your heart opening, extend your arms outward, unfolding your hands, like flowers blooming, until they come to rest comfortably at your sides. Notice breath. Soften belly. Open heart. With each inhalation, breathe in the fullness of life. With each exhalation, release any tension, relaxing more completely. Breathe in. Release. Focus inward and call to your Inner Shaman, your inner wisdom: "My heart is open to you. Be with me on this journey."

With your arms extended, lift your hands slightly, palms facing each other. Holding your hands about two feet apart, let your elbows bend and touch the floor so you are comfortably supported. With your palms still facing each other, reflect for a moment on the myth that is guiding the main character of Part One of your Fairy Tale. Imagine that this myth is being placed in one of your hands. Which hand more correctly represents that myth? What does the myth feel like as it rests in this hand? Is it hot or cold? Heavy or light? Rough or smooth? What color might it be? What other sensations do you notice? Take a few moments to explore the ways you experience this myth from Part One of your Fairy Tale.

Now reflect on the myth that is guiding the main character of Part Two. Imagine that this myth is placed in your other hand. What does this myth feel like? Is it hot or cold? Heavy or light? Rough or smooth? What color might it be? What other sensations do you notice? Take a few moments to explore the ways you experience this myth.

Notice the differences between your hands. Focus on the skin and muscles of each hand as you attend to these differences. Which myth is harder to hold, and which is easier? Which myth has a more pleasant feel? Are the edges of one more jagged than the edges of the other? Is one softer than the other? Do they differ in weight? Is one more buoyant? You might bring your hands closer to your face so you can imagine you are smelling or tasting each myth.

Explore the space between your hands. Be aware of any attraction, repulsion, or tension. What else do you notice as you bring your attention to the space between the myths?

Now reflect on what you have noticed about the sensations of the Fairy Tale Part One myth, the sensations of the Fairy Tale Part Two myth, and the space between them. What might this symbolize about the way these conflicting myths live within you?

Very gently, begin to rouse yourself. Move your fingers and toes, your hands and feet. Feel your circulation. Stretch your shoulders, your arms and legs, your neck and face muscles. Take a deep breath. Bring your attention back into the room. Open your eyes, refreshed, as if waking from a wonderful nap, alert and fully competent to meet the requirements of your day creatively.

In your journal, summarize the sensations you experienced, and reflect on their significance. If one myth was harder to hold, does that mean that it is too difficult to manage or that it is so new that it will take a while to accustom yourself to it? If one myth was rougher, does that mean that it is causing you trouble or that it is trying to get you to abandon attitudes that are soft or disempowering? If one myth was heavier, does that mean that it involves more problems or that it is more important? If one myth was more buoyant, does that mean that it is more inspirational or that it is impossible to achieve?

Next consider how you experienced the space between the two myths. Did they repel each other? Was there an attraction between them? Did one seem to overwhelm the other with its weight or power? When there is a conflict between myths, sometimes one of them has so much force that it appears invincible. Sometimes the two myths are equal in strength and clash so strongly that the two hands repel each other. In other instances, each has qualities the other needs, and the hands are spontaneously drawn together. Ann wrote:

> The energy between my two hands was very distinct. The left hand represented the girl in Part One of my Fairy Tale. It was weak and ineffectual. I had the sense it would not be of any assistance to me in a crisis or be able to hold firm under pressure.
>
> The right hand represented Part Two of my Fairy Tale. It was more confident and able, but I had the sense it was trying to overcompensate. Almost as if the physical strength of my right hand was actually greater than it needed to be. I felt a desire to strengthen the energy of my left hand by sharing with it the surplus energy of my right. In other words, to bring them into balance.

For Frank:

> My left arm became the old myth. I saw the old myth as keeping me restricted and weak and likely to stay that way because it didn't give me any confidence or impetus to push into new frontiers. That insight came when I noticed a parallel between my underused left hand and the way my old myth keeps me from developing. My left arm is not nearly so developed as my right arm, because whenever I have a choice between them, I don't use my left side. That's kind of how the old myth operates. The old myth keeps me weak by not having me use all of myself or having me put great effort into things I already do well, to the exclusion of those parts of me that call for new tricks. I don't take many emotional risks, and then I wonder why my passion is dampened.

On the other hand, so to speak, my right arm felt strong and sure of itself. It had no question of its competence. But as I put the counter-myth into my right hand, it did not feel right. While the sureness and strength in my right hand accurately represented the passionate qualities of the counter-myth, I was also aware that the myth itself was not well developed like my right arm. The old myth seemed to match the weakness of my left arm perfectly, but the counter-myth was not confident and well developed like my right arm. So I was having two opposing and confusing feelings about representing the counter-myth this way. In its content, the myth is strong like my right arm; in its development, it is still weak and immature.

It boiled down to a paradox: The old myth, which is very strong within me, was keeping me weak; the counter-myth, which is very weak within me, promised to make me stronger. I tried to make the two myths merge by bringing my hands together, but I couldn't get it to happen. The old myth stayed with my left hand just fine, but the counter-myth kept jumping away whenever the two hands would come close to each other. I guess that tentative passionate part of me doesn't want to have much to do with the long-standing restricted part.

DREAM FOCUS:

Identifying Obstacles to Resolution

PURPOSE: *To alert yourself to possible impediments as you formulate a new myth that embraces the best of your counter-myth and your old myth*

In the same way you have focused on specific dream themes in previous weeks, you will now be seeking insight into the roadblocks that lie on the path toward resolution of your conflict. Scan your journal looking for clues about the obstacles hindering an integration between your old myth and your counter-myth. With a tape recorder or a journal and pen next to your bed, write in your journal, slowly and mindfully: "I will sleep soundly and peacefully tonight while having a dream that reveals obstacles to the resolution of my mythic conflict. When I awake, I will recall my dream." Then, with deliberation, repeat several times before falling asleep, "I will have a meaningful dream, and I will remember it." If you don't recall a dream the first night, repeat the process each night until you do. After recording a dream, consider using Support Guide 2 to go more deeply into its meaning. Ann reported and reflected on the following dream:

I dreamed I was an assistant to a very strong, capable woman who was either an informer or a reporter in a war situation. She was taking me around on all of her assignments. I was aware all of the time that we were in danger of being discovered. She got a phone call saying there was something coming up and she had to go. We hopped into a very fast convertible car. I carried a telephone with me that had a very long cord. She said I couldn't bring the phone because it would get tangled where we were going. I said it would be impossible if we didn't have the phone. When I left the phone on the side of the curb and got in the car, I felt really anxious and wanted to get out of the car, but I didn't.

Associating the dream to my body metaphor, I am thinking of the other woman as the less fearful me—she is so capable and unafraid and she clearly had me under her wing. I was the weak arm and she was the strong arm, but I could feel that what she was doing was not altogether safe or right. It was energetically off. She was unnecessarily risking both of our lives.

Reflecting on how this dream comments on obstacles to the resolution of my conflict, I associate the telephone to an old and outmoded way of communicating, to my not having caught up to the fact that there are cellular phones . . . I thought I had to be tied to the phone line. Now I see a very interesting pun in my interpretation—"cellular phone" may be referring to communication from the cells of my body, learning to listen to the deep information inherent in my body and its cells, like when my body was telling me not to get into the car. Perhaps the obstacle to resolving my conflict would be if I ignore that information.

THIRD STAGE

Envisioning a New Mythology

Working Through Mythic Conflict

※

In the topside world, all is interpreted in the light of simple gains
and losses. In the underworld, all is interpreted in light of the
mysteries of true sight, right action, and becoming a person of
intense inner strength and knowing.

—Clarissa Pinkola Estés[1]

In the ongoing debate about whether evil is intrinsic to the human psyche or
traces to faulty parenting and insidious cultural influences, Rollo May portrayed the life force using the Greek term *daimon*: an urge in every being "to
affirm itself, assert itself, perpetuate and increase itself."[2] The daimon, the life
force, may be the source of destructive as well as constructive impulses. If fully
integrated into the personality, it can unfold with the creative vitality of life itself. But if a particular aspect of it is not integrated—which is inevitably the case
since human development always proceeds in leaps and bounds—that aspect
may become distorted, destructive, and dominant, sometimes taking over the
total personality.[3] This process can be seen in uncontrolled rage that periodically
erupts in someone who is normally serene and well-mannered, fervent patrio-
tism that serves unacknowledged bigotry, or heartless behavior coming from
someone widely perceived as "a very nice person."

Such qualities are often distortions of the life force that surge through an individual, aspects of the person's temperament that have been repressed, dissoci-

ated, or otherwise disowned. Disowned elements of the psyche may fiercely push for expression, eventually disrupting all psychological equilibrium. Carl Jung described these disowned aspects of the psyche as the *shadow*. While it can be incorporated in a manner that results in an expanded self-identity, the shadow is often the unseen source of a person's difficulties. Erich Neumann spoke of the necessity for a creative relationship between the shadow side of human nature and the conscious mind. He finds in the shadow the paradoxical secret of transformation itself; it is in and through the shadow that the "alchemy" of personality development occurs,[4] where the lead of disowned personal qualities is transformed into the gold of creative expression. Neumann explains: "At first, the figure of the shadow is experienced externally as an alien and an enemy, but in the course of its progressive realization in consciousness it is . . . recognized as a component of one's own personality."[5] This succession is illustrated in the following dream series:

Mary Beth was forty-six when her husband died, suddenly and tragically. Their youngest child had left home a year earlier, and they had been looking forward to peaceful years of retirement. Mary Beth had been an exemplary mother and homemaker, but she had never developed skills that could earn an income. She had enough savings and insurance benefits to carry her for about a year. After that, she would have to figure out how to support herself. Some six months after her husband died, just as she was starting to panic about her financial predicament, she had the first of three related dreams.

She dreamed she was at home sleeping in bed. It wasn't her actual home, yet she felt she was at home. In her dream she was awakened by the sound of pounding. She was petrified. Suddenly a masked man jumped through the window. He was a burglar, with a burglar's sack. When he saw her in bed, he approached her ominously. She woke up screaming as he began to rape her mercilessly.

Mary Beth had difficulty sleeping after this dream. Her sleeplessness led her into psychotherapy. About that time, she also came to a decision about how she would support herself. She enrolled in an intensive ten-week course that taught basic secretarial skills. She did well in the course and easily found a job in a small law firm. To her great relief, she was not fired during her probationary period. In fact, she had a sense that she was well liked. And she loved cashing her paycheck.

Mary Beth had a second dream. She was again in the same bed in the same room, sleeping. This time, she was awakened by a knocking on the door. She timidly opened it, and the same masked man pushed his way in. This time, however, she did not sense that he meant to harm her. He did not. He seduced her. She woke up with a sense of excitement.

About four months later, she had her final dream in this series. She had been flourish-

ing in her work. Not only were her basic secretarial skills more than adequate, she found that underneath her shy, effacing public self was a witty, good-natured woman who was able to understand others extremely well and to convey both empathy and good advice. To her surprise, she was made office manager. In that position, she started to enjoy a kind of power she had never even conceived of, and she gained increasing respect from the staff. In the third dream, she was in the same bed and the same room. But this time she had left the door ajar for her lover. In he comes . . . the same masked man, now with flowers and charm. She embraces him. As they begin to make passionate love, she looks at his mask, grabs it, and peels it off. There she sees her own face looking back at her.

Mary Beth's dream series shows how disowned aspects of the psyche may demand expression, particularly when circumstances beckon to them. Until you acknowledge such latent potentials, they may be more destructive than beneficial, eliciting powerful and contradictory emotions and generally wreaking havoc with your inner life. Mary Beth's identity was so removed from the competencies and independence required by her circumstances, and her shadow side so alien to her, that she was pushed into making radical internal adjustments. A terrifying encounter with a shadow element of the personality is illustrated in the following case:

Steve was a forty-seven-year-old Vietnam veteran whose life had been saved by a courageous medic during the war. After a six-year tour of duty with the Marines, he entered college at twenty-five, determined to become a doctor. While his original ambition was to serve as a mobile disaster-relief physician, he developed a fervent interest in the human mind and its sufferings. After medical school and a residency in psychiatry, he accepted a position in an upstate New York clinic that worked with veterans. Steve was thoroughly aware of the prevailing theories and treatment strategies for post-traumatic stress disorder (PTSD) when, after treating veterans and their PTSD for twelve years, he himself sought psychiatric help for that condition. "I wrote the book on PTSD," was his comment on entering therapy. His wife was weary of his periodic furious outbursts, hypervigilance, and sleep-disturbing nightmares.

"It's like he has this all-purpose, never-fail excuse for yelling and shouting," she complained. "Once he drove like a maniac with the kids and me in the car. One evening, while I was still at work, he broke into my office, raging at the security guard. I hadn't answered the phone when he had called earlier because I had been in the restroom."

By both their accounts, Steve was a devoted parent, dedicated husband, and devout Catholic—most of the time. His PTSD was triggered when he felt startled, abandoned, or when he perceived danger for those he loved. Fatigue was also a contributing factor.

Asked to describe these PTSD episodes in detail, he told his psychiatrist that there were no words adequate for the terror and his sense of being possessed by destructive forces far beyond his capacity to control. Following this lead, an art therapist who collaborated with the psychiatrist asked Steve to sculpt wordlessly, in clay, the "possessor." As he worked, he began to sob and gouge the clay; eventually he produced a diabolic face. He was overwhelmed with memories of retrieving decapitated, four-days-dead marines from a battleground under fire and with only the help of a sergeant he detested. At one point, Steve reexperienced his fury when the sergeant refused to help him gather into body bags the last several casualties. Suddenly a previously repressed memory flooded in. He collapsed in tears in the therapist's office with the words, "Oh, my God! I shot the son of a bitch. I killed another marine! Lucifer is in me!" Panic and guilt swamped him after twenty-seven years of repression.

This horrifying breakthrough was only the beginning of his therapeutic work. His psychiatrist eventually persuaded him to describe his crime to a priest, in confession. The priest came back with the judgment that twenty-seven years of suffering with PTSD was penance enough. Given absolution, Steve appeared dazed and disoriented. After several weeks of talking through his war experiences with his psychiatrist, during which several more potent though less devastating memories emerged, he was asked to work in clay again. This time, he produced a faceless blob, only faintly human. He called it "my vacant self." He surprised himself by observing, "Without Lucifer, I don't know what I am." Over months, his sculptures of faces became more and more realistic. One was a mask of a boy with large eyes. "That's me, at seventeen. I was scared the war would end before I could get there. Hard to believe!" Another was a mask of tragedy on the same face, just a bit older.

The final outcomes of Steve's strenuous efforts in therapy were marked relief from his PTSD symptoms and a striking increase in his vitality and effectiveness. Keying to the Latin meaning of Lucifer as "light bearer," the psychiatrist reflected on the irony that, for the past dozen years in his role as a psychiatrist, Steve had been bringing his own light to other veterans, while his shadow was lurking behind every corner, ready to assault him.

Steve's experience demonstrates how a disowned aspect of the psyche may become diabolical, not just filled with guilt and remorse, but evil and destructive, as when he endangered the lives of his wife and children. Until such latent forces are acknowledged, they are likely to be noxious, evoking powerful and contradictory emotions and generally wreaking havoc with a person's inner life. But when they are recognized, faced, and transformed, the whole personality may reorganize to incorporate their power constructively.

Jung observed that "one does not become enlightened by imagining figures of light, but by making the darkness conscious."[6] Among life's most curious paradoxes is that pushing away what is natural but seems negative *feeds* the negativity, while accepting in oneself what seems negative *maximizes* the chances of bringing its positive potential into being. As you work with mythic conflict in your own interior, shadow elements of your personality—parts of yourself that have been repressed or otherwise disowned—are likely to come within the reach of your awareness.

Rather than turn away or more vehemently stifle these aspects of your very human nature, such work provides an opportunity, as was evidenced with Mary Beth and Steve, to acknowledge and transform them from distorted and destructive forces into qualities that balance and empower you. To open yourself as much as possible to what you fear within, to stare down your own nightmares, disempowers malignant elements of your personality. This program may have already stirred the dark forces within, and as you proceed, we encourage you to enter their domain with the expectation of becoming stronger and wiser from the journey. A verse by Wendell Berry invites a courageous voyage into the dark night of the soul:

> To go in the dark with a light is to
>   know the light.
> To know the dark, go dark
> Go without sight, and find that the dark, too,
>   blooms and sings . . .[7]

The shadow is at the root of one form of counter-myth, where an aspect of the personality that is denied by the dominating mythology still finds insidious expression. But the shadow is not the only element of the unconscious. Another form of counter-myth is based on a personal quality that emerges out of a developmental readiness to make significant changes in the story you are living: an unwillingness to keep trading submission for love, a hunger for relationship over achievement, a yearning for artistic or spiritual expression. The counter-myth pushes you toward transformation while the prevailing myth acts to conserve ways that are known and established. The internal conflict between the two is mirrored at the social level in the perennial tension between conservatives and liberals.

Conservatives tend to defend a mythic vision that emphasizes and conserves what is of value from the past, even as the forces of change carry a society into the future. Liberals tend to focus on reform and progressive ideals, sometimes to the point of undervaluing the hard-earned achievements of previous generations. Both forces operate in each of us. Winston Churchill once said that the man who is not a liberal when he is twenty has no heart and the man who is not a conservative when he is forty has no brain. An appreciation of the conservative and progressive aspects of your own nature can help you better mediate the tensions between old and emerging myths.

When a counter-myth first breaks into your awareness, you may be overwhelmed by its power and make abrupt changes in your life. A college student may renounce a lifetime of religious observance in the space of a semester, while a nonbeliever may convert to a religious orthodoxy in moments. Adolescent rebellion, sexual infidelity, and impulsive divorce may each reflect the explosive appearance of a counter-myth. A man who has been a dedicated husband and father has an affair with a woman half his age. When he later enters psychotherapy to try to piece together the shambles he has made of his life, he is likely to discover that he was, with little self-awareness, acting out a counter-myth that challenged the dutiful but stifling existence he was doing little to rejuvenate effectively. A young woman who prided herself for academic excellence in high school abandons her college scholarship after she falls in with a religious cult that preaches total surrender and service to the organization and its leader.

In the remainder of the program, you will be encouraged to recognize the strengths and the shortcomings in both old myths and counter-myths, and to cultivate patiently a third, new mythic vision that transcends their limitations while incorporating the most vital aspects of each. Although counter-myths often operate unnoticed, they may break into awareness through dreams, daydreams, art, slips of the tongue, and other spontaneous expressions of your mythic underworld. The counter-myth is often imaginative, inspiring, forward-thrusting—yet lacking a practical realism. By focusing your attention on your counter-myth, you are able to be aware of its influence more readily and to participate in consciously developing and refining it.

SESSION 1:

Mapping the Effects of Your Conflicting Myths

PURPOSE: *To identify ways in which your mythic conflict affects your inner life and influences your experiences in the world*

By carefully observing personal conflict, new directions in your mythology may be revealed. In this ritual, you will create a map of the thoughts, feelings, and behaviors that are consistent with your old myth and those that are consistent with your counter-myth, and you will articulate the operating motto of each.

From this examination of how the old myth and the counter-myth function, you will be better able to recognize when each is dominating a given situation. You will continue to refer to this conflict map as you work toward resolving the conflict.

1. Review your journal to crystallize your understanding of the prevailing myth and the counter-myth.

2. Draw a line down the center of a blank sheet of your journal to make two columns. Label the columns "Old Myth" and "Counter-Myth."

3. You may wish to take a journey to your Inner Shaman at this point in order to request that new light be shed on your understanding of the old myth or the counter-myth. Use the methods you have found most effective for contacting your Inner Shaman, and raise any issues you would like to explore concerning your old myth or your counter-myth.

4. At the top of the "Old Myth" column, write a motto that characterizes your old myth; in the other column write a motto that characterizes your emerging counter-myth. If the motto for one or the other does not come to you easily, remain alert for it as you proceed with the instructions that follow.

5. Reflect on your actions, thoughts, and feelings during the past several hours. In the appropriate column, record which feelings, statements, or behaviors were guided primarily by one or the other of these myths. Next, reflect on the past couple of days. Then consider patterns of thought, feeling, or behavior that characterize the past year or two.

If the connections between your experiences and your myths do not readily appear to you, don't press yourself after giving it a fair try. Instead, carry your journal with you for several days, making new entries as they occur to you, or reflect each evening on your actions during that day. Your conflict map will describe specific thoughts, feelings, and actions that are connected with longstanding as well as emerging patterns in your life.

Meg's old-myth motto was "Adult life is a spoiler." Her counter-myth motto was "Life is juicy all the way through." The motto of Frank's old myth was "Be careful, try hard, look out," which he associated with his fears, uncertainties, and cautious approach to life. The motto of his counter-myth was "Follow the scent," and he associated it with the passion of a jaguar in the wild. The motto of Ann's old myth was "Kindness above all else. Power kills." The old-myth column of her conflict map described these feelings, thoughts, and actions:

Past Several Hours

I've supported my friend in his work.

I've dreamed that the work I am doing now will be of benefit to others.

I've felt the joy of loving and supporting others.

Past Several Days

I've forged on with a headache instead of going to bed.

I've made sure my family was well before leaving for this trip.

I've called my friends to make sure they were okay.

I've felt guilty for not wanting to be generous.

I've wept gratefully for the friendship of another.

I've seen my power intimidate another.

I've felt frightened that I am growing hard and unattached.

Past Several Years

I've worked to find a gentle way to restructure a relationship that was painful for me.

I've devoted my work to the service of others.

I've given financial assistance to many.

I've learned new ways of expressing truth in a nonhurting way.

I've felt ashamed by the growing power in my expression.

I've carried friendships that have felt burdensome.

I've said yes when I've wanted to say no.

I've given time to do things I haven't wanted to do.

I've undervalued my needs for time alone.

I've felt saddened by the heartbreak of another and comforted that person.

Ann's counter-myth motto was "In discernment, power; in blind kindness, cruelty." The counter-myth column of her conflict map read:

Past Several Hours

I've worked at a pace that is good for me.

I've said when I needed to stop.

I've felt excited by the precision of my thinking.

I've felt excited but afraid of the new clarity that is coming to me.

I've been realizing that the truth may be uncomfortable, but it is kinder than giving false illusions.

Past Several Days

I've spoken clearly and honestly to a friend, and she appreciated it.

I've written a letter ending a relationship that has not felt right for a long
time, in a loving and nonjudgmental way.

I've chosen to go on a journey for my own pleasure, and my family was
happy for me.

I've felt a brewing sense of strength as I speak what I actually feel.

I've thought that I actually might get free of my fears of harming others.

I've hurt a friend when I spoke the truth.

Past Several Years

I've written to everyone whom I felt I had hurt in any way.

I've said no to relationships that don't feel right for me.

I've realized that the breakdowns that have happened in my relationships
were not all my fault.

I've committed myself to enjoy the fruits of my labor more.

I've turned down requests for money from friends.

I've seen how horribly complicated life gets when I don't say what I need
to say.

I've set clear boundaries with people who want my time.

I've formed new friendships with people who enrich me.

I take more time to create.

I feel more whole and fully expressed with my family.

I am clearer with my discipline of my son.

Reflecting on the journey she took to her double-aspected Inner Shaman,
Ann wrote:

Under the gentle guidance of my Shaman's Madonna-like aspect, my old
myth has developed my compassion. But it has left me weak and ineffectual
in other areas. The counter-myth, which has been slowly surfacing for some
time under the guidance of the Dark Discerner, has been teaching me the
ways of power, clarity, and discernment. A New Myth will establish itself
when the two aspects of my self merge, the Madonna's kindly compassion
married with the powerful truth of the Dark Discerner.

Bringing Your Conflicting Myths into Dialogue

PURPOSE: *To personify your conflicting myths, giving each a character, a posture, and a voice*

In this ritual, you will be making each side of your mythic conflict come to life in a dramatic enactment. Ann used the names "Angel Girl" and "Slasher" for the characters representing her opposing myths. Here is a segment from their dialogue:

ANGEL GIRL: You are too aggressive.
SLASHER: You are too weak.
ANGEL GIRL: You don't take into consideration the fragility of people.
SLASHER: You underestimate their strength.
ANGEL GIRL: There is a coldness in your approach to life.
SLASHER: There is a false sentimentality in yours.
ANGEL GIRL: I don't like the way you discard people.
SLASHER: I don't like the way you patronize them.
ANGEL GIRL: I hate your puffed-up vanity.
SLASHER: I hate your false humility.

Meg chose the name "Proper Young Lady" for the character representing her old myth and "Born-again Child" for the character representing her counter-myth. Their themes corresponded with the contrasting mottoes that summarized her mythic conflict ("Adult life is a spoiler" versus "Life is juicy all the way through"). She had the two characters engage in a dialogue and transcribed the following from a tape of their conversation:

PROPER YOUNG LADY (scolding, shaking finger): Look at yourself! You're a
   disgrace to me and everyone around you.
BORN-AGAIN CHILD (puzzled): What are you talking about?
PROPER YOUNG LADY (pointing): Your clothes are worn, and they have
   stains and loose buttons. Your hair is unkempt, and (condemning, censuring
   tone) you're barefooted.
BORN-AGAIN CHILD (defensively): I'm playing.
PROPER YOUNG LADY (sighing with exasperation, shaking head, tightening
   mouth): Yes, I know. You play entirely too much. Life is serious, life is
   demanding. And you are missing the point.
BORN-AGAIN CHILD (on the attack): You just want me to be like you . . .
   neat, tidy, and emotionally constipated. Never a hair out of place or an

original thought. Your idea of an adventure is to ride the city bus. You've got too many rules, too many resented duties, too little imagination. You're scared of making mistakes.

PROPER YOUNG LADY (shocked and insulted): How dare you! You who won't do a moment's work unless you're having fun doing it! You who have no responsibilities! You who have no sense of history or future! You dare to mock me? I've lived and I've suffered. I know ten times as much about life as you. Do you dare reject what I have to say?

BORN-AGAIN CHILD (rolling down a long hill, getting grass stains on her jeans): Yep. I don't need what you've got to teach.

PROPER YOUNG LADY (frustrated): Sit down and listen to me. It's not polite to talk back to your betters. And look at how disheveled you've gotten yourself!

BORN-AGAIN CHILD (laughing): I'm never going to be polite. I'm going to be honest instead. I'll say what I think and feel, and I'll do what feels good. Like this. (Throws an imaginary water balloon at the conservatively dressed Proper Young Lady.)

PROPER YOUNG LADY (drenched and acting outraged): You miserable brat! You self-indulgent, inconsiderate, rotten child! I'll show you. (Starts toward Born-again Child, who skips away, just out of reach.)

In her journal, Meg reflected:

I had a good time with this one. People sometimes comment that I am "strong" or "sure of myself," and they are accurate to a degree. I often, however, feel stuck in the nonconforming posture of the child—as if that stance were a mold of its own and I were not truly free. And I choose my ground carefully, avoiding social settings where I will be in contact with traditional, conservative, establishment types, because I feel so unequipped to deal on that level. I do kind of wish I could "pass" as a normal person when I want to, just as black people who were light-skinned used to try to "pass" as whites. But that never worked very well, and I don't suppose it would work for me. Maybe what I need to do is accept myself as a slightly out-of-step person, be grateful for the love I get as an eccentric, and stop worrying about making myself fit in.

With these experiences, Meg's self-righteousness began to shed its rigidity and her defiance began to lose its anger. Later, reflecting on these two qualities in her journal, she noted: "They seem like perversions of two positive aspects of my personality—self-assurance and individualism." Frank used the names "Earnest" and "Jolly Green Giant" in his dialogue:

EARNEST: If you're not careful, you're going to get both of us hurt.

JOLLY GREEN GIANT: You little wimp! If I was as careful as you, we'd never get out of bed! You work so hard on the dumbest things so that you don't ever have to risk that there'd be a moment you might have to enjoy. It would make you feel too guilty!

EARNEST: You are going to get us in a lot of trouble. Consider the industrious ant who builds a giant hill despite his tiny size.

JOLLY GREEN GIANT: That's terrific if building anthills is your mission in life. Besides, if we go at your pace, rigor mortis will set in by April.

EARNEST: Well, what do you want me to do?

JOLLY GREEN GIANT: You might try smilin' sometimes. Or laughin'. Or playin'. Maybe just start with breathing fully, you constricted little worm!

EARNEST (haughtily): Fiddlesticks! All that nonsense is hardly necessary for a mature person.

JOLLY GREEN GIANT: That's the funniest thing I've ever heard! Your image of "maturity" is of a dried-up, convoluted, scared old bullfrog. The reason for life is to live! And with zest and vigor and joy.

EARNEST: I'd be embarrassed to be as audacious and brazen and vain as you, exuding all over the place.

JOLLY GREEN GIANT: Embarrassed, eh? I think you have exposed the chains that are binding you to your dreary, colorless existence.

EARNEST: Well, it's not just embarrassment. What people think matters for many reasons. It even holds consequences for my profession.

JOLLY GREEN GIANT: It's your profession you're worrying about? Let me tell you somethin' about what your profession's doin' for you. It's not only making you dead while you're still alive, it's gonna have you dead before the retirement years for which you think you're living.

EARNEST (befuddled): So you're trying to tell me that if I stop worrying about being embarrassed, I'm going to live longer?

JOLLY GREEN GIANT: Why, Earnest, I believe I finally have your attention.

EARNEST: Well, I'm not sure I believe you, but I must admit I've been feeling less than sensational lately. Maybe there is something to what you're saying.

JOLLY GREEN GIANT: Less than sensational, eh? You do flatter yourself with understatement. Listen, pal, you come along with me on my path. You're gonna like walking the first mile so well that you're never gonna wanna go back to your old ways.

EARNEST: Did you say come with you on your path? You, sir, are out of your mind! You are of the vulgar and unrefined sort whose sensibilities are barbaric. You'd zip me along into your uncouth ways so fast and blatantly that I'd be humiliated in a thousand ways. Besides, I'd be so terrified that I wouldn't enjoy a thing. Forget it!

As is evident, Earnest and the Giant still have some distance to cover before a constructive resolution is likely to occur. By personifying your old myth and your counter-myth, you will be exploring internalized "subpersonalities."[8] A subpersonality can be thought of as an aspect of the psyche that is governed by a particular personal myth. Choose a name for the subpersonality associated with your old myth and a name for the subpersonality associated with your counter-myth, such as Ann's "Angel Girl" and "Slasher," Meg's "Proper Young Lady" and "Born-again Child," and Frank's "Earnest" and "Jolly Green Giant." A forty-four-year-old community college instructor named his old myth "Altar Boy" and his counter-myth "Pioneer." A twenty-eight-year-old computer engineer used the names "Robot Woman" and "Flash Dancer."

Physically enact your dialogue, using appropriate gestures and wholeheartedly dramatizing it. This will engage not only your intellect but also your intuition and your feelings about these competing myths. It also will attune you to relevant "body memories" and other physical aspects of the prevailing and emerging mythic themes. Draw on your sense of humor in emphasizing and appreciating the differences between the characters. If you are not working with a partner, you might use a tape recorder as a sort of witness. New insights about the relationship between the opposing myths often emerge from reviewing the exchange.

Begin by finding a physical posture that portrays your old myth. What facial appearance is most fitting? Should you smile, grimace, scowl, laugh, frown, stare, twitch? What gestures would be most appropriate for this character? Should you point? Put your hands in your pockets? Hug yourself? Shake nervously? Dance? Applaud? Jump? Pray? Crawl? Having found this first posture, step out of that spot, face this "person," and assume a posture that represents your counter-myth. You might start by finding the posture and gestures that are the opposite of your old myth. Give yourself enough time to work your way into this role. Try out a few different postures so you may feel your way into the one best suited for this subpersonality. Note what is happening to your muscles and your sense of balance as you find your way into each posture.

Once you have established the postures and facial expressions that best represent each character, go back and forth a few times between them. Have each one begin to look at and size up the other. Either figure may evolve beyond its initial identity. This can be a valuable development—just keep the character consistent with the myth it represents. Begin the dialogue. Have one of the parts speak to the other. Alternate.

In each role, assume the characteristic posture and say the words that express your feelings and thoughts while looking at and reacting to the other character. Be deliberate in using a fitting tone of voice. Your speech may be smooth or raspy, loud or soft, high or low, rapid or slow, guttural or nasal, fluid or stuttering—whatever is appropriate for your character. After one of the characters offers some initial comments, move over to the other character's spot, assume the appropriate posture, and answer. Again find a fitting voice quality. Continue to move physically between the two characters while you let the dialogue develop. As these characters encounter each other, allow the words to flow out. Keep the dialogue going without long pauses or planning. Encourage your spontaneity. Simply move into one of the positions and assume the appropriate posture as that character begins speaking. Move out of that position and into a facing position whenever the second character responds. Keep your facial expressions, posture, gestures, and tones appropriate to the character you are portraying.

A good way to start the dialogue once you have established both characters, or to proceed when the discussion gets bogged down, is to have one side ask the other, "What do you want from me?" In the early part of the dialogue, focus your emphasis on the conflict and establish the differences between the two sides. As you continue the discussion, however, see if the communication between the characters spontaneously improves. Even if they do not begin to listen with more care and respect for each other, that is fine for now. They will have ample opportunity to work through their differences.

After completing your dialogue, re-create or summarize it in your journal. You may also want to draw each character. As you reflect in your journal, consider how the old myth and the counter-myth were expressed. Were some feelings or ideas disclosed that you did not know you held? Because it engages you at bodily as well as verbal levels, this exercise often reveals aspects of the conflict that were previously outside your awareness.

As you proceed in the program, have your characters engage in additional dialogue from time to time. You may find that after each of the rituals, their ability to communicate has been somewhat enhanced. Use the physical posturings when you extend the dialogue and record the highlights in your journal.

PURPOSE: *To release the psychological energies bound in a personal quality that is inhibiting your development*

The procedures medieval alchemists used for attempting to transform base metals into gold have been studied in the past century by such thinkers as Carl Jung and Mircea Eliade, who discerned profound esoteric meanings in the practice of alchemy. Alchemical methods are believed to have been the outer expression of a sophisticated transformative spiritual discipline. According to Ralph Metzner, "Chemical experimentation was like tantric yoga ritual: slow, deliberate, with a maximum of empathic awareness and sensitivity to the changes in matter."[9] Part of the challenge at this point in working with your personal mythology involves transforming the base qualities of old myths into the gold of the new.

Some personal characteristics may be so potently connected with the old myth that they become obstacles to changing it. In this ritual, you will identify a quality in yourself that you believe interferes with the constructive resolution of your mythic conflict, and you will call on your Inner Shaman to help you find ways to turn that obstacle into an opportunity. Reflect on a personal quality that may be keeping you trapped in your conflict. Perhaps your impulsiveness prevents you from creating a more prosperous lifestyle, your compulsiveness prevents you from enjoying the comfortable lifestyle you have created, your fearfulness interferes with your ability to take the risks required for professional success, or your insecurity causes you to push away relationships by clinging to them. Meg went through the ritual twice, focusing once on the self-righteousness of the Proper Young Lady and a second time on the defiance of the Born-again Child. Frank worked with his compulsion to achieve. Ann chose her difficulties with openly speaking the truth when it might hurt another.

PREPARATION: *Choose a quality you wish to transform. In the following instructions, you will be doing a ritual dance with your Inner Shaman to transform this quality into a resource. You may physically do the dance, which we recommend, or simply do it as a fantasy. You will need a single sunflower seed, almond, or similar food. Leave the seed where you can reach it easily. During the part of the ritual when you are doing the dance, you*

may also (if you do not have the prerecorded tape) have primal music with drumming play-
ing in the background.

Standing where you have some room to move, take a few deep breaths, plant your feet on the ground, and prepare to invite your Inner Shaman to visit you in your everyday world. Recall your Inner Shaman's appearance. Now imagine that your Inner Shaman has materialized in front of you. Whether or not you can actually see the form of your Inner Shaman standing before you, sense your Shaman's presence.

As you look at your Shaman, sense how you feel about offering up the quality you wish to transform. An imaginary bundle appears before you, and you begin to hold it with both your hands. You know that the quality you wish to change is inside the bundle. Examine the bundle. What color is it? Is it heavy? Does it have an odor? Are there sounds coming from within it? Present the bundle to your Shaman.

Explain the quality to your Shaman. Honor your dignity by describing the quality with compassion for yourself. Establish what it is about the quality that is not working for you. Now consider the ways in which you hope to trans-form the quality. Stubbornness may become a balanced determination. A quick temper may provide the zest for passionate involvement. Laziness may be the safeguard against frenzied overinvolvement. Find in the quality you wish to transform the kernels of a quality you would like to develop. Once you have described the change you are requesting, listen for your Shaman's response.

Your Shaman faces you and places his or her hands on the bundle. The bun-dle is between you, and both of you are holding it. Now your Shaman starts to move. You realize that you are to move in synchrony as you both hold the bun-dle. Begin to move, keeping in harmony with your Shaman.

The movement gains speed. The rhythms change. Soon it is a free form of dance with the bundle held between you. Your Shaman begins to chant: "Let the change begin!" You chant along.

Notice that the bundle is surrounded by a luminescent color, a bright light that almost obscures it. The change is occurring. You continue to chant. The movement becomes centered on the luminescent bundle you are both holding. You begin moving it high and low, to and fro. It becomes brighter with each additional motion. The dance continues. It works up to a frenzy. Now you are chanting very fast: "Let the change begin!"

Finally, you stop and look your Shaman in the eye. Both of you still have your hands on the bundle, which continues to glow. Your Shaman tells you that the quality in the bundle is being transformed, just as you requested. You are told to place the bundle on the spot where you have stored your seed. As you do so, the bundle suddenly disappears, and your Shaman tells you that all the energy of its bright light has gone into the seed. As you look at the seed, you sense more deeply just what this new quality is and how you would feel if it were fully developed within you.

Your Shaman tells you to pick up the seed and slowly chew and swallow it. Put the seed into your mouth and begin to chew. As you chew, feel yourself consciously ingesting the new quality.

As you finish chewing this sacred morsel, savor the taste and savor the knowledge that a seed has just been planted for an important change in your life. This ritual marks a turn in your path. While the changes may not be immediate or radical, the shift in direction at this point will make an increasing difference as you go further down the road. Say good-bye to your Shaman, and watch as he or she fades back into your inner world.

Reflect on the experience in your journal. Consider whether, like Meg, you wish to repeat this ritual a second time, concentrating on another characteristic. In her journal, Ann wrote:

My dance with the Shaman felt strong and connected. I knew I no longer was alone in my commitment to transform various aspects of myself, but I had a true ally. Her strength felt wonderful. As we carried the bundle, it began to glow. What I had considered to be a problem had miraculously become the altar from which new life would grow. When it became a seed and entered my body, I felt that from it I would create a new life.

The most important thing I gained from this experience is that a quality for which I might judge myself harshly is merely a stepping-stone toward a richer way of seeing. The inability to openly speak the truth is not only a weakness, it is also an expression of my deep empathy and compassion.

Can I be strong enough to keep my heart open and still speak the truth?

At any time in the future, you may use the seed to reactivate the transformed personal quality it carries. In your imagination or with another seed, place the seed in your mouth. Slowly, deliberately begin to chew. Ingest it with a maximum of sensitivity to the physical transformation of the seed as the quality it carries infuses itself into your being.

DREAM FOCUS:

An Integration Dream

PURPOSE: *To enlist your dream life in further resolving the discord between your old myth and your counter-myth*

You will be incubating a dream where the two sides of your mythic conflict lend each other their strengths, show each other how to be more effective, and discover how they can work together. Scan your journal for clues about difficulties between the two sides and ways they might achieve greater resolution. With a tape recorder or a journal and pen next to your bed, speak or write in your journal, slowly and mindfully: "I will sleep soundly and peacefully tonight while having a dream in which the energies of the two sides of my inner conflict begin to integrate into a single, unified energy. When I awake, I will recall my dream." Then, with deliberation, repeat several times before falling asleep, "I will have a meaningful dream, and I will remember it." If you don't recall a dream the first night, repeat the process each night until you do. After recording a dream, consider using Support Guide 2 to go more deeply into its meaning. Ann reported and reflected on the following dream:

> I am in a theater, and people who are followers of the Maharishi are having an evening. The show begins and then the main chap leaves the stage and comes to get me to join them. I feel slightly annoyed that they would use me in this way, but it feels like I would be making too big a scene if I refused to go up. When on the stage, instead of doing something profound and spiritual, as they are expecting, I create a song that fits the situation perfectly, but it is light and funny. It crescendos to an unbelievable operatic climax, and dramatically I sing the last words—"Brown toast!" The audience cheers. A folksinger comes on the stage singing with his guitar; it is clear that they want me to sing along. I do, and the harmonies are quite beautiful. While the audience is clapping, the man says, "Why don't you come back after I've established my own self with them." I can feel his sense of competition and decide that I don't want to participate in it. I say, "Go for it. You're on your own." I leave the stage.
>
> Backstage I am sitting beside the Maharishi's right-hand man, when two friends of mine join us. We chat a moment, and Marion and I comment on the beautiful light that is reflecting off Mike. Suddenly she begins to weep and says that his health has not been great. She asks if I believe that the HIV virus could also cause cancer. I say, "They seem to be related. Yes." She weeps in my arms, and says, "How could I ever live without him?" I say, "Live with him now." That's the end of the dream. I will use the creative projection technique to reflect on it.

I Am "Brown Toast": I am brown toast. I am an ordinary, simple human pleasure. I am a staple of life. I have been made stronger through the fire and yet am unassuming in my ways.

I Am the Lyric "Brown Toast": I will not be coerced into assuming false airs for the sake of serving the beliefs of others. I would rather make people laugh by making myself basic and amusing than give voice to what pretends to be spiritual.

I Am "Mike": I am a man with a purpose. My whole life is lived to transform the planet. I always have a new project on the go that will make a huge difference. I am exhausted, and I am dying.

I Am "Marion": My heart is always focused on how I can be of service. There is a place where I do not exist, for everything I do is in response to another. I am worried, I am tired, I weep easily, and fear change.

I Am the Folksinger: I fear that I will be overshadowed. I fear that I will go unnoticed. I am competitive but do not want anyone to know.

I Am the Main Chap: I will use anyone or anything to further my beliefs. I am insensitive to the true feelings of others. I am flaky and ungrounded and opportunistic.

There is a simple quality in me that doesn't care about fame or fortune but longs for the wholesome, simple world of "brown toast." I realized how much I live my life serving causes that I'm not one hundred percent sold on and giving people what they want, even if I have to do it halfheartedly. Mike is that aspect of myself that is being sacrificed to the service of the whole. Marion is that aspect of myself that feels helpless and unable to do anything about it. What I seem to be saying in this dream is that there is no healing possible, cancer is a deadly disease, there is no resolution possible, do the best that you can, and live with him now. Some resolution dream! But it shows me how hopeless my inner self feels in compulsively trying to change things that cannot be changed. As I reflect further, I also realize that some things in the dream that I accepted as hopeless can be changed or at least fought, such as Mike's cancer. Perhaps a key to the resolution is to be able to discern what is and what isn't worth my effort.

In the next weeks, those things I feel I must do, even though I don't want to, I will find a way of doing that is truthful to me. I will hold steady in letting go of the relationship that no longer serves me. I will not engage with acts of competition from one friend in particular, but will back out gracefully.

Conceiving a Unifying Mythic Vision

Each successively higher-order structure [of consciousness] is more complex, more organized, and more unified.

—Ken Wilber[1]

Mythic thought generally moves from an awareness of contradictions toward their resolution.[2] Through the creation of unifying symbols, your psyche reconciles the opposing tendencies that inevitably exist within you. Jung referred to this unifying property of symbols as their "transcendent function." Ann's glowing tree and Mcg's abalone shell each served as a force for inner unity, providing a larger context that could incorporate previously incompatible visions. Meg's abalone shell symbol, for instance, helped her reconcile the part of her represented by the shell's drab and ordinary exterior with the part of her represented by its iridescent interior. Because life challenges you to find a constantly evolving balance of inner polarities, *unifying symbols* are the guiding stars that orient you toward greater harmony and wholeness.

Myth and Perception at War. Perception is a match-mismatch process.[3] If what you see in the world corresponds reasonably well with your guiding mythology, a basic psychological equilibrium will tend to be maintained. But if your myths and your experiences do not match, you will be spurred toward thought and action that replaces the mismatch with a better fit. A man we know who "had to marry" his high school sweetheart because of an unwanted pregnancy while both were in their teens secretly believed himself to be an irresistible Casanova, leashed only by the bonds of his marriage. While faithful, he was resentful and inattentive, until his wife left him when they were in their mid-thirties. Unbound and free to pursue his fantasies, he was consistently rebuffed by the women he tried to lure. His myth and his perceptions went to war.

Your unending stream of experience flows in a feedback loop with your existing mythology. Your myths guide you toward particular actions, and the consequences of those actions either reinforce or challenge the guiding myth. When your experiences and your myths do not correspond, two basic possibilities emerge for handling the contradiction: You can alter your perception of the experience, or you can alter your myth. Our Casanova interpreted his first rejections as confirmations of his myth, modifying his perceptions to fit his self-image. He concluded, for instance, that his magnetism was so overwhelming that the women who rejected him simply could not cope with it, and they were forced to make a hasty retreat, selecting instead less manly suitors who did not intimidate them. After numerous rejections, he was forced to adjust his self-image, abandoning his Casanova identity. Similarly, you may unconsciously distort your perceptions so they can be assimilated into the mythology you hold, or you may, also often unconsciously, revise a guiding myth to incorporate new or freshly perceived experiences. Your mythology gradually evolves as it adjusts to experiences that do not fit its premises.

Myth and Counter-Myth at War. When a long-standing myth becomes too rigid or entrenched to adapt itself to new information, the psyche begins to formulate alternative ways of organizing experience. Counter-myths provide an impetus to expand beyond the limitations of the mythology you have been living. They can hasten development or ravage stability, depending partially on the awareness and skill with which you meet them. They may be modeled after the myths of others who have an influence on you, they may be rooted in a developmental readiness to accept the more enlightened myths of your culture, or they may be patterned after an intuitive perception of untried possibilities. In any realm of life that requires important decisions—from your relationships to your career to your use of leisure time—both the tendency to find comfort in familiar myths and the impetus to discover fresh ways of understanding are in continual play. From this dynamic tension, you adjust and you evolve.

William Blake observed that we have the option to fight mentally within ourselves or physically between ourselves.[4] People do not necessarily recognize both sides of a mythic conflict, though it rages within them. The tendency is to perceive the world through the eyes of a long-standing mythology, even as a counter-myth waits at the gate to your awareness, champing at the bit. When a counter-myth does break into your awareness, the tension between the two is a battle waged between your ingrained adaptations to the past and your recognition of a need for new strategies. The old myth is familiar, but its limited vision grew out of a world that no longer exists, a past that could not anticipate what would become possible. The counter-myth promises a more fertile but untested future.

The promise of the counter-myth sometimes ignites an individual into making a radical change—quitting a good job, leaving a viable marriage, moving to a new locale, joining a cult—which, in the long view of his or her life, proves to have been somewhere between self-defeating and disastrous. Many people report the experience of having left a difficult marriage only to select another partner with whom they create a painfully similar relationship. Unresolved issues with a parent may be at the core of the mythology that attracts a person to an emotionally equivalent situation. While a counter-myth may have emerged with enough strength to make it untenable to stay in the first marriage, the old mythology still prevailed in the selection of the next mate.

When your mythology is being challenged by a counter-myth, the possible outcomes range from living out the conflict unconsciously, and repeatedly, to working it through and moving on. Changes that are rooted in an *integration* between the worthwhile features of the old myth and the inspiration of the counter-myth are fostered by developing a larger mythic perspective that is attuned to the meaning of the change and its long-term consequences.

Myth and Counter-Myth in Concert. Several scenarios are possible at the points of conflict between an old myth and a counter-myth. You may consciously identify primarily with the old myth or with the counter-myth, become increasingly torn or confused, or work out a compromise that sacrifices some desirable elements of each; or, as the inner resolution becomes more complete, a new myth may emerge that incorporates the best qualities of both while transcending many of their limitations. Fostering such a constructive resolution of the conflict is the focus of this and the following chapter.

The conflict between a prevailing myth and a counter-myth was poignantly evident in Philip, a successful young sales manager who sought counseling because, in his words, "I am failing as a husband and I am afraid that my marriage is not going to survive." Philip's highly religious parents had placed heavy emphasis on family loyalty, and his father, whom he admired tremendously, was like a television caricature of the 1950s "family man"—a dedicated, trustworthy, and quietly self-sacrificing provider. The son not only attempted to emulate his father in his own marriage, he upped the ante by selecting a wife who was so insecure and demanding that no matter what he did, she was unsatisfied. She expected his unwavering attention during every free moment he had away from work, she expected him to be in the car and headed home from work every day at 5:01 P.M., and she was prone to debilitating psychosomatic illnesses when he would balk at her demands. Given the structure of the personal mythology that was defining Philip's role as a husband, he could only sympathize with her illnesses, take extra special care of her while she was sick, and amid great guilt and self-recrimination, pledge himself to show greater devotion the next time so he would not again disappoint her. But of course, she was always disappointed. That was the unwritten contract of their mythology à deux. Her dependency was interlocked with his prodigious efforts to keep her happy.

As is often the case, when Philip came for help, he was scrutinizing the problem through the lens of his old myth. He believed that his marital difficulties were caused primarily by his failure to live up to his father's example, so patient and giving a husband that, Philip believed, he could have made any woman happy. Just beyond Philip's awareness, however, another image of the role of a marriage partner was being kindled, and it was fanned as he witnessed successful give-and-take relationships in the lives of his acquaintances. In attempting to make sense of the contradiction that although he was all give and his wife was all take, yet she was still unhappy and resentful, he began at some level to generate another view of what was required in a marriage. This counter-myth gave credence to his needs as an individual, separate from the marriage. But such impulses seemed unthinkably self-indulgent to him, and he batted them away from his awareness like flies at a picnic.

The inclination to attend more to his own needs, however, and to expect more from his wife kept cropping up in subtle ways and became increasingly difficult for Philip just to shoo away. It was particularly evident in a growing anger and resentment that he could not control. Sometimes, after feeling quite satisfied with the marriage, he would suddenly swing pendulumlike to an exaggerated selfishness and blatant spite toward his wife. Then, as if the counter-myth were eclipsed by a revival of the old myth, he would again find himself in the grips of guilt and remorse. As he began to explore his anger in his therapy sessions, he was challenged to find a larger mythic vision that would retain the wholesome values from his old mythology while supporting a more vital personal life for himself and a more realistic relationship with his wife.

To summarize, sacrificing the familiarity, self-understanding, and worldview associated with a prevailing though outdated myth can be so painful that you fight dearly to reject the emerging myth. On the other hand, you may be so distressed with the problems the old myth creates for you that you attempt to sever yourself from it and clutch at a counter-myth. But the counter-myth, which was in part developed to compensate for the old myth, inevitably has its own distortions and limitations. Understanding these polarities can help you achieve a balance when you find yourself on a seesaw between old and emerging myths. Paradoxically, in order to grow beyond an old myth, it is often necessary to accept the role it played in your life, understand the reasons you needed it at one time, and appreciate the valid messages it still holds. The old myth and the counter-myth will naturally, and often outside your awareness, compete to influence the way you make sense of your world. While both support partial and often seemingly incompatible directions for your development, resolving their inevitable conflict will ultimately serve to expand your sense of who you are and the options your world offers.

PURPOSE: *To further the cooperation and understanding between the figures personifying your conflicting myths*

This is the second of three personal rituals that involve dialogue between your old-myth and counter-myth characters. You may find that after performing the ritual for transforming obstacles into opportunities, a new pathway of communication has opened between the two sides. In addition, where the first dialogue was intended to accent the differences between the sides, in this dialogue you will encourage them to begin to understand and accept or at least respect each other's position. Both sides are aspects of who you are, and each benefits when they can exist together in better harmony. You will set up the dialogue much as you did earlier, alternately embodying the posture of each side. At this point in the program, Meg's "Proper Young Lady" and her "Born-again Child" were able to express only more animosity toward each other and made little movements as Meg extended their dialogue. Ann's "Angel Girl" and "Slasher," however, were able to enjoy some progress:

ANGEL GIRL: I would like you to honor my pace and not push others too fast.
SLASHER: I hear that, and I would like you to realize the importance of
    speaking the truth at all times.
ANGEL GIRL: I ask for your patience if I find it difficult in some areas.
SLASHER: You will have my patience, as long as you promise that you will
    listen to me so we can find a way to say, however long it takes, what has to
    be said.

ANGEL GIRL: I can do that. It's hard for me sometimes to be able to distinguish between when I'm being discerning and when I'm just shutting people out.

SLASHER: I can understand that. If you will always check in to your body and see if your body feels comfortable with what you are saying, you will discover whether or not you are actually telling the full truth.

ANGEL GIRL: If I am having trouble speaking the truth bluntly, are you willing initially for us to find a way to say what is needed to be said as gently as possible?

SLASHER: I can do that, as long as I am sure you and I have an agreement that you are going to strive to be able to always speak the truth to people.

ANGEL GIRL: I can do that. I can say I truly will strive, but I may hit some times when I'll find it very, very difficult. At those times, you'll bend?

SLASHER: I'll bend.

ANGEL GIRL: Thank you.

You can see how the two figures personifying Ann's conflict are gradually becoming more able to cooperate. Extend your own dialogue after reading about the second round of Frank's:

JOLLY GREEN GIANT (responding to Earnest's last outburst after the invitation that he try Giant's path): Calm down, little man. I can understand that you're scared. Maybe we can find a pace that will keep me feelin' like we're still alive without scarin' you to death.

EARNEST: Well, you talk like I wouldn't have anything to offer even if I wanted to do something with you.

JOLLY GREEN GIANT: One thing you certainly know how to do is to apply yourself, although you generally have the imagination of a goldfish in the choices you make for those precious efforts. I propose that you apply yourself to some of the things I might get a kick out of, too.

EARNEST: Such as?

JOLLY GREEN GIANT: I thought we might try downhill skiing this month and white-water rafting in the summer.

EARNEST: That does it! You go your way and I'll go mine. I find your proposed endeavors totally terrifying, and I find you, sir, to be an insensitive, reckless boor.

JOLLY GREEN GIANT: Your oversensitivity certainly balances any insensitivity in me, but I guess I can understand your fears. What if we start with your takin' some time off to go cross-country skiing? You enjoy that, much as you hate to admit it.

EARNEST: But before we can go off on this wildly irresponsible odyssey of passion and flight, we must be sure that someone is minding the store.

JOLLY GREEN GIANT: I don't mind bein' sure the store is bein' minded, but if we must be certain that no speck of dust that lands may light in its resting place for more than seventeen seconds, such as is your custom, we shall have precious little time for anything else.

EARNEST: But if I do not attend to the store in the exquisite manner to which I, along with anyone with any class, am accustomed, two complications may be foreseen. First, all our excess and idle time might soon become dreadfully boring unless your program is quite magnificent. Second, I would surely lose the opportunity of being this year's recipient of the National Broom Society's Best-Kept Shop Award. If I am to forgo that honor, then this trip had better, pardon the expression, be damned good.

JOLLY GREEN GIANT: Trust me, Earnest. Take a deep breath, lean back, and enjoy the ride.

EARNEST: I think this is rather insane, but I shall retain an open mind about your idiotic scheme.

PURPOSE: *To experience in your body a symbolic resolution of the conflict between your old myth and your counter-myth*

This personal ritual is designed to deepen further the integration you have been cultivating between your old myth and your counter-myth. Just as you saw in an earlier ritual how your body may be a battlefield for the conflicts in your personal mythology, it may also be a temple for the resolution of those conflicts.

PREPARATION: *You have already associated your old myth with one hand and your counter-myth with your other hand. Review in your journal the entry for Week 5, Session 3, the sentence describing your old myth and the sentence describing your counter-myth. You will begin here by again representing your conflicting myths in your hands. This time, however, you will not stop with the conflict but transform it, imagining a physical integration of its two sides and finding a phrase that symbolizes its resolution. Sit or recline comfortably, take a deep breath, and close your eyes.*

As you tune in to your breathing, listen for your inhalation and your exhalation. Notice how your belly and chest fill . . . and empty. Your breath becomes slow and deep. Tensions release as your mind and body relax more completely.

Sense again which hand you associate more with your old myth and which hand you associate more with your counter-myth. Are they still represented on the same sides as they were earlier? Focus on the hand that represents your old myth. Notice the sensations in the same side of your body as this hand.

Now focus on the other side of your body and notice the sensations. Compare the two sides. Is one warmer than the other? Lighter? Heavier? Darker?

Notice where in your body the two sides meet. Is the line jagged or straight? Do the energies of the two myths repel each other along this boundary line? Do the energies blend? Is one side reaching or pushing over into the other side?

Mentally communicate with both sides. Set the intention that you are inviting the energies of the two sides to mingle and integrate into a single energy.

Place your hands so your palms are facing each other, about two feet apart, and let your elbows bend so your arms are comfortable. Again tune in to the hand that represents your old myth and the hand that represents your counter-myth. Notice any sensations you can feel in the space between your hands.

Sense or imagine an energy pulling your hands together, as between opposites attracting. Allow this energy to increase with every breath. Feel the energies of each side of your body begin to blend with each other. Know that the instant your hands touch, a new symbol will emerge that represents an integration of your old myth and your counter-myth. At the same time, you will feel a merging of the energies between the two sides, and a single unified feeling will wash over your hands and permeate your body.

As the energies of your hands and the two sides of your body blend and integrate, take a deep, relaxing breath. Imagine the spirit of the old myth and of the counter-myth mingling, synthesizing, integrating, becoming a single energy that retains the best qualities of both. Allow them to harmonize further with every breath.

As the integration between the old myth and the counter-myth deepens, sense the changes they suggest, the new direction your life may take. As this mingling of the two myths permeates your body, allow a phrase or motto that symbolizes this sense of resolution and integration to come to you. With each breath, this phrase becomes more vivid and memorable. If a phrase has not yet come to you, make one up now. Lower your hands. Sense the energies between the two sides of your body flowing into each other and becoming a single unified energy.

You may bring back this feeling of integration anytime you wish by using a technique you are about to learn. Whenever you wish for a booster that furthers the integration of your old myth and your counter-myth, place your hands in front of you, palms facing each other. Recall your new myth motto. Then with three deep breaths, feel the space between your hands; slowly allow your hands to be drawn together, squeezing them as they meet. Sense the energies of the two sides of your body mingling and integrating in harmony and wholeness.

With three more deep breaths, feel this new integration wash over your body. Place your hands in front of you, palms facing each other. With three more deep breaths, feel the space between your hands and slowly allow your hands to be drawn together, squeezing them as they meet. Sense the energies of the two sides of your body mingling and integrating in harmony and wholeness. With three more deep breaths, feel this new integration wash over your entire body. You may repeat this sequence anytime you wish to evoke the energy of your new myth.

When you are ready, take another deep breath and return to your ordinary waking consciousness, refreshed, relaxed, and alert.

Describe this experience in your journal. In what ways did you feel an integration between the two sides? Of what obstacles were you aware? What new directions seemed to emerge for you? What was the motto of this newly integrated energy? Describe the steps for deepening the integration between your conflicting myths or injecting yourself with the energy of their resolution (taking three breaths, bringing your hands together, and squeezing them while recalling the motto).

Ann wrote:

As my hands drew toward each other I could feel an anxiety, a fear that something within me would have to die for the new to be born. What if I became cold and unfeeling? What if I became grandiose? But I could also feel a sense of longing to begin the journey. As my hands finally came together, there was a sense of relief, a coming home, a greater sense of safety. The motto was spoken by both myths together: "Love without Truth is chaos. Truth without Love is cruel."

PURPOSE: *To generate a reverie that points the way toward further resolution of your mythic conflict*

You have, through this program, been tilling the symbolic soil of your inner life, finding the roots of existing mythic images, generating new imagery, and exper-

SESSION 3:
A Resolution
Fantasy

imenting with novel combinations. From here, you will be cultivating a single guiding vision that points you in a new and more fulfilling direction—toward a meeting of your most valued potentials and the opportunities your world presents.

As you did when you requested an "integration dream," you will be inviting symbolism that further resolves your mythic conflict. In the previous personal ritual, you represented your mythic conflict in your body. Here you will create a fantasy—a symbolic journey—whose purpose is to further the integration between old and emerging mythic forces within you. You will be seeking a unifying symbol that assists you in resolving their discord.

PREPARATION: *With your Personal Shield and journal nearby, sit or recline comfortably, take a deep breath, and close your eyes.*

Settling into this safe, secure spot, focus on your breathing. Place your closed hands over your chest. Notice breath. Soften belly. Open heart. As you sense or imagine your heart opening, extend your arms outward, unfolding your hands, like flowers blooming, until they come to rest comfortably at your sides. Notice breath. Soften belly. Open heart. With each inhalation, breathe in the fullness of life. With each exhalation, release any tension, relaxing more completely. Breathe in. Release. Focus inward and call to your Inner Shaman, your inner wisdom: "My heart is open to you. Be with me on this journey."

Recall your earlier feelings as you explored the sensations in each of your hands. Starting with the hand that represented your old myth, re-create in this hand the sensations associated with that myth. Tune in to the energy and feeling of these sensations. Ask for a symbol to emerge from this energy that in some way reflects your old myth. The symbol may occur to you logically. Perhaps it would be an article of clothing from a memory of a time when your old myth was forming, or the face of a person, or an object that represents an experience from your past, or a symbol you have already worked with, such as the Paradise Lost drawing on your Personal Shield. Or the symbol may occur to you intuitively. As with a dream symbol, you might not know what it means at first. Your symbol may be very abstract, like a geometrical design on a colored background, or it could be very concrete and familiar. With your next several breaths, allow a symbol for your old myth to take form in your imagination. Remember this symbol. If you still have not come upon a symbol, make one up now.

Focus on your other hand. Re-create in it the sensations you associated with your counter-myth. Tune in to the energy and feeling of these sensations. Ask for a symbol to emerge from this energy that in some way reflects your counter-myth. Again, the symbol may occur to you logically or intuitively. It may be abstract or concrete. With your next several breaths, allow a symbol for your counter-myth to take form in your imagination. Remember this symbol. If you still have not come upon a symbol, make one up now.

Imagine that you have entered a large theater, and you are the only one in the audience. Take a comfortable seat wherever you wish. You are about to see your conflict dramatized on the stage. The play will have two acts. Act I is called "The Conflict." You know that when the curtain rises, the symbol of your old myth will meet the symbol of your counter-myth. However logical or illogical this may be, the stage will also have a setting that provides a context for their interaction. The lights dim and the curtain is about to rise. As it comes up, the two symbols are on the stage, and the conflict between them begins to unfold. Be alert as the story emerges.

In a few moments, the conflict will reach a climax. Allow your breathing to be slow and deep as you calmly take in the drama. The curtain is about to fall on Act I. As it does, breathe out any tension from your body and allow yourself to relax during this intermission.

Act II is called "The Resolution." In it, the two symbols will be supported to find an outcome that is favorable for each of them. Their relationship and their understanding and appreciation of each other will improve. You may already be wondering how your inner playwright is going to work this one out. Will the two symbols speak their new understanding and appreciation of each other? Will the resolution be expressed in their movements? How will the energy between them harmonize? What turn in the plot of the play will bring about the resolution to their conflict?

You are intent as the curtain rises for Act II. There again are the two symbols. As the action unfolds, they interact with each other in an increasingly harmonious, positive, and mutually supportive manner. Watch how they accomplish this.

The play is about to end. Allow your breathing to be slow and deep as you observe how the differences between the two symbols are settled. Examine the closing scene. As the curtain falls, tune in to your reactions about your play.

Prepare to return to your ordinary waking consciousness. You will be able to remember all you need of this experience. Very gently, begin to rouse yourself. Move your fingers and toes, your hands and feet. Feel your circulation. Stretch your shoulders, your arms and legs, your neck and face muscles. Take a deep breath. Bring your attention back into the room. Open your eyes, refreshed, as if waking from a wonderful nap, alert and fully competent to creatively meet the requirements of your day.

Describe in your journal the play as you experienced it. Two of the techniques presented in Support Guide 2 for deepening your understanding of your dreams can be particularly useful for examining your play. The first is called "vital focus." Reenact the play in your imagination, first Act I, then Act II. At vital moments—for instance when a scene changes, a new character appears, or the emotional tone shifts—freeze the action, making a still photograph or a short film clip of the scene in your mind. Take a deep breath. Scrutinize the scene, registering every detail you can. Attend to expressions, postures, props, and scenery you may not have noticed earlier. Sense the emotion of each character on the stage. You may also question the characters and even the scenery and props about their roles in the drama, as if they were actors, and allow them to answer you in your imagination. Examine in this manner two or three such moments in each act. Be open to your intuitions and insights about the meaning of the scene as well as of the entire play as you move through this process. Explore these insights further in your journal.

The second technique you will be using is based on the method of "extending the dream." Again envision the play unfolding. This time, however, rather than stop with the end of Act II, extend it in your imagination. Add a final scene that carries the play further and in the direction of even greater resolution between the two symbols. Register this final scene deeply and describe it in your journal, along with your associations and insights about its meaning. Here are Meg's reflections:

> I imagined my left hand (Born-again Child) playing with my dog (a golden retriever named Gud Dawg), fooling around with his muzzle, letting him mouth my hand with his potentially destructive but oh-so-gentle jaws and teeth, feeling his glove-leather ears, scratching under his chin. The energy between us was lovely. My right hand (Proper Young Lady) held a leash attached to a collar. It was smooth and strong, with a pivot attachment and a heavy hand grip. My hand felt occupied and useful but limited. It's laughably simple to see the symbolism in this fantasy. Gud Dawg is utterly trusting, has great yet gentle strength, and is the epitome of innocence and charm. He is also lacking in judgment in the ways of the world and would

quickly be hurt or killed without the limits I put on his freedom. I love him and in many ways he is a teacher for me, but I must look out for his in-the-world welfare, providing him with proper food, shelter, and fences in order to keep him safe. In return he shows me pure joy, forgiveness, generosity of spirit, and nobility of character. The leash is an instrument that limits Gud Dawg's activities and the distance he can move. While it is effective and life-preserving, anytime I can, in my responsible judgment, leave it off him, I do. I let him run freely in the forest. I restrict him in the city. I could punish him by use of the leash, and sometimes he reacts as if I had. It is important that I keep it clear in my mind what my motive is when I use it. If I am controlling for the sake of control, that's wrong and an insult to his character. If I use it to protect him from pain or confusion, then I am justified, whether he understands or not.

Meg saw herself as a character in her resolution fantasy:

I am skipping and turning, running in broken circles on the beach. Gud Dawg is leaping and frolicking beside me. The wind is crisp but without chill, the waves are beautiful, not stormy. He takes the leash I'm carrying and tugs on it with his mouth, inciting me to pull back, to whip him around before he drags the leather out of my hand. I have a good grip and know he can't take it from me, but neither can I pull the other end out of his mouth. We are both enjoying the contest. It occurs to me that if I can use the leash playfully and responsibly, it will become a valuable part of my life, saving me endless grief and difficulty. The innocent part of me needs the experienced part, and vice versa—I'm not so much at war as I was.

Ann's old myth was symbolized by an open hand, in a gesture of greeting. Her counter-myth was symbolized by a hand with the index finger pointing upward, as if making a point. In her imagery, the two symbols drew together and repelled apart. She was struck by her ambivalence about resolving their differences. She observed, "I could feel my urge to blend the two myths, and I could also feel my fear of the power of the counter-myth."

Frank reflected on his symbolism:

This time, as if to show how confused I am about which myth is stronger, my right arm became the old myth. I see it as a massive, cold stone wall.

My left arm is also a wall. But this wall seems ethereal and is very fragile. Next I see a knight on a horse. The knight has incredible muscles, kind of like the strong man in a circus. I see him reaching across so he is touching both walls, and he is going to pull them together. I see him struggling to pull them closer together, but something is stopping him. It seems he is realizing that the fragile wall will just crumble when it meets the stone wall, and that is not what he wants. So he builds a latticework structure into it so that even if it does crumble, it will retain its character. And then, through some magic spell, he brings heat to the other wall, and it begins to soften. It becomes transformed from cold blocks of stone into mounds of some warm, inviting, doughlike substance.

Then, as he pulls the two sides together, the fragile wall does indeed crumble, but that's okay because the latticework and the ethereal quality remain. When the two walls have merged, the lattice framework brings a magnificent sculpted form to the dough, which remains warm and soft. It was like I was being shown that for my two myths to come together, I have to soften the structure of the old myth and give more structure to the counter-myth. When I took the fantasy further, the new wall came to life and became animated. It actually became like a cartoon character of a mammoth elephant with the lattice becoming its skeletal structure and the doughlike substance its massive flesh. It started to walk around and do little dance steps and sing and play. The creature was very funny as it hobbled around, but then it caught my eye and knowingly winked at me, and it suddenly struck me that this colossal, playful creature was somehow very wise.

DREAM FOCUS:

Dreaming Your New Myth

PURPOSE: *To glimpse, in your dreams, the shape and complexion of a new guiding myth*

Review your journal for any recent dreams that provide a glimpse into a new myth that synthesizes the best qualities of your old myth and your counter-myth. Use one or more of the dream interpretation techniques in Support Guide 2 to work with any dreams that you identify. To incubate a "new myth" dream, ask for a new myth that resolves your original conflict. Before falling asleep, take a few deep breaths, think about your conflict, affirm your desire for a new direction, and write slowly and mindfully in your journal a statement such as: "I will sleep soundly and peacefully tonight while having a dream that reveals to me a new, more wholesome, guiding image. When I awake, I will recall my dream." Then, with deliberation, repeat several times before falling asleep, "I will have a meaningful dream, and I will remember it." Immediately upon waking, record and explore your dream. If you don't recall a dream the first night, repeat the process each night until you do. Here is Ann's "new myth" dream and her analysis of it:

Dwayne (my partner) and I were in a battleground. He was stabbed in the back and fell into my arms. I lowered him gently to the ground and placed the pin he had made me in the wound, and I very strongly said, "You must not die! You must not leave me!" I turned a couch over so that he was protected under it. I then found a powerful sword and stood between him and anyone who moved toward us. I fought and killed about forty knights. I fought with tremendous ferocity. When all the opponents were dead, I hurried and lifted the couch off Dwayne. He was white and almost dead. I took hold of his feet and began to pour into his body all the energy that the fight had created in me. Again I said, "You must not leave me!" Energy returned to him. He sat up, and we embraced.

I Am Dwayne's Back: I am open and unprotected. I don't see danger. I am wounded by my blindness.

I Am the Pin: I am a testament of the balanced union of masculine and feminine love. I have the feather of an eagle which gives me freedom and vision; the talon of the osprey which makes me strong and bold; and a crystal that gives me clarity and insight. I bring these qualities of clarity, strength, and sight to the blindness of Dwayne's back.

I Am the Forty Knights: I am the competitions of the world. I am the power seekers. I am the hostile elements.

I Am Dwayne: I am kindness. I am enthusiasm, artistry, innocence, joy.

I Am Ann: I am capable, protective, resourceful.

I Am the Energy: I am the power of justice, the force of truth, the life urge to survive.

I Am the Embrace: I am the union, the coming together, the safety, the love.

This dream seems to be telling me that the aspect of me that shares Dwayne's qualities needs the protection of the strength, clarity, and vision of the other aspect of me. It feels as if the new myth that is seeking to arise in me is a place of balance where I have the capacity both to protect and to be protected, to bring forth power and to be receptive to my needs.

It is entirely possible that your imagery, dialogues, and dreams, rather than leading to resolution, seem to be telling you that the two myths are not yet ripe for integration. Some people find this so discouraging that they force a resolution for which they are not ready. But even the successful integration of conflicting energies into a single, unified image does not erase the fact that there are two forces at play. Because each side has its own strengths, you probably would not want to lose either completely. In most cases, the constructive resolution of the competing myths resembles teamwork more than the dominance of one side by the other. In that teamwork, the two sides begin to operate as one, so you may eventually feel a unified inner voice on issues about which you once felt deeply divided. The opening personal ritual of the following chapter directs your energies toward further building such teamwork.

FOURTH STAGE

From Vision to Commitment

——————— ✥ ———————

Committing to a Renewed Mythology

✵

The future is not out there in front of us, but inside us.
—Joanna Macy[1]

Mythic images organize your perceptions, thoughts, feelings, and behavior into the repetitive patterns that are the constants of your life. They have a magnetic force that pulls you to conform to them. Psychologist David McClelland and his colleagues identified relationships among the imagery in popular literature and subsequent societal events, including economic output, political violence, and participation in warfare.[2] For instance, the amount of achievement imagery (based on a standardized scoring system) found in fairy tales and children's readers predicted the society's level of productivity twenty years later, when that generation had become the labor force. Aggressive imagery in popular literature foreshadowed warfare. Such relationships were found in a wide range of cultures throughout much of recorded history.

How can you assess the long-term consequences of the new mythic image you have been cultivating in this program? Have the qualities of life-enhancing guiding myths been established? What are the characteristics of personal myths that are harmful? Habits of thought that sustain personal happiness and fulfillment have been studied by psychologists, along with habits of thought that tend to impede them. Your happiness depends more, for instance, on your capacities to set realistic expectations, appreciate your blessings, and savor small day-to-day pleasures than on your age, gender, race, location, education, or, assuming you are living above the poverty level, material wealth.[3] Does your current guiding mythology prompt you to revel in small delights? In this chapter and the next, you will be assessing and refining your new mythic vision in the light of contemporary psychological knowledge, and you will advance a commitment to manifest that vision in your world.

People inevitably project, habitually and unconsciously, their inner images onto the ambiguous situations life continually presents. The way your mythology organizes your psychological life determines a great deal about your happiness and effectiveness in the world. Does your new mythic image make it easier to like yourself? Research shows that people with strong feelings of self-worth are "less vulnerable to ulcers and insomnia, less likely to abuse drugs, more independent of pressures to conform, and more persistent at difficult tasks."[4] Does your new mythic image usher you toward more fulfilling relationships, more rewarding social activities, greater social support, a present-centered absorption in the flow of life, physical fitness, and enough rest and personal solitude, all of which are also associated with happiness?[5] Does your new mythic image realistically highlight that which gives you greater control over your future? Extensive social science surveys have found that "having a strong sense of controlling one's life is a more dependable predictor of positive feelings of well-being" than many of the more "objective conditions of life."[6]

Martin Seligman, the psychologist who coined the terms "learned helplessness" to describe one of the central dynamics of depression and "learned optimism" to describe one of the dominant characteristics of people whose lives are highly effective, has persuasively demonstrated that the inner templates you place on your experiences can have a profound impact on your welfare. In brief, his studies show that if you *feel* helpless, you will be less effective in the world than if you feel optimistic.[7] Along the continuum from "learned helplessness" to "learned optimism," depression and despair decrease while life satisfaction, personal effectiveness, and overall happiness increase. People whose internal explanatory schemes—their personal myths—lead them to believe mistakenly that the sources of their misfortunes and disappointments are permanent act far less effectively than people who (within limits) err in the other direction.[8]

Another bias that works against personal effectiveness, according to Seligman, is the routine attribution of failures to general rather than *specific* causes, prompting you to assess your problems as being more pervasive than they actually are. Seligman's research also suggests that your effectiveness is compromised if you blame yourself too much for outcomes over which you have no control. In addition, Seligman targets rampant individualism without a commitment to the common good as another strategy of thought that is ultimately a source of "increased depression, poor health, and [life] without meaning."[9]

Dan McAdams, who has conducted the most compelling research to date specifically on "personal myths," has identified six standards that modern adults might employ in critically evaluating the stories they create to make sense of their lives:[10]

1. The first is *coherence,* the extent to which the characters of the story are consistent with the context of the story, the culture, and human nature; the extent to which events in the story follow in a logical manner; and the extent to which the parts of the story do not contradict one another. If your personal mythology lacks coherence, it leaves you wondering why life turns out in such an inexplicable, puzzling manner.

2. The second criterion of a life story that supports mental health is *openness.* Some personal myths are too coherent, striving for a level of consistency that does not account for the instabilities and ambiguities of life—particularly of modern life—does not allow for the consideration of alternative futures, and does not support the need for change, growth, and development. The requirement for openness and flexibility in a personal mythology must be balanced against the requirement for coherence, commitment, and resolve.

3. *Credibility* is McAdams's third standard. While we modern adults consciously participate in the creation of our identities to a greater extent than ever before in history, "we do not create them out of thin air, as we might a poem or a fiction."[11] An adaptive guiding mythology takes into account the facts of the person's abilities and circumstances.

4. The fourth standard is *increasing differentiation.* As you develop and as you assimilate new experiences, your personal mythology will naturally become richer, deeper, and more complex.

5. At the same time, an effective mythology leads to the *reconciliation* of conflicting internal forces, opposing subpersonalities, and contradictory aims and visions.

6. In McAdams's final standard, which he calls *generative integration,* the inner story leads toward "a creative involvement in a social world that is larger and more enduring than the self."[12]

In the early part of the program, your efforts fostered the *differentiation* of a prevailing myth and an emerging myth. In the middle part you were working toward their *integration*. The task from this point on is to advance this integration further so that the most functional, most adaptive, most positive elements of your old myth and your counter-myth are incorporated into a new myth that is attuned to the above principles. The program has been designed so the new mythology that emerges from the steps you are following will be slanted in just those ways.

SESSION 1:
Extending Your Dialogue with Your Inner Shaman's Support

PURPOSE: *To engage the deep wisdom of your Inner Shaman in resolving remaining discord between your old myth and your counter-myth*

In the following personal ritual, you will be advancing the dialogue between the characters representing your old myth and your counter-myth, but this time you will also bring into the process a personification of your Inner Shaman. Here is an example of how the conversation unfolded for Meg:

PROPER YOUNG LADY (yelling to Born-again Child, who has again gotten away): Your obstinacy is going to keep you from becoming a mature and responsible adult!

BORN-AGAIN CHILD: Seems to me that the people who you call "mature and responsible" are just bored, and they are certainly <u>boring</u>. They think that now that they are mature, everything is all settled, finished, with nothing new to learn. I am happy that I'm always growing and learning new things.

PROPER YOUNG LADY: Well, I was taught all I need to know by my parents and my Sunday-school teachers. But sometimes I do ask if I'm being the full person I was meant to be.

SHAMAN: Good question. I want to congratulate you on asking one of the seminal questions of all time.

BORN-AGAIN CHILD: Hey, I can ask that same question! I'm the most curious of the lot.

PROPER YOUNG LADY: I never thought I'd hear you admit to being anything but completely satisfied with your total self-indulgence.

BORN-AGAIN CHILD: I hate giving in to the stuffy likes of you, but the fact is I am somewhat attracted to pretty clothes and would like to learn how to earn a living. I would even like it, I think, if someone courted me.

PROPER YOUNG LADY: Fat chance.

SHAMAN: Now, now . . . see what you can do to behave like loving sisters. Otherwise, you are each always going to feel incomplete.

BORN-AGAIN CHILD: Oh, my! I don't want that.

PROPER YOUNG LADY: Me neither! Let me, since I'm the more mature, make the first concession. I would like you to teach me to build a sand castle. Some I've seen are very pretty.

BORN-AGAIN CHILD: You'd get all sandy and feel like you'd lowered yourself.

SHAMAN: You must give each other the benefit of the doubt. If you do that, you are much more likely to be believed yourselves.

BORN-AGAIN CHILD (enthusiastically): You're really willing to learn from me, Proper Young Lady? No kidding? Wow! I do much better when I'm treated like an equal instead of a defective piece of machinery.

PROPER YOUNG LADY (looking old and tired): I need you because maybe you can help me feel alive, robust, excited. Without you, I get caught up in competition, sickness in my spirit and my body. I bog down, feel heavy, on the brink of death. Can you teach me to play again?

BORN-AGAIN CHILD: I will teach you all about sand castles and dams! How's that?

PROPER YOUNG LADY: And I will give you the pink dress with the lace collar I've seen you looking at enviously. I'll even throw in some satin hair ribbons. But you're sure you can teach me how to play?

BORN-AGAIN CHILD (taking her hand): Hey, it's just like riding a bicycle. Come on, I've got a golden retriever puppy I want you to meet.

SHAMAN: I'm pleased with both of you. It is time now to consider how you are going to work out living together.

PROPER YOUNG LADY: It makes sense for me to be in charge during the school and business day. Maybe when we're out in public too. And I hope you, Born-again Child, will be in charge of our free time, when we can have sensations, be loud, ask questions, and be free of constraints.

BORN-AGAIN CHILD: You bet. Good plan. Could I wear your eyelet petticoat with the pink dress too?

Your Inner Shaman's aid may be of special value in finding creative solutions to the problems that are still of concern to the characters governing each side of your conflict. In previous rituals, you have seen your Shaman's wisdom and love.

The Inner Shaman is also rugged and disciplined, fully recognizing that at times difficult decisions, compromises, and sacrifices must be made. Strength must also be developed, and this strength must be creatively, and in certain circumstances, forcefully, applied. You can expect your Shaman to be a fair but tough moderator in this next dialogue. As in the previous ones, you may wish to have a blank tape available so you can record the encounter.

Begin by finding the stance, posture, and facial expression of the figure who represents your old myth. Next step back, face that image, and find the stance, posture, and facial expression of the figure who represents your counter-myth. Then step out of that role and move into the position of the Shaman, forming a triangle as you face the other two figures. Take all the time you need to find the stance, posture, and facial expressions that correspond with your Shaman. Next, as the Shaman, ask the other two figures: "Where are you not in agreement?" Then have the figures representing your mythic conflict engage in a dialogue about this question. Continue until they reach an agreement or an impasse. Whenever they reach an agreement, you will return to the position of the Shaman, comment on the resolution they reached, and ask, "Are there additional areas in which I may assist you?"

If the two figures come to an impasse, return to the position of the Shaman; consider the desires, needs, and intentions of each; and address one or both figures. Then allow them to engage each other in further dialogue, until they reach some level of agreement or need further assistance. Continue by moving into all three of the positions as needed, until the most important issues have been addressed and the highest degree of resolution possible for the three of you, combining your resources, has been achieved. When you are finished, from the position of the Shaman, invite both figures to contact you, through imagination or through another enactment like this one, whenever your help is needed. Recreate or summarize this discussion in your journal. Here is Ann's conversation:

SHAMAN: I've brought the two of you here to see if we can bring peace
    between you.
ANGEL GIRL: I want nothing but peace.
SLASHER: I want the truth.
SHAMAN: So what we are looking for here is a way that we can have peace
    and truth and love living in one body.
ANGEL GIRL: I still feel that the truth is too difficult to marry with love.
SLASHER: If you don't get it together, we're going to have endless chaos on our
    hands.

SHAMAN: Perhaps what can happen here is that if the two of you look at the two aspects of myself, you could each align with one of the parts of me. Angel Girl, join in with the Madonna aspect of myself. Slasher, join in with the Dark Discerner. Who I am is your new myth.

ANGEL GIRL: I can feel fear at the thought of giving up my power here.

SLASHER: Your sentimentality could undermine my power here. I don't like it!

ANGEL GIRL: I've seen the truth be so cruel to so many people.

SLASHER: I've seen us wounded over and over again by your not letting me have my say.

SHAMAN: Can you see how impossible it is—the two of you must work together.

ANGEL GIRL: I do see that, and I will do everything I can to relinquish my hold on the kingdom here.

SLASHER: And I will do everything in my power not to steal power from you, but to share the throne with you.

SHAMAN: Whenever you are in doubt, hold back, go slowly, and check in with me.

I've known for years and years and years how incredibly hard it is for me to tell the truth if it is going to hurt someone. I've put myself down for it so deeply, and it's only through this inner work I'm doing that I've seen the thing I've disdained in myself as in fact a great beauty. If I can acknowledge my kindness as beautiful and add to it rather than do away with it, that's where the power is going to come from. To be that compassionate with people, and then to add the truth and discernment, is a much better way to go through life. I'm not suddenly going to become cold and cruel. By combining my basic urge to be kind with discernment is true kindness.

At the end of Frank's last dialogue, the two figures had reached a tense agreement about taking time off to go cross-country skiing. This segment of the dialogue begins with Earnest having second thoughts:

SHAMAN: With what disagreements may I help you?

EARNEST (to Jolly Green Giant): I've been reconsidering the prudence of our pact. I believe you want me to all but drop out of my work and my responsibilities. I do not believe you have seen to all the details to ensure that everything will be kept in Proper Condition.

JOLLY GREEN GIANT: If we wait until your good time to start enjoyin' ourselves, we'll still be in the office at midnight on New Year's Eve in the year 2020! I'm _tired_ of waitin' for you, and if you won't make some major changes right now, I'm goin' to quit cooperatin' with you at all. You need me in ways you don't know about. If I weren't taggin' along in the dreary life you have carved out for us, you'd have dried up and died years ago.

EARNEST: You always want to move so fast! How about if we take off to play one time this year to see if we like it? An experiment. If we like it, maybe we'll do it again next year.

JOLLY GREEN GIANT: One time this year—perhaps again next year! My, you are gutsy! I don't think this discussion is goin' anywhere except to bog us down in your characteristically obsessional and boring ways. I appeal to our wise old friend here to get us out of this endless rut you keep draggin' us into.

SHAMAN: I have comforting news for you, Earnest. You truly can afford to relax. You have my assurance that you are not going to be so powerfully swept away that you cannot return to the ways with which you are so familiar and comfortable. Should you stumble, you need only stand up. You can take many more risks than you have ever imagined would be within the limits of conscientiousness.

And Giant, you must be much more appreciative of the steps Earnest does take. Rather than continually pointing out to him how much further he has to go, you can relax, and immerse yourself in the small new freedoms that are offered by the changes he has sincerely begun to make. He will blossom only if you reward him for what he does correctly instead of continually criticizing and ridiculing him for not doing enough.

I ask each of you to alter your attitudes in these ways, and you will reap the gifts you have for each other more fully. You will each find the other to be less of an enemy and more of a friend.

EARNEST: Okay, Giant, I will trust you to lead me to take _small_ steps. That much of an invitation, I offer. But if you _dare_ to force me to go too fast, or say another _word_ about downhill skiing or white-water rafting unless _I_ bring up these horrific subjects, it will be seven years and seven days before I will even discuss so much as a vacation with you again.

JOLLY GREEN GIANT: Okay, Earnest, that is fair. And I do appreciate the efforts you are makin' to increase the enjoyment each of us has in his life, however cautious they may be.

SHAMAN: Watch that sarcasm, Giant.

JOLLY GREEN GIANT: Okay, okay. I know that each step you take into my territory is frightening for you, and I will acknowledge your efforts, and yes, even your courage for takin' them.

SHAMAN: That's better.

JOLLY GREEN GIANT: Well, I guess that's about as much fun as we can hope to have for today. Let's shake on it.

EARNEST (extending his hand, playfully): Aren't you getting to be the gentleman!

SHAMAN: This is a good beginning. I must warn you not to expect too much from each other. Each of you will make mistakes in learning the ways of your until now distant counterpart. I encourage you to treat what you have agreed on as an experiment, to approach it with goodwill, and when you have difficulties, to return to me and to continue our deliberations.

You can see that, with his Inner Shaman's assistance, each of Frank's competing subpersonalities began to recognize the strengths of the others' positions and to find more room to experiment with ways that had seemed foreign. Use your Inner Shaman to teach the figures representing your conflict to cooperate in a way that makes the resources of each more available to you.

PURPOSE: *To prepare the way further for a more vital guiding mythology by going to the source of a dysfunctional myth and using your imagination to transform the conditions that established it*

Some experiences from your past leave a residue of trauma and fear that inevitably hampers your development until they are, in one way or another, understood and healed and the emotional residue is released. Here, as in some of the previous rituals, you will be selecting a moment of wounding from your childhood.

PREPARATION: *Review the Paradise Lost section of your Personal Shield and the earlier journey to childhood roots of your mythic conflict, looking to identify a time of personal wounding. Or perhaps a totally different scene will occur to you now. With your Personal Shield and journal nearby, sit or recline comfortably, take a deep breath, and close your eyes.*

Settling into this safe, secure spot, focus on your breathing. Place your closed hands over your chest. Notice breath. Soften belly. Open heart. As you sense

SESSION 2:
Rewriting
History
Through the
Emotionally
Corrective
Daydream

or imagine your heart opening, extend your arms outward, unfolding your hands, like flowers blooming, until they come to rest comfortably at your sides. Notice breath. Soften belly. Open heart. With each inhalation, breathe in the fullness of life. With each exhalation, release any tension, relaxing more completely. Breathe in. Release. Focus inward and call to your Inner Shaman, your inner wisdom: "My heart is open to you. Be with me on this journey."

In a moment you will be reflecting on a scene where you were wounded in a way that has had reverberations in your mythology and in your way of being in the world. Recall the Paradise Lost drawing on your Personal Shield. Recall your journey to the event that led to some of the beliefs and codes of conduct you took on in your childhood. In the next few moments, choose one of these events or allow another memory from which a healing would be personally beneficial. Allow the scene to become more and more vivid with your next three breaths. If a scene of a time of wounding has not yet come to you, allow it to emerge now, or make up a plausible scene in your imagination.

Examine the scene closely. Notice who is there and what is occurring. In a moment, you in your adult form will go back in time and magically enter the scene. As you magically come into the scene, you have the respectful, in fact, awed, attention of those who are there and who have just watched you materialize. You are fully aware of what is being done that is hurtful to your younger self, and you can see the deepest motivations of whoever is causing the suffering. You can understand the person's distortions, difficulties in life, and shortcomings. You can see it all. If your younger self's wound is caused by something out of anyone's control, such as a death or an accident, you can observe how others respond and whether they help the child effectively adapt to the trauma.

In this fantasy, you are able to change the scene. You may be able to shift the behavior of someone who is causing the wound by bringing new awareness to that person. You can bring out a deeper truth or a more humane response. You can find someone to protect your younger self better, or you can teach the child better methods of self-protection.

Select one person who might be able to improve the child's circumstances. Use the full force of your creativity to bring this person to make choices that are more humane and compassionate and beneficial for your younger self.

If you are able to show or persuade this person to take more constructive action, allow the fantasy to unfold so the person does things differently, perhaps more lovingly, perhaps more wisely. To the extent your imagination allows, have the person who is doing things differently also shower tremendous love on the child. If you are not able to enlist one of the actual participants in the scene to do things in a better way, then you, in your adult form, may step into the fantasy and nurture or protect the child in just the way the child needs. In any case, speak to the child. Give the child information or advice that might be helpful. And also shower the child with your affection.

Move into the experience as the child receives this love from you in your adult form as well as from any other participant from the scene who can extend compassion to your younger self. Experience the love coming into you. Receive it with your inhalation. With your exhalation, release the sorrow and pain stored up from this period of your life. Receive the love; release the sorrow. As you survey this scene, if you would like to say something to any of the characters in order to complete this visit to your past, go ahead and say it now. When you have finished the conversations, take a deep breath, and move forward in time to the present.

Prepare to return to your ordinary waking consciousness. You will be able to remember all you need of this experience. Very gently, begin to rouse yourself. Move your fingers and toes, your hands and feet. Feel your circulation. Stretch your shoulders, your arms and legs, your neck and face muscles. Take a deep breath. Bring your attention back into the room. Open your eyes, refreshed, as if waking from a wonderful nap, alert and fully competent to creatively meet the requirements of your day.

Remaining deeply relaxed, make a commitment to yourself that every day, for as long as you find it useful, you will set aside a few minutes to relive this scene, to make it more and more a reality for yourself. In a manner similar to the way dreams can heal emotional wounds, this fantasized revision of your personal history, deeply experienced, can have an emotionally healing impact. Ann wrote the following:

The scene I went back to was an evening in the living room when I was about eleven or twelve years old. I was entering the room when I heard my father say, "Well, Ann is a real sweetie, and we all love her, but everybody knows that she is bone from the neck up." I can remember being stopped in my tracks. If I was retarded in some way, there's no way that I would know I was retarded. I felt a chill go through me. I went up to my room and sat on the bed in shock. I felt profoundly shaken and humiliated. So this was why I was doing so terribly in school. This was why so many things made no sense to me and seemed so difficult.

As I entered into the scene as an adult, I first spoke to my father: "Dad, you need to see that Ann has a way of seeing that is not natural to you.

Your way of thinking represents a patriarchal view that has shamed the feminine way of being in the world. Your daughter Ann is incredibly creative. Her mind works in ways that you cannot conceive. She is stifled in the confines of the school she attends. She learns best with acknowledgment, support, and trust in her creative force."

I also realized how much I wanted to comfort the girl. I wanted to help her know what was happening, and why her way of thinking did not fit in. I knelt down beside her and looked into her eyes. I told her that it was impossible for most people to understand the way she thinks because the way she gathers information is unique. I told her that though she couldn't see it now, the very sense of failure that she was feeling was part of the training that would give her richer ways of seeing. I told her that in years to come she would be prized for the fresh and creative insight she would bring to things and that some of the best minds in the world would enjoy her company and find it useful. I told her she needn't fear that she was not smart enough to handle the gifts and influence she would have, for she was bright and intelligent. She was extremely relieved to hear my words and to feel my love.

This was very powerful for me. I feel this to be very related to why I fear the truth. If I were ever to say something that blocked another person like that, I would be horrified. Plus, Dad's comment planted the nagging doubt that I am "bone from the neck up" and that whatever I speak will not be true or wise and could therefore do damage. This exercise puts an old fear to rest.

SESSION 3:
Consulting Your Power Object

PURPOSE: *To find guidance about your new myth in the patterns of nature*

The natural environment is rich in symbols and metaphors that can instruct you on attaining greater rapport with your inner nature. In this ritual, you will use a natural object as an ally to teach you about harmony and balance as you envision your new personal myth. Go outdoors and find a Power Object—a stone, a flower, a milkweed pod, a piece of wood, a leaf—that draws you to itself, or select something you already possess. One man found a stone near his driveway that was smooth on one side and rough on the other side. Meg chose a geode (a stone in which there is a cavity lined with crystals) that she had treasured for a long time. People often select something that grows. Meg reflected in her journal:

My Power Object is my geode. It has been cut in half, and the cut surface has been polished. The outside is rough and looks uncompromising. The cut surface has many shades of cream, gold, and honey in frozen rings. At the center is a heart of crystal. The crystal catches and refracts the light with its tiny prisms. The whole thing is wonderfully complex and beautiful.

I see that it took a major change—cutting the geode in half—to expose the magnificent center. I realize that the process must have been violent and intrusive to the raw stone. I see that the polishing has exposed remarkable intricacy and subtle beauty. I imagine that the crystal center is grateful to be exposed, after millennia, to the light.

I think the lesson for me is that I can trust that if I move deeper, beyond my mundane surface, I will expose the valuable and pleasing potentials hidden within me.

PREPARATION: *After you have selected your Power Object, find a quiet space where you will not be interrupted. With your Power Object nearby, sit or recline comfortably, take a deep breath, and look at your Power Object.*

Sink into the stillness and concentrate on your Power Object. It can answer questions for you about your life and about your personal mythology. This object from nature is a teacher, a guide, a gentle witness about life. Look closely at your Power Object and get to know it: touch it, feel it, smell it, taste it if you like. Ask, "What do you have to teach me about myself?" Allow the answer to bubble up in your mind while you are touching it or gazing at it. Perhaps you and the object are similar in some ways. Perhaps your Power Object contains certain qualities that you are trying to develop. It may instruct you about how to overcome the obstacles that are facing you. Discover what your Power Object has to teach you about yourself.

Shifting the focus of your question, ask your Power Object what it has to teach you about formulating a new myth that resolves the conflict between your old myth and your counter-myth.

Now ask your Power Object what it has to teach you about life and about living with a more vital mythology.

Once you have examined your Power Object and learned something of what it has to teach you about yourself, your mythology, and your life, turn to your journal and record your reflections.

Ann wrote:

My Power Object is a bone carving of an African goddess of fertility. She is strung on a string with copper and wooden beads. She speaks to me: "Your power lies in the ancient feminine, in the mystery of the Earth Mother's deep history. You carry a wound in your side, as all those do who follow a path with a heart. Your connection with people and animals is through the body as well as the spirit. You are connected by bone and mystery. You are an artist carving your life into a sacred design—fertile, creative, and generative. You are sustained on the wisdom, the precious and useful metals that you have mined for yourself out of the depths of the earth.

"Your new myth lies in the ancient Dark Discerner quickened to compassion by her own wound. Powerful and deep-seeing, with arms open wide in welcome of all. Your future lies in the freedom of your nature. Do not be afraid to let her come."

Frank's Power Object was an intricately layered piece of bark that came from a fire-scorched tree:

My first observation when I asked what it had to teach me about myself was that wherever the dead bark had fallen away, the bark underneath it was more beautiful. This suggested to me the importance of letting go of past restrictions and of trusting that my deeper parts will have more vitality than my outer "bark."

When I asked what it had to teach me about my new mythology, I received the same basic message. Parts of me through which I once made contact with the world, such as my dedication to my work, have now become veils. I must learn to drop away what is dead, what does not enhance life, and to trust that what is beneath it will serve me better. I also noticed that beneath the top layer, which the tree was so freely discarding (there were chips all over the floor), fresh healthy bark was hidden. So when the dead bark dropped away, new strength and beauty appeared. This suggested that I keep cultivating the inner parts I want to develop, rather than get too bogged down with trying to peel off the dead bark (my hardness and drivenness), which will fall away on its own.

When I asked the bark what it had to teach me about life, I saw how much that death is part of life, natural and inevitable. But I am oriented to fight death, not just with my terror when I think of dying, but in my fear of losing whatever I have. If I am willing to risk the death of certain habits and patterns that are very familiar to me and very comfortable, other vital but latent inner parts will have room to flourish.

When you have finished asking your questions of your Power Object, keep it in a special place, perhaps near your Personal Shield, where you may easily consult it for further guidance. If your Power Object is perishable, you may wish to return it gently to the earth, where it can rejoin the cycle of change. Be prepared to find a new Power Object whenever you need one.

PURPOSE: *To bring greater clarity and focus to your vision for change*

Following the same general procedure you have been using, take a few deep breaths as you settle into bed, contemplate your vision of a renewed direction, and write slowly and mindfully in your journal a statement such as: "I will sleep soundly and peacefully while having a dream that deepens my vision of my new guiding myth. When I awake, I will recall my dream." Then, with deliberation, repeat several times before falling asleep, "I will have a meaningful dream, and I will remember it." Immediately upon waking, record and explore your dream. If you don't recall a dream the first night, repeat the process each night until you do. Ann wrote:

DREAM FOCUS: Deepening Your Vision

> I dreamed Dwayne and I were invited into a hall of mirrors. It turned out to be a medicine circle built on a hill made of sixty-four large stones. They were a soft luminous yellow with translucent blue markings. We went and stood in the center of this circle and one by one we approached each stone. When we were standing in front of it, a mirror would appear in the air and we would glimpse a vision from the other side. I must have seen fifty such images. A few I can recall are a man and woman squatting together in a prehistoric cave; two knights standing beside their horses, one knight in soft blue and the other in pinkish armor; two androgynous beings from the future; a peasant couple with ragged clothes; a king and queen, regal and dignified.
>
> The yellow-and-blue stones were luminous like the sun and the moon. I feel this is a statement of the coming together of the masculine and feminine principles: love and truth, surrender and power, night and day. As we looked into the mirrors, it was as if they represented all the different aspects of this male-female principle trying to find its way to harmony.

Deepening Your Vision

❧

Myths are manifestations of fundamental organizing principles that exist within the cosmos.

—Stanislav Grof [1]

Can you realistically hope your life will one day conform to your new mythic vision? In an examination of the scientific foundations of psychotherapy, psychologist Michael Mahoney notes that at the core of planned as well as spontaneous human changes are shifts in the *personal organization of experience* [2] or, in our terms, in a person's guiding mythology. Mahoney observes that psychological development involves periods of disorder and disequilibrium in the organization of experience (the breakdown of long-standing myths), leading to a fresh (driven by a new myth) ordering of a person's inner life. He poses three critical questions:

1. Can humans change?
2. Can humans help other humans to change?
3. Are some forms of help better than others?

Mahoney cites evidence supporting a qualified yes to each of these questions: People can and do change, but there are limits to human plasticity; people can help others change, but they can also interfere with constructive change; some forms of help are more effective than others, but scientific understanding about specific influences is still rudimentary.[3] A belief in the human capacity to change is central to American myth and ideology. Improvement, observes Martin Seligman, is in fact the *end* for which Americans believe freedom is the *means*. Yet this is a relatively new concept. According to Seligman:

> Traditionally, most people in the West have believed that human character is fixed and unalterable, that people do not and cannot improve. The change from a deep belief in the unchangeability of character to an equally deep belief in the capacity to improve is recent, and it represents one of the most fundamental and important revolutions in modern thought. . . .
>
> When a society exalts the self, as ours does, the self, its thoughts, and their consequences become objects of careful science, of therapy, and of improvement. This improving self is not a chimera. Self-improvement and therapy often work well, and it is a belief in human plasticity that underlies these strategies. The [modern self] believes that it can change and improve, and this very belief allows change and improvement.[4]

Seligman surveys the findings of scientific investigations of the problems therapy can and cannot change.[5] Panic, phobias, and sexual dysfunctions are highly responsive to psychotherapeutic approaches that have been correctly selected and properly applied. Social phobias, agoraphobia, and depression are moderately responsive. More intransigent are obsessive-compulsive disorders, chronic anger, persistent anxiety, and alcoholism; sexual orientation is probably unchangeable. Seligman identified three factors[6] that influence the degree to which a psychological condition is susceptible to change:

1. The stronger its *biological underpinnings,* the harder a psychological condition will be to change. (Conversely, the greater the degree to which it is learned, the easier it will be to change.)

2. The easier it is to confirm the *beliefs* underlying the psychological condition, the harder it will be to change the condition.

3. The more the beliefs underlying the psychological condition are entwined with a person's *worldview,* the more difficult it will be to change that condition.

Personal myths are deep-seated beliefs and organizing frameworks entwined with your worldview—your larger mythic system. This program has been targeting those myths that are dysfunctional, even if long held and consistently confirmed by the logic of long-standing beliefs. To the degree you are able to bring about constructive changes in such fundamental perspectives, positive shifts in your life will tend to follow. We all, according to William Irwin Thompson, continually create our guiding images. Like lure-casting fishermen, we cast them before us, and then reel ourselves into them.[7] In this chapter you will be further refining the personal myth that you will, in subsequent chapters, be casting out in front of you.

PURPOSE: *To examine imaginatively how your new myth might unfold into the world*

Creating Part Three of your Fairy Tale is a way of consciously and deliberately casting in front of you a metaphorical image that you may then "reel yourself into." Recall Part One and Part Two of your Fairy Tale. Consider the two contrasting approaches to the problems in your life. Also review the work you have subsequently completed toward resolving the conflict between your old myth and your counter-myth. Here is Part Three of Meg's Fairy Tale:

> After the porpoise delivered Juanita Margaret to shore, the first thing that happened was that she saw a broken Annie Green Springs wine bottle bouncing in the surf. The second thing to happen was that her caretaker, Prudent, was appalled at the condition of her clothes and hair. The third thing was that her schoolteacher, Rational, heaped contempt on her wild story that she had ridden a porpoise to the depths of the sea.
>
> Juanita Margaret decided that the first lesson she could practice was to retreat to Nature, and this she did until her head and heart settled down and even ceased to ache. "Aha," she thought. "It works! When I am hassled, a retreat to a peaceful, timeless space is indeed healing. I will remember that."
>
> Being as flexible as the kelp had never been easy for her. She was undoubtedly a stubborn, even rigid, child, in that she usually could see only one way to accomplish anything. That lesson came one day when she, a devoted health-food nut, was offered a hot fudge sundae with whipped cream, three cherries, chopped pecans, and a little American flag on the summit. Her conflict was truly epic. "I want it! I want it! I want it!" cried her impulsive, reckless part, with visions of sweet shudders passing through her mouth and limbs. "Oh, no—never, ever, under any circumstances!" proclaimed her righteous, rigid self, snapping mouth closed, tight as an

abalone on the reef. Fortunately, at that moment a vision of the flexible kelp came to Juanita Margaret. "I will stay rooted in my beliefs, but I do think I will eat this sundae. After all, it's only six weeks until my birthday!"

Being secret about her good works had never been Juanita Margaret's way. Keeping silent about her talents was not her strong suit. It is true that she often did genuinely good things for high motives. She had many skills and assets. But there is just no nice way to deny that she was a big mouth, often blowing her own horn in the town square. It wasn't so much that she was full of herself; it was more that she was actually rather empty inside, having been sent out to play so often. One day, while she was caroling her own virtues, she saw someone yawn. "Oh, my," thought Juanita Margaret, "I am becoming the worst sort of a bore. Even I am bored. Boredom is a dreadful sign; it means I am sick of my own company. What to do?" She thought of the abalone with his boring exterior and palace-of-lights interior. She thought, "I believe I should pay attention. It seems to me that if I save some of my good stuff, my very best good stuff, and keep it inside, silently, it may serve me better. I will have to wait for someone to notice me to have the attention I love so much, but I can be occupied with adding lovely nacre designs to my interior canvas. I believe I will try this as a cure for boredom." It worked so well that no one ever yawned in her face again, and the people she invited in to see her mother-of-pearl rainbow painting came to love her deeply.

Here is Part Three of Ann's Fairy Tale:

And so it came to be that the girl left the grove of trees and returned to her native land. As she traveled, she vowed that no matter what life brought her, she would keep the golden pebble glowing brightly in her heart. She met strangers along the way who wanted to douse her light, yet she also met strangers who rejoiced with her in the gift that she bore. She found that it was not the mockery of others that stifled her light, but her own fear of being laughed at.

One stormy night she came to a crossroad and there at the turnstile sat a boy from her village, huddled in the dark. It was the same boy who had thrown the stone at her so long before. The night was dark, but the light from her pebble grew bright and she smiled at him in the light of its glow. He was embarrassed and so he merely said, "Where are you going?" She said she was returning home. The boy felt very relieved, for, you see, he had lost his way, although it was impossible for him to admit that it was so. And so for a while they traveled together, with the light from the golden pebble leading the way. As the boy grew familiar with the girl, however, he began to want the light for himself, as he had once before. When he found that it belonged to her and could never be his, he began to mock the very light that was guiding them through the night. The girl felt the sting as she had felt it years before, but she did not dim her light this time. She stood up as straight as an oak tree, lifted her head, and quietly but firmly said, "I do not know why this light was given to me, but it is sacred to me. Why do you need to mock it?" The boy was not quite sure what to say. The girl looked him right in the eye, the light grew brighter and brighter, and suddenly the girl knew she would never be frightened again. She could not, in fact, even remember what had made her so afraid.

Just at that moment the boy disappeared and the girl found herself at a cottage door deep in the forest. The door opened, and there standing before her was a family of people, their arms open, beckoning for her to come in. The room was filled with a sense of joy and light she had never known. And suddenly she realized she was in the company of others just like her. The light in the room was emanating from them just as it did from her. And she knew that she would never be lonely again.

Frank's Part Three:

Frankie had learned by this time that he was not destined to be a King as he had once believed, and he had learned that to continue to wish he could be a King would bring him much unhappiness. On the other hand, he had reason to believe that if he could accept his own ordinariness, he would be successful as a citizen and could have much the kind of life that he wished. What surprised Frankie when he looked in the crystal ball was that he envied the King not for his crown but for his vitality.

Frankie saw that he had made many choices that led him away from such vitality. He realized, for instance, that the only thing requiring him to do everything Just Right was his belief that he had to, no matter what the personal cost. He also knew he could succeed when he set his mind to something, and he decided that his desire to regain his spontaneity should be no exception. As he went about this, however, he found that in one sense this project was an exception. His style of persistently pushing toward a goal actually interfered with the goal of being free in the moment. Still, he harnessed his persistence even in learning how to let go.

By the time Frankie had become a grown man, he was comfortable living in an ordinary home in an ordinary village. He had an ordinary wife, ordinary children, and an ordinary job. But his favorite word was "extraordinary." Every day he would look in wonderment at his world. His children were miracles to him. He would spend hours playing with them, and he would delight in their curiosity and enthusiasm for life. He cherished his wife—so different from him, so mysterious, so exquisite, so lovable. They would look in each other's eyes for eons and make up poems about what they saw. He loved his work. He would become absorbed in the challenge of doing things a bit differently every day, always finding a creative twist. For this, he was appreciated by his colleagues and valued by his employer. He took great satisfaction in the job he did, and he did not confuse his work with his worth, so when he went home, his job responsibilities stayed at the office. Frankie did not grow up to be King, but he lived happily ever after with the wealth and power supplied by his rich inner life.

Here we see Frank adjusting what he values, what he will pursue, and how he will pursue it. While his insistence on relaxing and enjoying the moment may seem somewhat frivolous when you think of the profound life choices governed by personal myths, Frank's ability to relax and enjoy himself affects critical issues in his life. He was particularly concerned about chest pains that had been increasing in frequency in recent months, and he was allowing himself to feel sad about having grown distant from his wife over the years. While he was not certain that the obsessive style supported by his old myth was responsible for either of these problems, it clearly had dominated his life and eclipsed his vitality. He became determined to change it.

Your Fairy Tale will also suggest a new direction for you that draws on the inspiration of your counter-myth in correcting at least some of the problems inherent in your old myth. The following instructions will lead you into Part Three of your Fairy Tale by invoking the mood and energy of the bodily resolution of your conflict you achieved in an earlier personal ritual. Then, as you did in your resolution fantasy, you will see Part Three enacted on an imaginary stage. Finally, you will retell the story to another person or in your journal.

PREPARATION: *Review Parts One and Two of your Fairy Tale. Part Two taught the main character an important lesson about life. Describe this lesson in your journal. Also review your new-myth motto (Week 7, Session 2). Then, with your Personal Shield, Power Object, and journal nearby, sit or recline comfortably, take a deep breath, and close your eyes.*

As you tune in to your breathing, listen for your inhalation and your exhalation. Notice how your belly and chest fill . . . and empty. Your breath becomes slow and deep. Tensions release as your mind and body relax more completely.

Once more, place your hands in front of you, palms facing each other. Recall your new-myth motto. With three deep breaths, sense the space between your hands and slowly allow them to be drawn together, squeezing them as they meet. Feel the energies of the two sides of your body mingling and integrating in harmony and wholeness. With three more deep breaths, experience this fresh integration wash over your entire body.

Surrounded by the energy of your new myth, imagine that you have entered the same large theater where you experienced your resolution fantasy. You are the only one in the audience. Take a comfortable seat wherever you wish. You know you have come here to witness an enactment of Part Three of your Fairy Tale. You know that when the curtain rises, the main character of your Fairy Tale will be in the same dilemma as he or she was when Part One ended. Recall the way Part One of your Fairy Tale did end. But now that character will be wiser, having been instructed by the experience of Part Two. Recall Part Two of your Fairy Tale. In Part Three, you are about to see the main character use that experience to resolve the earlier dilemmas in a new way.

As the curtain rises, the final scene from Part One of your Fairy Tale is portrayed. In this play about Part Three of your Fairy Tale, the problems faced by the main character will be approached in a fresh manner. As the curtain rises, examine the opening scene in detail. Allow your breathing to be slow and deep as you watch the drama. Stay present as it unfolds.

Part Three of Your Fairy Tale is now coming to its conclusion. By the time the curtain falls, the initial conflict will have been resolved in a new and creative way. Allow your breathing to be slow and deep as you watch the closing scene.

As the curtain falls, tune in to your reactions about Part Three. Reflect for a few moments about the drama. When you are ready, take another deep breath and return to your ordinary waking consciousness, refreshed, relaxed, and alert.

Write Part Three of your Fairy Tale in your journal, perhaps after first speaking it into a tape or sharing it with a partner. Allow it to change and evolve with each telling or writing. The remainder of this chapter will provide opportunities to review this portrayal of your new myth, make appropriate adjustments, and translate it into language that is directly applicable to your current life.

SESSION 2: Completing Your Personal Shield

PURPOSE: *To condense into a single image a symbol representing your new myth that draws on all the work you have done up to this point in the program*

When you created your Personal Shield, you did not complete the fifth section, which will contain a symbol representing a renewed vision of Paradise Regained. Here you will fashion that symbol and complete your Shield. For Meg, the abalone shell from her first Paradise Regained image returned as an element of her new image. But rather than an isolated piece, it became part of a delicate, butterfly-shaped necklace made of silver and abalone shell, hanging from a fine chain. She drew this necklace on the final section of her Personal Shield, reflecting, "I can always quietly carry this totem of my great teacher."

PREPARATION: *Review the initial image of Paradise Regained from your Personal Shield and your journal reflections about it. That image represented an ideal you have followed, probably since you were quite young. Your subsequent life, as well as the work you have done until this point in the program, possibly have challenged that image. In creating your resolution fantasy (Week 7, Session 3), you established a symbol for your old myth and one for your counter-myth. Review those symbols now. With your Personal Shield and drawing implements nearby, sit or recline comfortably, take a deep breath, and close your eyes.*

As you tune in to your breathing, listen for your inhalation and your exhalation. Notice how your belly and chest fill . . . and empty. Your breath becomes slow and deep. Tensions release as your mind and body relax more completely.

Sense one more time which hand you associate with your old myth and which hand you associate with your counter-myth. Are they represented on the same sides as they were earlier?

Imagine that the symbol of your old myth, from the earlier ritual, or one you create now, is sitting on one shoulder, and that your counter-myth symbol is sitting on your other shoulder. Sense how each symbol feels, and explore the sensations on both sides of your body.

Once again hold your palms facing each other, about two feet apart. Sense or imagine an energy pulling your hands together. Allow this energy to increase with every breath. As your hands slowly draw together, imagine that the symbols on your shoulders are moving down toward them. Before your hands touch, the symbols have come all the way down your arms. When your hands do touch, a new symbol will appear that represents a deep resolution of the conflict between your old myth and your counter-myth.

When you allow your hands to touch now, this new image becomes more vivid with each breath. If an image hasn't come to you yet, make one up in your mind. When you are ready, draw it on the Paradise Regained section of your Personal Shield, knowing that it may continue to develop even as it is being drawn.

Ann wrote:

The symbol includes the symbols of my old myth (an open palm welcoming all) and my counter-myth (a hand decisively pointing to what it sees). The open hand supports the other hand, making it clear that Love must always be the foundation on which Truth stands. And from the center of them both, a small gold pebble of light emanates. It is the Mystery beyond all Mysteries that lights my way.

For Frank:

When the symbols touched, the background was all pink and I kind of slipped back in time to feelings from a very early age. Suddenly there was this warm, pink soft-plastic toy I haven't thought of since I was maybe two or three. I had deep, rich, warm feelings as I remembered this toy (I couldn't quite see the toy, I just remembered its pinkness and how good I felt playing with it). It seemed to represent a time in my life when my spontaneity was uninhibited, my appetites were honest and unrestrained, and my experience of the world was sensual and innocent. When I brought the image into my body, it suddenly became my heart, pulsating, pink, vibrant, alive. I felt myself reclaiming my childhood enthusiasm, happiness, and bubbling laughter, and this newly enlivened heart was the image I drew on my Personal Shield.

SESSION 3:

Seeking
Confirmation
from
the "Powers
That Be"

PURPOSE: *To evaluate and refine your new myth according to both logical and intuitive sources of knowledge*

You have been generating within yourself a new vision, and you have a notion of how this vision might translate into your life. By the nature of the process, however, this territory is unfamiliar. You are considering taking a step into a way of being you've never fully experienced before. Until this point in the program, you have been distilling your vision, but you have not yet tested it in your life. That will be the final focus of the program. Before fully committing yourself to your vision, you will in this personal ritual further evaluate it and its merits. Though this is a challenging assignment, adjusting your vision through inner reflection is typically a great deal easier than having to adjust it after it has caused problems for you in the world. On the basis of the research summarized in the opening discussion of Week 8, you can reflect on the way your new mythic vision compares with the characteristics of personal myths that promote happiness, maturity, and well-being. While your new myth will not directly address all of these qualities, you can sense whether its *spirit* is consistent with each of them. Consider—briefly reflecting on one quality at a time—whether your new myth

- prompts you to revel in small delights
- makes it easier to like yourself
- promotes more fulfilling relationships, more rewarding social activities, and greater social support
- enhances physical fitness, rest, personal solitude, and a present-centered absorption in the flow of life
- highlights that which realistically gives you g   ...er control over your destiny
- supports "learned optimism" rather than "learned helplessness"
- balances openness and flexibility with coherence, commitment, and resolve
- accurately takes into account the facts of your abilities and circumstances
- paces your development as you mature
- reconciles conflicting internal forces, opposing subpersonalities, and contradictory aims and visions
- leads to a creative involvement in your social world that is larger than your self-concerns
- retains the most functional, most adaptive, most positive elements of your old myth

- retains the most functional, most adaptive, most positive elements of your counter-myth
- creatively transcends the limitations of both your old myth and your counter-myth

Once you have considered your new myth in terms of these guidelines, carefully consider any alterations that occur to you, and describe them in your journal. Frank added a phrase to his new-myth motto emphasizing that self-worth is based on being, not doing. In addition to this logical analysis of your mythic vision, in this ritual you will open yourself to intuitive sources of wisdom to help you refine and revise your new myth, inquiring of your highest self and of forces that are beyond you.

When people reflect on the most far-reaching powers that human consciousness can begin to conceive—the realm referred to by words such as God, Nature, the Tao, or the Ground of Being—they may relate most strongly to a picture, a concept, or a voice. Although it is beyond the human intellect to comprehend fully the ocean of which it is a single sparkling drop, many rites, prayers, and meditations are designed to elevate human perception and feeling to reach toward this realm. In this ritual, you will be asked to open yourself to this sphere—however you conceive of it—and to present, for confirmation or modification, the new myth you have been formulating. Your Inner Shaman, who dwells close to this domain, will be your guide.

PREPARATION: *After reflecting on the relationship between the above qualities and your new myth, prepare yourself for the possibility of being touched by transcendent forces. Recall the method you have used to contact your Inner Shaman, as you will be making another visit. As in an earlier ritual, you will need a nut or a seed that you can chew and swallow. With your Personal Shield, Power Object, seed, and journal nearby, sit or recline comfortably, take a deep breath, and close your eyes.*

Settling into this safe, secure spot, focus on your breathing. Place your closed hands over your chest. Notice breath. Soften belly. Open heart. As you sense or imagine your heart opening, extend your arms outward, unfolding your hands, like flowers blooming, until they come to rest comfortably at your sides. Notice breath. Soften belly. Open heart. With each inhalation, breathe in the fullness of life. With each exhalation, release any tension, relaxing more completely. Breathe in. Release. Focus inward and call to your Inner

Shaman, your inner wisdom: "My heart is open to you. Be with me on this journey."

Journey to the place of your Inner Shaman, drawing on the method you have used before. Greet your Inner Shaman. Feel the power and the love that meet you. Let it be known that you wish to be transported to a realm where you will be blessed by God, or by the Great Spirit, or by the higher forces of nature that affect human destiny—use a concept that is fitting for you.

Your Inner Shaman smiles approvingly and bids you to be seated. You are given a sacred herb (the nut or seed). You put it in your mouth. As you chew slowly, you know its sacred ingredients are beginning to flow through your body. You lie back and relax. Soon you are entering a powerful state of non-ordinary consciousness. You feel yourself entering the realm of Spirit. Your sense of a powerful Intelligence all around you intensifies as you continue to breathe deeply.

You recall your purpose for this journey. You are to review your new myth. Sense the wise and benevolent forces that are present. Surrounded by the sacred powers you have evoked, find a phrase or sentence that conveys the essence of your guiding myth. State it out loud.

Imagine your statement being registered by the surrounding Intelligence. This Intelligence hears you and reflects your statement to you. You have been received.

You will hear a series of questions. As each is posed, sense how the surrounding Intelligence answers it:

- Does this guiding myth call to the best and the highest within you?
- Is the myth built on grandiosity?
- Does the myth lack in ambition?
- Is it limited by your fears and apprehensions?
- Will the new myth cause difficulties you have not yet anticipated?
- Is it reasonable to attempt to implement the new myth in your life at this time?
- Should any adjustments be made before you begin to shift your life in the image of this myth?

Sense the spirit of the responses that come to these questions, and restate your new guiding myth. Know that you are surrounded by sacred energies that will assist you. Listen as this expression of your new myth enters your awareness. When you are finished, attune yourself to the wisdom and compassion that surround you. Be open to other visions or insights. Again find your way to your Inner Shaman. Describe your new myth to your Shaman. Listen for a response. When you have completed your conversation, bid your Shaman farewell.

Prepare to return to your ordinary waking consciousness. You will be able to remember all you need of this experience. Very gently, begin to rouse yourself. Move your fingers and toes, your hands and feet. Feel your circulation. Stretch your shoulders, your arms and legs, your neck and face muscles. Take a deep breath. Bring your attention back into the room. Open your eyes, refreshed, as if waking from a wonderful nap, alert and fully competent to creatively meet the requirements of your day.

In your journal, under the heading "My New Guiding Myth," describe your new myth in terms of its guiding principles, along with any other reflections on this experience.

Ann wrote: "My first statement was: 'I am a conduit for Divine Love.' But I've been saying that forever. The new myth is simply: 'I live my life in truth and with love.' " Frank, recognizing that he was burdened by feelings of inadequacy that traced to his old myth, and that he longed to live with greater trust in his primal being, rather than deferring to his highly controlling old myth, wrote: "I am whole; I am complete; and I am expanding perfectly as my passion moves through me!" Meg also summarized her new myth in a single, guiding sentence: "Serenity is gained through loving, thoughtful action." She described the essence of the myth: "I am part of Creation. I, and all my relationships, are, just like Creation, continually evolving and growing more interconnected through the forces of Love."

As Meg comes to identify herself with spheres larger than her isolated inner world, you can sense how the self-centeredness that characterized her earlier mythology (the product partially of needing so early to be self-reliant and partially of being an only child) is changing. Up to now, the collective "other" had seemed so oppressive to Meg that she could come only as far as allowing it to serve as an object of her love, with little room for the intermingling of the other's wants, needs, and myths with her own. Now, as she is beginning to integrate opposing elements of her inner being, she seems better able and more willing to engage in the give-and-take of interpersonal relationships as well. She is also beginning to appreciate that her need to be alone in nature provides a balance to social life instead of serving only as an escape from it.

As Frank listened to these instructions, he was reminded of the feelings of inspiration that had transported him to a sense of spiritual appreciation a dozen years earlier when he had visited a magnificent cathedral in Cologne, Germany. Elaborating on his new myth, he wrote:

> My new myth instructs me to affirm all within me that is passionate and life supporting—to appreciate it, attend to it, make room for it, and enjoy it as I move through life. I am to be particularly alert to my tendency to lock myself into unnecessary or high-paced activities that crowd out spontaneity and passion. And while I am taking the time to affirm what joy and creativity may be mine, I am not to judge what is not there; I am not to focus a searchlight on every inner event and sit in judgment should it not live up to hopes or expectations.
>
> I am to use this principle in both work and play. I am to use it in looking backward and in looking forward. When I look back on events that have occurred, I am to immerse myself in what was life-affirming, and to align myself with such experiences. I am not to keep focusing on times that were limited by my obsessions and deficiencies. Such analysis has been my pattern, based on the belief that I can only learn from my mistakes, but beyond a certain point this has had only the effect of dragging me down. Looking in the forward direction, I am to project this same life-affirming emphasis into my future. The expectations I send out for myself are to be confident and encouraging. Specifically, my new myth assures me that I will activate the more vital and passionate ways of being I have been exploring throughout the program. I can see this; I can expect it; I know it will come to pass.

As you can sense, this statement is expressed neither in the form of a story (as in his Fairy Tale) nor as a rule of conduct (as would be found in ethical systems such as the Ten Commandments), but simply as a reminder, in Frank's own language, of how he intends to monitor certain thoughts that affect his passion. Some people, for instance Meg, use more poetic language in stating their new myth ("I am part of Creation. . . ."). Make your statement in the language most fitting for you. You will see in the following chapters how even an abstract or poetic statement of your new mythic vision can be translated into concrete steps for living by its guidance. In closing this session, we want to caution you against being overly critical of yourself as you refine your new myth. Embrace your best efforts. As Linda Schierse Leonard has observed, "In order to create we must continually forgive ourselves for our inability to embody the perfect vision."[8]

PURPOSE: *To evaluate and refine your new myth through the wisdom of your dreams*

Mentally review your new-myth statement before going to sleep, and ask for a dream that will in some way confirm its validity for you. Using the same general procedure before falling asleep, take a few deep breaths, reflect on your new myth, and write slowly and mindfully in your journal a statement such as: "I will sleep soundly and peacefully tonight while having a dream that affirms or alters my new guiding myth. When I awake, I will recall my dream." Then, with deliberation, repeat several times before falling asleep, "I will have a meaningful dream, and I will remember it." Immediately upon waking, record and explore your dream. If you don't recall a dream the first night, repeat the process each night until you do. Ann wrote:

I was on a train going somewhere and looked back to discover that the end of the train was on fire. People were running through the flames and panicking. Someone said, "This is what we all fear could happen if we get too enclosed." We unhooked the end of the train and began to labor up a steep hill. I wondered if we would make it to the top. Somehow the train makes it.

I find myself walking beside a woman and she says to me, "I have lost everything in the fire, and I have no insurance. How will I ever support my daughter?" I tell her not to worry, that we will all help her reestablish herself. She is very relieved. Another person comes and asks me to follow her. She takes me into a room that is circular, with many windows. We look through one of the windows to a small parking area under some trees, and she says, "The parking lot is usually full, but the workers are all gone." I say, "I'll help."

I am suddenly on a frozen lake with skates on. I am with a friend and we share how we were both ice-skaters at one time. Two men with a strange canoe-type boat come onto the ice. They are all dressed in black, and it appears that this boat, which has circles cut in the bottom through which their skates contact the ice, is very uncomfortable to operate. But they appear not to care. They get in and with tiny steps move out onto the lake. My friend and I laugh, and say, "Well, they like it." I then do a graceful pirouette, but when I try to finish the turn, I realize that the point on the front of my skates is not there, and I wonder how I will learn to maneuver with no brakes or pivotal point. I feel quite content to be in this dilemma. I awaken.

The confirmation I feel from the "Powers That Be" has to do with an acknowledgment of the sword of truth that knows I cannot make it up the hill if I am pulling the extra weight of past chaos. In cutting away from myself that which is burning and out of control from the past, I am able to move on. There is an affirmation that though there is no "insurance" that would be able to fully compensate for the loss, it is made clear that I will be cared for from unexpected sources. I am told that though the lot where the workers park is bare, it is not always this way. There is a sense that they will return and that in the meantime I will do whatever is needed. I am also told through the ice skates that though I don't know how to use these skates, I will find a way. I feel confirmed that I am in transition, but that there is nothing to worry about. I am equal to the task.

FIFTH STAGE

Living from Your New Mythology

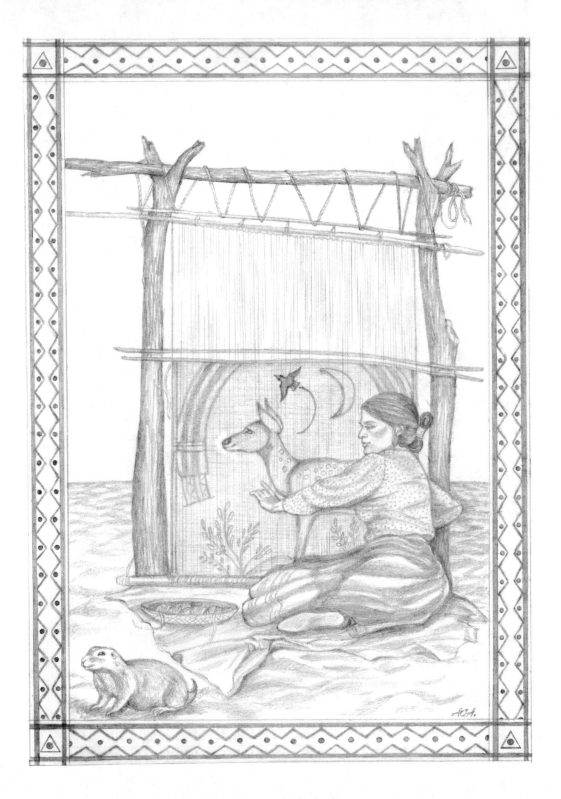

Weaving a Renewed Mythology into Your Inner Life

✦

At the moment of insight a potential pattern of organized behaviour comes into being.

—Rupert Sheldrake[1]

To this point in the program, you have identified a core conflict in your guiding mythology (First Stage—Weeks, 1, 2, and 3), you have examined each side of that conflict (Second Stage—Weeks 4 and 5), you have worked toward a unifying vision that incorporated the most desirable qualities of each side of the conflict while transcending their limitations (Third Stage—Weeks 6 and 7), and you further refined this vision and developed a commitment to live from it (Fourth Stage—Weeks 8 and 9). Here, you will begin the final stage of the program, which involves translating this vision into your life. With this chapter you will be weaving your new myth into your inner life. In the following chapter, the focus shifts to the outer world.

When you attempt to create a lasting change in your inner life, exactly what are you trying to change? Beliefs, feelings, motives, brain cells? In this chapter we are going to present a theory that may seem very radical to at least some readers. We believe that "fields of information" influence consciousness and behavior. We suggest that just as a magnetic field will line up iron filings, informational fields, as real as magnetic fields, exist in the physical world and exert a tangible influence on your feelings, beliefs, and behavior. Your personal field is as decisive for your subjective life as the field carried by a magnet is for the iron filings. The information coded in your personal field corresponds with your personal mythology. By understanding this relationship, as you will learn to do in this chapter, you can use procedures for influencing your personal field as you shift deep and elusive patterns in your guiding mythology.

Spiritual practices such as meditation provide an auspicious path for influencing your personal field because the energy with which your field resonates when you meditate can be quite pure and curative. Other ways of directly influencing your personal field introduced in this chapter include guided imagery, altering self-statements, and the use of ritual and behavior rehearsal. Shifting the personal field that is the physical underpinning of an ineffective guiding mythology is a potent way of supporting its transformation.

Personal Myths as Fields of Information

One of the enduring mysteries of nuclear physics is that if two photons are separated under certain conditions, regardless of the distance that may come between them, a change in one creates a simultaneous change in the other. These *distant effects* at the subatomic level are difficult to explain, but they are no more mysterious than the way in which people may be sensitive to distant influences in such phenomena as telepathy. Visualization, prayer, and meditation have each, under experimental conditions, exerted measurable effects on the health, comfort, or temperament of people who may be any distance away.[2] Focused attention has even been shown to directly influence mechanical devices.

You have probably heard anecdotes, for instance, about an old clock's stopping at the moment its owner died. Numerous studies have shown that by focusing their attention, individuals can reliably influence mechanical systems such as random-number generators. Researchers from the School of Engineering at Princeton University found that the output of random-event generators was also affected when the devices were simply placed in the presence of organized groups of people. The effect was strongest during periods when the group's attention was focused, the group's cohesion was high, or the group's members were sharing a common emotional experience. In experiments with ten separate gatherings, ranging from business meetings to scientific research conferences to ritual religious events, this effect of the group's collective behavior was so strong that the probability against its having occurred by chance was about 5,000 to 1. The researchers conclude: "If sustained over more extensive experiments, such effects could add credence to the concept of a consciousness 'field' as an agency for creating order in random physical processes."[3] Independent studies at the Consciousness Research Laboratory in Las Vegas corroborate these findings.[4]

Fields of Information. Several features are shared by reports of telepathy and the influences of visualization, prayer, meditation, and group activity on distant events: (1) Each seems to involve information gained in a manner whose physical mechanisms are difficult to explain within conventional frameworks; (2) evidence suggesting the existence of each of these phenomenon, while not unequivocal, has been accumulating; and (3) each could be explained if "fields of information" are at play.[5]

A field is an *area of influence,* presumed to exist in physical reality, that cannot be seen, but which is inferred through its *effects.* Neurologists,[6] physicists,[7] engineers,[8] psychologists,[9] biologists,[10] physiologists,[11] healers,[12] and systems theorists,[13] on the basis of findings from within their respective disciplines, have postulated the existence of physical fields that might influence consciousness and behavior.

Biologist Rupert Sheldrake has formulated a field theory that encompasses biology as well as mental processes, culture, and the mythologies of individuals and nations.[14] Sheldrake defines a field as a region of influence, for instance electromagnetic, gravitational, or quantum-matter fields, that cannot be seen, but which, like all fields, is known through its effects.[15]

Every living system, every unit of the physical world—from the molecule to the mind—has its own unique "morphic" (i.e., form-giving) field, according to Sheldrake, which contains information about the system's potential form and behavior. The acorn holds the morphic field of the oak; the tadpole that of the frog. The information held in a field is similar to genetic information *(inform* means, literally, "to put into form"). Morphic fields are regions of influence that hold in-*form*ation. The morphic field of the frog is the top-down counterpart to its genes, which work from the bottom up in encoding its physical form and instinctive behavior.

The morphic field, according to Sheldrake, complements genetics as nature's way of "carrying" a species' memory. In addition to governing the form of biological systems, morphic fields organize animal and human behavior, social and cultural systems, myths and scientific hypotheses, and other mental activity. Three characteristics of morphic fields as conceptualized by Sheldrake are that (1) morphic fields, like gravitational or electromagnetic fields, are "physically real," though too subtle to be detected by standard mechanical instrumentation; (2) morphic fields affect physical, mental, and social forms by *resonance* (as in a tuning fork) rather than through an *exchange* of energy, where one gains what the other expends; and (3) morphic fields are "comparable in status" to quantum-matter fields, explaining some of their characteristics such as "nonlocality," the quantum property whereby an effect is *instantaneous* and *unaffected by distance.*

Sheldrake believes that family, group, and cultural morphic fields exist, and that such fields are able to "store" and "transmit" information from one generation to the next. As new members grow up within or enter a social group, "they tune in by morphic resonance to the fields" that maintain that group's traditions.[16] Morphic resonance—instantaneous and unaffected by distance—could also plausibly be the physical mechanism in paradigm-stretching instances of information transmission, such as telepathy and the distant effects of visualization.

Preliminary attempts to verify scientifically the existence of morphic fields have been reported by investigators in different parts of the world. Some of the results have been statistically significant, while others have not. Studies that seem to support the hypothesis have been criticized for flaws in their experimental design.[17] Some advocates of the morphic field hypothesis, on the other hand, maintain that using current research strategies to study such elusive phenomena is tantamount to squeezing them into a Procrustean bed, force-fitting these subtle fields into limiting, preconceived concepts. When morphic fields operate in nature, they are believed to serve a purpose associated with the survival or enhancement of a species, a critical feature that is not easily built into laboratory and other contrived experiments.

Sheldrake has identified naturally occurring phenomena[18] that lend themselves to "field of information" explanations. The abilities of homing pigeons, for example, defy other rationales. Homing pigeons have been able to find their way eighty miles back to the nest even after their vision was impaired by experimenters using frosted contact lenses.[19] Other homing pigeons found their way over long distances after their ability to orient themselves to the earth's electromagnetic fields was blocked by magnets or Helmholtz coils attached to their bodies.[20] Plausibly, homing pigeons tune in to a field of information that is distinct from an electromagnetic field and imperceptible to human senses and existing instrumentation.

Sheldrake sees a direct relationship between morphic fields and the brain, where "characteristic rhythmic patterns of activity within the nervous system" may resonate with a particular morphic field.[21] While the morphic field hypothesis is highly controversial, the concept corresponds well with our observations of the way personal myths naturally develop, and we find ourselves increasingly referring to it in our thinking about how to work with a person's evolving mythology.

Personal Fields and Personal Myths. A *personal field* is the field of information counterpart to the physical body. A sensitive observer, even without visual or auditory cues, can often detect an altered "energy" or "vibration" in another person ("Before I even pulled into the driveway, I could feel that he was angry"). While relatively stable, personal fields may be influenced by perceptions, feelings, thoughts, behavior, and interactions with the fields of information that exist in the environment. A *personal myth* is a symbolic representation of the individual's personal field.

For instance, a competent and powerful woman regularly becomes insecure and accommodating when her amiable husband walks into the room. The personal myth governing her identity as a strong and independent woman is displaced by a personal myth that transforms her posture into that of a subservient wife. Measurable shifts in the neurophysiological activities that determine perception, affect, cognition, and behavior have occurred. Both field and neurology have changed; her "1950s housewife" and her "woman who runs with wolves" personal myths symbolize the two states. Each state of consciousness emerges from bottom-up influences, such as genetics and neurology, and top-down influences, such as a particular constellation of her personal field. Here, in a very brief and speculative outline, is the way we understand the relationship of personal fields and personal myths:

1. While personal fields of information are generally too subtle to be detected by the senses, they constitute the top-down dimension of your personal mythology, complementing your neurophysiology, which can be thought of as its bottom-up dimension.

2. The personal myth activated in you at a given moment, whose symbolism can be investigated using techniques such as the personal rituals presented in this program, can be thought of as a psychological map of your personal field at that moment.

3. The vibration of your personal field is affected by at least three sources:
   - your physical body
   - psychological processes
   - external fields, such as those in the physical environment, as well as what Sheldrake refers to as family, group, and cultural morphic fields

4. Strategies for directly embedding a new mythology into your personal field can build on the presumed influence on your personal field of:
- setting an intention
- visualizing the qualities of the new myth
- imagery journeys to the past to rework old trauma
- imagery journeys seeding the future with a new myth
- shifts in self-statements
- behavioral rehearsals
- personal rituals
- repetition

In rituals such as "Saying Good-bye to an Antiquated Myth," "Transforming Obstacles into Opportunities," and "Rewriting History Through the Emotionally Corrective Daydream," you were using such techniques to extricate yourself from the murky, tarlike qualities of your old myth and the field it activates. In this chapter will be performing three additional rituals—each designed to build and strengthen a personal field that corresponds with your new myth—one through imagination, one through words, and one through action. This spectrum of approaches could conceivably influence you at many levels, and fields of information would seem particularly responsive to their impact. In brief, recognizing the "field" as well as the neurological dimensions of your personal mythology promotes an understanding of both the top-down and the bottom-up influences on your psychological and spiritual development.

SESSION 1:
Invoking Your New Myth in Your "Subtle Body"

PURPOSE: *To translate your new myth into an information field that influences your physical body, emotions, thoughts, and behavior*

Various traditions in both the East and the West hold that each person possesses at least one secondary body, referred to variously as the "aura," "subtle body," "pranic body," and "etheric body." Whether you think of this secondary body as no more than the authors' fancy, as a metaphor, a morphic field, or the energy-level infrastructure of the physical body, we encourage you to experiment with the concept because it is possible that:

1. personal myths create distinctive "vibrations" in your secondary body, which in turn influence your perceptions, feelings, thoughts, and behavior;
2. your old myth and new myth create markedly different vibrations in your

secondary body, influencing your perceptions, feelings, thoughts, and behavior in correspondingly different ways;

3. you can directly modify this vibration at any moment through the skillful use of concentration, focused imagination, and ritual;

4. because the habitual vibration in your secondary body is attuned to your long-standing mythology, your intention to make a substantial change in your mythology can be bolstered significantly by using such methods, as will be presented in various ways in this and the next chapter.

Buddha taught that "with our thoughts we make the world." To an extent, psychological research supports this counterintuitive assertion. In addition to the effects of thought on the physical world and human interaction, discussed above, imagined performance can improve actual performance. Mental imagery has been shown to be effective in assisting people in situations ranging from performing in a play to competing in the Olympics. According to Jeanne Achterberg, "The mental rehearsal of a sales presentation or a marathon race evokes muscular change and more: blood pressure goes up, brain waves change, and sweat glands become active."[22] The free-throw percentage of basketball players increased after they imagined themselves practicing perfect shots.[23] Studies of students, ranging from elementary school to university level, who were taught to use guided imagery and visualization demonstrate that these activities can facilitate highly desirable gains in cognitive skills, creativity, and self-esteem.[24]

Your mental images can also directly influence your physical body.[25] Numerous research studies suggest that "vividly experienced imagery that is both seen and felt can substantially affect brain waves, blood flow, heart rate, skin temperature, gastric secretions, and immune response—in fact, the total physiology."[26] People can be taught imagery that results in a statistically significant increase of their white blood cell counts. Moreover, depending on the imagery they choose, they can specifically increase one kind of white blood cell (e.g., neutrophils) or another (e.g., lymphocytes).[27]

The following brief exercise provides a concrete demonstration of the impact of imagination on the body:[28]

1. Stand erect, facing a wall with your shoulders parallel to it, and rotate your head to the right as far as it will go without moving your shoulders and without straining.

2. Measure the degree of rotation by precisely noting the farthest point you can see to the right. Memorize that point.

3. Come back to center and raise your right arm, and stretch toward the sky. With your right arm overhead, extend the fingers on your right hand and bend it back at the wrist.

4. Next, stretch all the way down your right side: right arm, right side of your chest, right hip. Lowering your right arm, stretch your right thigh, right knee, right calf. Extend the toes of your right foot as you bend it at the ankle.

5. Come back to center, and again without straining, measure the degree of rotation by turning your head to the right.

Most people find they can see farther to the right on this second attempt, which may be readily explained by the mechanics of the stretching exercise. Next try the experiment on your left side, along with one specific shift in the instructions, as follows:

1. Return to the same starting position. Rotate your head to the left as far as it will go without moving your shoulders and without straining.

2. Note precisely the farthest point you can see to the left, and memorize it.

3. Come back to center. This time, without moving a muscle, *imagine* you are raising your left arm. Imagine you are extending the fingers of your left hand and bending it back at the wrist.

4. Imagine you are stretching all the way down your left side: left arm, left side of chest, left hip, left thigh, left knee, left calf. Still not moving a muscle, imagine you are stretching your left foot, extending the toes as you bend it back at the ankle.

5. Relax. Come back to center, and again without straining, measure the degree of rotation by turning your head to the left.

Most people report that their heads rotated farther after this sequence, even though there was no physical stretching, "only" mental imagery. To convince yourself that this effect is real, you might repeat the experiment at another time, varying the order and switching the side of your body you physically stretch and the side you stretch in your imagination.

Since your new myth *is* new, your body has not developed the neural and energetic pathways that summon it as easily as it will after you've lived with the myth for some time. Sheldrake's observation that a morphic field is strengthened through repetition is a guiding principle for fostering a new myth. In the same way that you imagined stretching your muscles, you will in this ritual, using your imagination, "stretch yourself" into your new myth. Invoking your new myth in your "subtle body," or in whatever the concept of a subtle body actually denotes, you can "live" the myth in a subtle dimension of reality, eliciting it, practicing it, and strengthening it.

PREPARATION: *Review the Renewed Vision symbol from your Personal Shield and the statement you came to about your new myth with the assistance of the "Powers That Be." Then stand in a comfortable position, take a deep breath, close your eyes, and begin to relax.*

Recall the statement you made when you contacted the Powers That Be. Also bring to mind the image you drew on the Renewed Vision portion of your Personal Shield. Sense the "energy" of the statement and of the vision. While the energies of the two may be identical, each may carry different aspects of the myth. Imagine that these energies unite into a larger energy and that this larger energy fills you, permeating every cell in your body.

Move your body into a posture that symbolizes this energy. In this posture, your new myth and your body resonate, until every cell, muscle, and organ vibrates in harmony with your new myth. This vibrational field will evoke the behaviors, the ways of seeing, and the ways of knowing that grow out of your new myth, the vision you have painstakingly cultivated through your work to this point in the program.

Breathe deeply into this field of energy and invite your body and your mind to invoke it more and more frequently. Inwardly state an intention that this field be evoked in all situations where it can serve your highest purposes, even without your consciously requesting it. Take a few deep breaths, anchoring this field of energy in your body and your being.

When you are ready, prepare to take a step forward, maintaining the posture as much as possible, and consciously carrying with you the field of your new myth. As you take this step, you are taking a step back into the world, with your new myth more fully seeded in your subtle body.

Slowly and deliberately describe in your journal your experience of setting this field. This in itself can serve as another way of anchoring your new myth into your subtle body and your consciousness.

Meg used the image of her abalone necklace as a catalyst for evoking her new myth. Ann wrote: "As I stood in the energy of the new myth, 'I live my life in love *and* truth,' I realized that the gesture of my renewed myth absolutely mirured the words I had said: one hand in an open gesture of loving welcome, the other upheld in a gesture that spoke of clarity and the power to speak truth. I allowed the gesture to grow larger until I felt that I was stretching and making room for the power of the new myth.

Frank had his relationship with his wife in mind: "I'm much too somber, serious, and negative with Diane, and I decided to create, in my subtle body, more feelings of joy around her. At first I had difficulty activating these feelings. Then I imagined there was less pressure on me in other parts of my life, and I had all sorts of extra energy. I could feel the aliveness of my new pulsating pink heart flowing throughout my body, and the aliveness infused my subtle body. I liked this preview of how our relationship might change if I were less pressured and more open to that pulsating pink heart."

SESSION 2: Self-Talk That Supports Your New Myth

PURPOSE: *To translate your new myth into habitual internal statements that will influence your subtle body, perceptions, feelings, thoughts, and behavior*

Humans are motivated by what they say to themselves—whether critical or compassionate, wise or absurd. Your attitudes, beliefs, and plans are expressed in your *self-talk*—internalized, subvocal, self-directed statements. Consequently, a powerful way to facilitate desired changes in your mythology is to identify the self-statements or automatic thoughts associated with the old, dysfunctional myth and to replace them consciously with more constructive self-statements that reflect the new myth. Deeply felt self-statements tend to evoke and maintain the morphic fields that give form to your lived mythology.

If you can change your automatic, largely preconscious self-statements, new patterns of feeling, thought, and behavior will follow. Among the types of irrational self-statements, expressions of dysfunctional personal myths, that people frequently use are: "I need everyone to love and admire me," "Whatever I do, I must do it perfectly," and "I don't deserve to enjoy myself while others are suffering."

One way of accelerating the process of moving out of an old dysfunctional myth and into a new vision you sincerely wish to live is to go beneath the surface of your usual ways of thinking and to adjust the internalized statements. In this ritual, you will begin by reflecting on habitual self-statements that tend to maintain the dysfunctional myth you have been examining. You will bring these self-statements up to the surface so you can examine them, and just as wildlife scientists put tags on the fins of fish so the fish can be recognized when they come up from the deep, you will be putting mental tags on the self-statements that are the fins of your old myth.

Look inward to identify two or three self-statements that help maintain your old myth, that enforce its premises and support its values. Describe them in your journal under the heading "Self-Statements That Support My Old Myth."

Frank noted that when he thought of a creative project, or even a feasible project, he automatically started to instruct himself subvocally to begin work on it. His free time was always being crowded out with such projects, which he initiated without considering their cost to his overall well-being. Among Meg's self-statements were: "If I'm pleasant to people who don't see things my way, I'm giving in to the codgers and the emotionally constipated. If I restrain an impulse in a particular situation, I will be killing my spontaneity and my spirit. If I carry out a task in the routine and established way, I will be inhibiting my self-expression and stifling my growth."

Ann identified the following statements:

The truth is dangerous. Love is the only way. Choose love over truth.

I already take up too much space in the world, so I always need to give others what they want rather than take more for myself.

Loving people always put others first, need nothing for themselves, will accept whatever is dished out to them, and never say anything that might wound another. I am, at all costs, a loving person.

In order to put such self-statements behind you, it is useful to become clear within yourself that they do not structure your reality in a way that serves you. Identify a self-statement that still has a fairly good grip on you and examine (1) the evidence that supports it; (2) the evidence that disputes it; and (3) what would happen to you if you no longer lived according to it. You could do this in a number of ways. For instance, you could simply write about those questions in your journal, you could invite the characters that represent your old myth and your counter-myth to discuss the questions, or you could journey to your Inner Shaman and ask for help in coming to terms with these old statements.

Frank did not think he would easily be able to ignore the inner voice that told him that if he were to remain respectable and successful in his profession, he was continually required to master the tiniest details and exert his full effort at all times. When he challenged this belief, he came to see that success and status were not nearly the concerns for him that they once had been. Both were well established; he was proud of his career achievements and continuing to expand, and people consistently responded to him with respect. He realized he had much more license than he was using simply to relax his obsessiveness and "enjoy the ride."

Once you have unearthed your old myth's habitual self-talk, examined it, and committed yourself to finding a way to change it, an effective next step is to establish a way you can recognize these self-statements whenever they rise to the surface. For instance, you can tag them by experiencing them in a sensory way. You might find a color or a taste or an odor or a feeling that helps you recognize when a self-statement supporting a dysfunctional myth is activated and is influencing you. For each of the harmful self-statements you have identified, find a quality you associate with it: a color, an image, a feeling, a sound, a smell, or a taste. Now exaggerate whatever may be negative about that quality. Make it large, ridiculously large, so it becomes a parody of the original quality. Whether the quality you associate with the self-statement is a disagreeable smell, a discordant sound, an unpleasant taste, a negative feeling, or a repulsive color, make it so disgusting and memorable that your consciousness will be jogged if it sneaks in under your radar.

After you have articulated a few self-statements that you associate with your old myth, identified a negative quality you associate with each, and exaggerated that quality, describe these associations in your journal. Then, like the wildlife warden tagging the fin of the fish, firmly establish the association between each self-statement and the exaggerated negative quality. One at a time, bring each self-statement into your awareness and vividly imagine the quality. Also, place where you will see it every day a list of the self-statements you associate with your old myth to help you recognize when the old myth is engaged. After about a week, evaluate whether the list is assisting you to recognize self-talk associated with your old myth, and either reaffirm your use of the list or develop a new strategy that will better alert you to such self-talk.

Self-statements can also support your new myth. Mentally review Part Three of your Fairy Tale, the Renewed Vision symbol on your Personal Shield, and the phrase or sentence that states your new myth. Make a heading in your journal labeled "Self-Statements That Support My New Myth." Formulate two or three self-statements that would support this myth and the beliefs, attitudes, and behaviors you associate with it.

Meg's list included: "Understanding the other person's point of view will increase my effectiveness and equanimity. Saying no to some impulses is in my interest and leaves energy to invest in other ways. Moderation allows me the self-control to develop skills and understanding I once thought impossible."

Ann wrote:

Love is the truth in action. The truth is love made manifest. The two together are a force of Divine healing.

Every being takes up just the right amount of space in the Divine play.

Loving people can discern what to accept from another and what to let pass. They speak the truth with compassion, and because they take care of their own needs, they are capable of discerning what is truly called for in a situation.

Revise your self-statements until each gives you a clear instruction. Ann's three statements above were further developed into:

I live with a balance of love and truth.

I am at peace knowing I take up just the right amount of space on the planet.

I speak the truth with compassion, discerning what to accept of another and what not to accept.

As you reflect on your new self-statements, you may realize that some of them will be difficult to believe or to follow. If so, consider these three questions as you examine their validity: (1) What evidence supports the self-statement? (2) What evidence disputes it? and (3) What would happen if you actually lived according to it? You might invite further dialogue between the characters that represent your old myth and your emerging myth, or visit your Inner Shaman, as you refine these self-statements. It may be necessary, on the basis of these reflections, to revise some of the statements.

Frank, for instance, could not rationally support one of the statements on his list: "I bolster my enthusiasm for life by seeing only the positive elements when I review a situation." Yet he was able to revise it to: "When I find the positive elements in a situation, I accept them and enjoy them, and I no longer discount them by measuring them against what might have been possible."

Continue formulating and revising your list until you have a set of self-statements that offers you sensible guidance for living from your new mythology. The more you can habitually and concretely build these self-statements into your automatic thought patterns, the more quickly your behavior will align itself with your new myth. One useful technique is to imagine, for each statement, a situation in which you would feel good acting in accordance with that statement. Construct the situation fully—see pictures, hear words, and feel your physical sensations in the scene. Self-statements that have been linked to images, feelings, and sensations are more potent than thoughts alone. Another aid is to write the list in large and colorful letters and place it where you will regularly see it—on a mirror, on the refrigerator, on your bedroom wall. Repetition strengthens the influence of a self-statement. Use the list as an opportunity for frequently reviewing your new self-statements.

When you have settled on two or three statements you wish to change, memorize one of them. You will be using it in a procedure called *thought stopping,* a technique developed by cognitive-behavioral therapists. In thought stopping, you interrupt an objectionable self-statement as soon as you recognize it (such as the ones you "tagged" earlier) and immediately replace it with a self-statement that is in line with your intentions, such as the one you just formulated. When you recognize a habitual thought or self-statement that supports your old myth, take a deep breath. As you exhale, imagine yourself releasing the thought and releasing the field of the old myth from your subtle body. With the next inhalation, replace that thought with the self-statement that supports your new myth. With the next several breaths, imagine this statement imprinting itself on your subtle body.

Frank began to pause in instances when he normally would have reflexively told his wife he was too busy to do something they would both enjoy. He would then note automatic thoughts that were operating to keep him bound to his work, whether the activity was essential or not. When he identified such thoughts, he replaced them with the self-statement, "When I can play, I do play," and then made his decision. He also recognized that one of the ways he cut off his passion was by "not being fully present to what is." He realized that he devoted a great deal of his mental energy to ruminating about whether one thing or another was going to go wrong. He made a commitment to himself that whenever he recognized that his mind had drifted into obsessive worry, he would immediately take a deep breath and say to himself, "Notice breath. Soften belly. Open heart." Frank found it useful at the end of each day to log in his journal the old self-statements he had recognized and the new ones with which he replaced them.

Ann found the thought-stopping technique cumbersome. Instead, she wrote the word "Locate" on brightly colored pieces of paper and placed them where she continually ran into them. She put them by her telephone, on her steering wheel, on her refrigerator door, in her checkbook, in her underwear drawer, on the bathroom mirror, and on the front door. Whenever she would see the word, she would focus in on "what my thinking was doing." She would "locate which myth I am in." She would ask herself, "Where am I emotionally? Am I living in the present or in the old myth?" The notes were a continual visual reminder to keep her attuned to her new myth.

One additional technique for internalizing self-statements that support your renewed mythology is called the *temporal tap*. We were taught the temporal tap by Donna Eden, a healer who works with the body's energy fields, when we asked her if she could suggest a self-help technique for intervening in a person's energy field in order to shift automatic self-talk. Begin with the same self-statement you selected for the thought-stopping procedure. Reformulate the statement using negative terms such as "don't," "won't," "no," or "never," but without changing the statement's meaning. Frank's statement, "When I can play, I do play," was restated in the negative as, "I don't miss opportunities for play." Meg's new myth self-statement, "I understand the other person's point of view," was stated negatively as "I don't forget to receive the other person's point of view." The meaning, however, whether expressed in positive or negative wording, is a *positive* affirmation of the new myth.

Write your new-myth statement in both its positive and its negative forms. With your left hand, tap around the half-circle above your left ear, lightly but firmly enough that your fingers bounce off your head, beginning from your temple and down to the top of your neck. As you tap, say your new-myth statement in its negative wording. Repeat this four or five times. Then with your right hand, tap around the half-circle above your right ear, beginning from your temple and down to the top of your neck. As you tap, say your new-myth statement in its positive wording. Repeat the tapping and the statement four or five times. Repeat the entire process four or five times each day.

The rationale for the temporal tap,[29] very briefly, is that (1) the central nervous system, by necessity, filters out most of the sensory stimuli that reach it; (2) the tapping temporarily interferes with the filtering mechanism, making the mind particularly receptive to the statements; and (3) the need for positive and negative wordings is related to differences in how the left and right brain hemispheres process information, with the left hemisphere functions more critical and skeptical and thus more receptive to negative formulations. While the neurological explanations we have seen for the temporal tap are incomplete, the procedure has proven effective for each of us personally and with numerous clients. Whether the main mechanism of the temporal tap is simply repetition or whether the positive and negative wordings and left/right tapping actually influence the nervous system in the desired manner, it is a pleasant, ritualistic way to internalize further a self-statement that supports your new myth.

SESSION 3: Ritual Enactments of Your New Myth

PURPOSE: *To translate your new myth into patterned behaviors that influence your subtle body, perceptions, feelings, thoughts, and subsequent behavior*

This session involves three separate rituals: a behavioral rehearsal, a daily personal ritual, and a public ritual. In the first, you will be imagining yourself invoking the field of your new myth in your subtle body, physical body, feelings, movements, and words. It is borrowed from a technique used by behavioral therapists called *behavior rehearsal.*

Behavior Rehearsal. To begin, imagine a situation in which it might be difficult or a bit of a stretch to live according to your new myth, and see yourself living within its spirit nonetheless. For instance, you might imagine yourself expressing a dissenting opinion in a delicate circumstance, making a difficult request of an employer, or enjoying a quiet moment amid the pressures of a busy afternoon. Meg wrote:

> I have made an agreement with an acquaintance that he will do something for me. I have made several commitments and accommodations based on that understanding. Then he fails to follow through, and I am left in an awkward and compromised position. This always has elicited feelings of abandonment, betrayal, and anger on my part. I've tended to feel punished and punishing. I would withdraw to such a degree that the person would have absolutely no access to me. There would be no way he could ever have anything from me again. I would also feel like a fool that I was misled by the other person. Operating from my new myth, I see myself redirecting this energy, giving the best possible interpretation I can find for understanding the person's behavior. I don't take it as a personal affront. I stay rooted in my principles, but I also stay flexible like the kelp and consider all that might have caused the other's actions and all the possible ways for me to respond other than withdrawal. I feel good as I imagine myself operating from this position.

The situation you choose may be one you have directly encountered or one that you imagine. Bring it to mind now. Once you have chosen the situation, come into a standing position.

1. Begin by recalling or imagining the feel and field of your new myth. Imagine that with each deep breath, your subtle body is vibrating in resonance with your new myth.

2. Next, find a physical posture that embodies the spirit of the new myth. Allow yourself to experience, from this physical posture, the feeling of your new myth.

3. From this posture and feeling, sense in your body what it would be like to go through the situation you just selected, acting according to your new myth. Allow the scene to come to you now. Notice where you are, who else is there, and how you are being challenged.

4. Create a mental rehearsal, going through the scene in detail.

5. Open your eyes and "step into" your fantasy, creating a pantomime. If you need to change your posture to fit the situation, change it now. Find the gestures that fit. Physically but silently enact the pantomime.

6. When you are finished, come to center and take a deep breath.

Now move through the pantomime once more, this time adding words. The words might be those you would actually use in the situation you are imagining, or they may be a more universal or general expression of your new myth. Form the words in your throat and mouth. Speak them out loud. Practice living from your new myth in your imagination and your subtle body. Allow the enactment to evolve. With this behavior rehearsal, you are building your new mythology into your subtle body. Describe this experience in your journal. Ann wrote:

> I am imagining the time soon when I will be needing to tell someone I have supported financially for a long time that I will not continue to do so. I know that if I keep giving the help, not only do I cripple him, but it goes against what I need for myself. I must find the courage to allow this dear lifetime friend to flounder. Imagining us both in the same room, I am hearing all the arguments and strategies that have gotten me to maintain the arrangement this long. I can feel the discomfort in the pit of my stomach. I can hear my own internal arguments that it wouldn't hurt me to help just a little longer. But in spite of all my discomfort, like an addict giving up smoking, I fortify

my energy and do not succumb. I take on the posture of my new myth and simply say, "I do wish it could be different, but I have made my choice and I need, for myself, to stand by it. I wish you every blessing."

Frank imagined himself intensely involved in a project when his wife came to "ask for my car keys because she has misplaced hers again. Where I am usually irritated by such interruptions, I remind myself, 'When I can play, I do play.' I get up, take her by the hand, whirl her around twice, and dance her across the room."

Daily Personal Ritual. Repetition is one way to establish a new myth firmly in your subtle body, neural networks, and conscious thoughts. Describe in your journal a ritual you can perform each day that will help establish your new myth in your personal field and in your life. A daily ritual might involve meditating for a few moments before each meal with gratitude for that which sustains you and a recognition of the opportunity to live from your new myth. It might mean ceremonially repeating your pantomime every evening. You might translate your mythic vision into a behavior you can regularly repeat. For instance, to implement a myth that allows you to receive help and support from others, you might each day ask a different person to do a small favor for you. At the end of the day, you could ritualistically mark on a special chart the requests you made that day and the results of having made them. One woman, who was trying to become more responsible, took her Power Object, a beautiful stone, and committed herself to carrying it and exploring it every time she went up or down the stairs in her home. The stone was to accompany her on every trip. If she forgot it, she would interrupt whatever she was doing to complete the rite. In so doing, she was continually renewing her commitment toward greater responsibility. With each trip up or down the staircase, she was making personal responsibility a stronger quality in her personal field, and she had built in the secondary gain of communing with her Power Object on each trip as well.

Meg created the following personal ritual:

I will get a package of colorful balloons and choose one whose color matches a quality I want to develop. I will slowly blow it until it is plump and pretty, and I will write on it the name of a quality. When there are several balloons, I will hang them carefully from my bathroom mirror until there is a wreath of words: patience (soft blue), kindness (warm pink), humor (red), forgiveness (deep blue), learning (green), and honor (white) surrounding my face in the morning and night when I brush my hair and teeth.

Ann's personal ritual was to take her earlier stance, with her left palm open in a gesture of loving welcome, and the right hand resting on the open palm in a gesture of pointing, as in making a point. Her statement was, "I have the strength to know and lovingly claim what is of highest priority for me." Since Ann already was in the habit of a morning ritual, she added this to the very end of it. At that point, she would also clarify her priorities for the day, and she committed herself to living from them.

Frank, who found it difficult to get going in the morning, decided to start each day by standing in front of a mirror and finding a posture that symbolized his old myth. He would then meditate on the feelings he associated with the new pink heart and would let those feelings pulsate throughout him until they filled him so completely that he was moved to stretch his body to make room for them. He would imagine he was stretching his whole being into harmony with his new mythology, until he relaxed into a posture that for him was a physical statement of his myth. Finally, he would identify one situation he anticipated that day which was likely to trigger his old myth, and he would envision himself handling it according to his new myth.

Frank's ritual was a variation on the following instruction: Each morning, in front of the mirror, direct the feeling you associate with your new myth into your subtle body, assume the posture and the facial expression that represent this myth, summarize its guidance in a single statement, and hold a one-minute discussion with the mirror anticipating this day from the perspective of your new myth. In your journal, design a single ritual you are willing to perform daily during the following week. You will be given further suggestions for a daily personal ritual in the next chapter.

Public Ritual. We also suggest that you plan a "ritual of transition" that marks a *public* declaration of your new myth. A public ritual involves at least one other person. Choose people who care about you and who are not likely to be so threatened by the changes you intend as to be unwilling to support you in implementing them. One element of a ritual of transition is ceremonially to leave the old myth behind. You could, for example, begin with a photograph of yourself during a period when you were in the grips of the old myth or a drawing that represents that period. In the ritual, you might burn the photograph or drawing with a friend there to witness, scattering the ashes and drinking a toast to your new myth as it is symbolized on your Personal Shield.

At the most basic level, your public ritual could involve simply having someone who cares about you witness your daily ritual or the behavioral enactment you performed earlier. In a more ambitious ceremony, you might design an evening with candles, flowers, song, incense, holy objects, and sharing the sustenance of food—portraying your new myth in a way your friends are likely to register deeply. You might, for instance, have several friends take on the roles in your behavioral enactment, so that it becomes more like a skit or play. Another ceremony might involve making a statement of your intentions at a gathering of certain intimates or sharing an artistic rendition that captures the spirit of your new myth, such as your Personal Shield, your Fairy Tale, a painting, a poem, or passages from your journal. If you are anticipating a special event, like a reunion of friends you've not seen for a good while or a graduation party or a retirement party or a wedding, you may find that it empowers both the ritual and the event to combine them.

Meg's public ritual used the balloons from her private ritual: "I will be the 'balloon lady' at the next Summit Summer Festival. I will write one nice word on each balloon, and the children will be surprised to find qualities like Love, Beauty, and Truth dancing over their heads on a string. I will enjoy the sight very much, and I will lovingly offer each child an understanding of their special quality. If anyone is curious about why I did it, I will answer in a way that reflects my new myth: 'Serenity is gained through loving, thoughtful action.' "

Ann already had a beautiful altar set up in her home. She and her partner chose a night when they were alone. They placed flowers on the altar, lit candles and incense, and sat facing each other on cushions. She shared with him all that she was discovering of the myth she was leaving and the one she was moving into. She then danced her ritual to his drumming.

Frank brought a dozen pink roses to his wife, along with a letter he had just written turning down a new account he normally would have accepted, because it clearly would have overtaxed him. He showed her the new enlivened pink heart on his Shield, which happened to be the identical shade as the roses. He also promised to say yes to her next three invitations to do something fun together.

A poignant ritual was carried out by a woman whose mythology had grown out of a childhood that was afflicted with sexual molestation and parental alcoholism. In her new mythology, she had come to an integration of toughness and compassion. She timed the ritual to coincide with a Thanksgiving gathering in which her husband, brother, sisters, nieces, nephews, and children were all present. After announcing, as they gathered in the living room after dinner, that she was performing a ritual to commemorate a change in the mythology she was living out, she showed them her Personal Shield. She used the symbolism on her Shield in describing her life as an emerging drama whose purpose was to teach her both the compassion and the toughness that characterized her new myth. She described how the critical events of her life opened her to the wisdom of this new mythology, and she told her personal Fairy Tale, emphasizing how the theme of the entire adventure was to help the heroine learn the new mythology. Everyone was deeply moved, and some were stunned, as she metaphorically disclosed family secrets that had been concealed for decades. With everyone's rapt attention, she potently ended the ritual by presenting her eldest daughter—as a legacy for her future offspring—with her Personal Shield, a tape recording she had made while telling her story that evening, and a letter to a male descendant and another to a female descendant, four generations in the future, describing her new myth and how she had come to it.

Once you have designed a public ritual that seems appropriate and pleasing to you, make plans in your journal for carrying it out. Be aware of the mood you wish to create, design the event with that mood in mind, and, in advance, convey to the participants the importance the event holds for you.

PURPOSE: *To try out your new myth in the safety of your dreams*

Reflect on the spirit of your new myth and consider how your life might change if you were already living according to it. Using the same general procedure, before falling asleep, take a few deep breaths, think about your new-myth statement, and slowly and mindfully write a statement such as: "I will sleep soundly and peacefully tonight while having a dream that shows me how to bring the spirit of my new myth into my life. When I awake, I will recall my dream." Then, with deliberation, repeat several times before falling asleep, "I will have a meaningful dream, and I will remember it." Immediately upon waking, record and explore your dream. If you don't recall a dream the first night, repeat the process each night until you do. Ann wrote:

> I dreamed I was with my friend Mahara. We are sitting cross-legged sewing metal grommets onto a doe hide. There is a feel of Native American spirit in our work. The grommets keep the hide from tearing if you hook something onto it. The two of us are totally content in a green meadow, naked in the sunshine, sewing together. The dream leaves me with a feeling of elusive potential, a sense that I could someday have this kind of contentment, but probably never will.
>   I Am the Hide: I will tear if something is hooked on to me. I am

DREAM FOCUS:
Your New Myth in Action

unfortified. I am fragile. I am natural, but not strong enough to withstand the daily rigors of life without reinforcement.

I am Mahara: I am kindly, positive, committed to inner growth, love, and wisdom.

I Am the Green Sunlit Meadow: I am potential, I am freedom, I am contentment, I am vast, open, and bursting with life.

I Am a Metal Grommet: I am a sacred circle, a symbol of power, superimposed strength, help, and support. I had to be fashioned out of something that is hard, unbending, and fixed, and made into something self-contained and useful, and then sewn into the fabric of what is natural.

I Am the Elusive Potential: I am the absolute simplicity of the act of sewing without all the stresses of modern life. I am elusive because bringing together the doe skin and the metallic indifference of modern life seems impossible.

This dream is telling me that I am a work in progress, that I am having to develop and bring into myself aspects that are not natural to me. My new myth in action is that I can take with me the gentleness and natural kindliness that Mahara represents and yet bring in the strength and fortification that the grommets represent.

Translating Your New Mythology

into Daily Life

❧

Myth is the bubbling lifespring of our consciousness . . . of our
highest creativity as well as of our worst delusions, and the secret
is all in how it is tended.

—Stephen Larsen[1]

Steven Covey speaks of the "hard moments" each of us face every day, and
of the critical space between stimulus and response—the interval within
which we can determine our actions.[2] He describes these hard moments
as intervals where the gap between stimulus and response is saturated with old
habits and temptations toward the "lower road." The way we handle our hard
moments sets a tone that permeates our lives. With such choices, we calibrate
our automatic pilot to take either the higher road or the lower road, to follow a
soul-affirming or a soul-negating guiding myth. Frank, for instance, was able to
identify an underlying theme in many of his hard moments. Whenever there was
a choice between doing something that satisfied his need for accomplishment
and having time for his inner life—to meditate or smell the roses—he automatically went after the accomplishment. As a result, his zest for life was being con-
fined and force-fit into projects that were not in alignment with his deeper
nature. It was not surprising that his primary complaint was that his passion was
shriveling. By focusing on his hard moments, he could see how his choices at

those times were having the net effect of suffocating his spirit. Reframing his hard moments as skirmishes in his battle to regain his passion made them, at the very least, more interesting, and he used this awareness to build the psychological muscles that, at appropriate times, steered him toward being rather than doing.

To live in concert with your mythic wisdom, as you have been discovering, involves astute inner observation. "Carefully observe which way your heart draws you," counsels an Hasidic proverb, "and then choose that way with all your strength." *To observe carefully which way your heart draws you* is a fair summary of the first nine chapters of this program. With the previous chapter, the focus shifted to *choosing that way with all your strength.* Even bringing about desirable changes in your mythology can require the full strength of your will. Habits of thought and behavior that grew out of an old myth may hang on tenaciously.

On the other hand, bringing a measure of inner resolution to the mythic conflict you identified early in the program and formulating a new guiding vision have in themselves set into motion some shifts in your thought and behavior. Deliberately incorporating your new myth into your life involves both an inward focus and an outward one. The previous chapter emphasized the inner focus, highlighting the images that regulate you, the words you say to yourself, and physical, psychological, and behavioral ways you can incorporate the spirit of your new myth into your subtle body. This chapter emphasizes the outward focus, inviting practical changes in your habits and priorities. Both chapters draw particularly from the contributions of cognitive and behavioral psychotherapists for bringing about changes in thought patterns and behavior. The personal rituals in this chapter are designed specifically to increase the harmony between your new myth and the way you live your life.

You will, for instance, analyze your psychosocial environment, determine how it does and does not support your new myth, and how you can bring about changes that make it more supportive. You will project your new myth five years into the future and envision the changes you can make now that will lead you in the direction in which "your heart draws you." You will create a "behavioral contract" with another person or with your Inner Shaman that specifies the steps you will take, week by week, to "choose that way with all your strength." By the time you have performed the personal rituals presented in this chapter, you will have laid out a practical plan for anchoring your new myth into your daily life.

PURPOSE: *To analyze the reinforcement patterns in your environment and make changes so they better support your new myth*

One of the most venerable principles in modern psychology is that people tend to repeat behaviors that are rewarded and avoid behaviors that are punished. You are more likely to change maladaptive behavioral patterns when they are no longer reinforced. You may welcome your new myth, but if your world is organized in a way that reinforces the old behavior and punishes the behavior that corresponds with your new myth, you will be less likely to perpetuate it. In this ritual, you will identify the rewards and punishments that maintain your old myth and promote your new myth. By making changes that favor your new myth, you will prepare an ecology, a balance of relationships within your environment, in which the new myth is more likely to flourish. Consider, for instance, how your family, friends, co-workers, or acquaintances sustain your old myth or inhibit your new myth. To have the desired behaviors more frequently reinforced, you might spend more time with people whose behavior supports your new myth or ask others to provide similar support.

A woman who wanted to change her tendency to "mother" other people asked her friends to stop praising her for being so helpful to everyone. Frank started to form friendships with people who knew him outside his professional identity, hoping to reinforce the development of other parts of his personality. Ann's old myth had her putting the needs of others far above her own, but when she attempted to prioritize her needs, she found that while some of her friends were highly supportive of her intention, others could not separate their need to use her from her need not to be used any longer. She found that the friends who could not support her new myth tended to drop away. In this manner, the atmosphere around her shifted so that it better supported her new myth. Enlisting people who care about you to support behavior that is consistent with your new myth helps establish it in your life.

Another way of changing the reinforcers acting on you is to shift your commitments. If your new myth instructs you to make more time for your inner development, but in addition to your work and family responsibilities, you coach a soccer team, are organizing a recall drive against the local mayor, sit on three community boards, are in a group that watches and discusses a new movie every week, and subscribe to and keep current with a dozen magazines and professional journals, your new myth encouraging unstructured time for reflection gets buried. Once your priorities have been set, they often become embedded in the structure of your life and exert a force long after the myths and values that originally supported them have shifted. You may, for instance, spend many hours every week happily doing tedious chores for a cause in which you passionately believe, but then find yourself resenting the time and effort as your passions change. Your commitments reflect the myths you held when you established them. As you evolve, however, unexamined commitments can quietly keep you locked in a mythology you have outgrown.

Many reinforcers and punishments are symbolic, meeting psychological rather than practical needs. Western culture teaches us to attach our sense of adequacy and self-esteem to particular kinds of symbols, such as those conferring status, fame, or power. As the qualities to which your sense of self-worth is attached shift from those conditioned by your culture to those chosen by a deeper voice, your life is likely to deliver richer satisfactions. A man whose self-esteem is contingent on the number of women he can attract may find that as he becomes more psychologically mature, he begins to derive an unanticipated sense of fulfillment from the depth of his relationships rather than the number of his conquests.

A resource that was working to support Meg's new myth was her "incredible richness of close friends who are marvelous models of goodness." Another was that she lived in a beautiful rural setting "that has less commotion than most people have to endure." She also recognized that her own hope, insight, determination, desire, experience, and faith were factors working in favor of her new myth. Influences she identified as working against her new myth included old habits, fears, spite, suspicion, jealousy, and neediness.

Use what you have learned through this program about creating personal rituals to invent a ritual that will lead you to construct a "List of Reinforcers." The list will specify the rewards and punishments that cause your life to be more or less aligned with your new myth. Consider aspects of your family life and your work life and other areas that reinforce your old myth, and also consider changes that might be possible for you to make that would shift the circumstances to support your new myth better. Identify not only the positive and negative reinforcers in your environment but also the symbolic reinforcers that operate within you, reinforcers like Frank's formula that he would earn the right to enjoy himself only after achieving an unspecified (but certainly unattainable) degree of success.

You might sit down and simply make the list, carrying with you an attitude of sacred ritual to elevate the activity; you might take an imagery journey where your list is revealed to you; you might consult your Inner Shaman before completing the list; or you might meet with a friend who can help give you perspective as you analyze the forces in your environment that are influencing your efforts to implement your new myth. Give serious consideration to this important task of identifying the factors that strengthen or obstruct the development of your new myth. In the final personal ritual of this chapter, you will use your List of Reinforcers as you decide where to focus your efforts for making changes in your life so daily behavior in line with your chosen myth is rewarded more and punished less.

Ann identified several internal and external conditions reinforcing her new myth, among them:

My home is truly a sacred temple for my work.
My urge and passion for creative expression are powerful.
I have reached a point in my career where I no longer have to prove myself.

Conditions negatively reinforcing Ann's new myth included:

Some of my friendships do little for me while requiring me to do much for them.
Some of my artistic projects do not aesthetically excite me and do little for my well-being.
I am so busy that I often can't find the time to feed my hunger to be creative.

Positively reinforcing Frank's new myth were:

The playful presence of my wife.
I've distinguished myself enough so that I no longer have to struggle for professional recognition.
I am increasingly restless with tasks that don't hold meaning for me.
I know that beneath my shyness and obsessiveness is a very passionate and playful man.

Conditions that negatively reinforced Frank's new myth included:

I feel I don't have a right to enjoy my life if I'm not achieving prodigiously.
I do receive additional recognition and income when I overwork.

When I try to have fun, I usually feel awkward and the experience seems empty.

Most of my friends are also high achievers whom I know mainly through my work, and I haven't developed other kinds of friendships.

SESSION 2:
The Sequel to
Your Fairy Tale

PURPOSE: *To project your new myth five years into the future and consider how the changes you are implementing now are likely to unfold*

A sequel is a literary work, complete in itself, that continues a preceding work. In the Sequel you are about to create, the direction taken by your Fairy Tale will intersect with the anticipated direction of your life. You may stay within the metaphor of your Fairy Tale (Ann's approach, as you will see) or set the context in your own life, as did Meg:

> I'm sitting at my word processor, writing a book, smiling. No one is with me physically, but I am very conscious that loved ones are within reach. I take time out every day to go out of my house, into the woods, to be in the forest and by the creek. I have found the theme and the method to communicate my ideas about Nature and life effectively, and I feel useful and competent. I'm very aware of a growing edge of freshness and novelty and discovery in my life. But I'm not so subject to the storms and the emotional violence that once plagued me constantly. My relationships with people are deep and real and enduring. I'm contented with the direction of my growth and my changes, and I don't see any end to them.

Ann wrote:

> And so it came to be that the young girl matured into a wise and beautiful woman. She shared in the companionship of others like herself and together they embarked upon a journey to bring the light of the golden pebble to the hearts of many. They wrote books for others to read. They sang songs for others to hear. They created works of art for others to see. But most important of all, they lived lives that resonated with the light of the golden pebble shining within their own hearts. They became beacons that lit and inspired the hearts of all they met, and there came to be great rejoicing in the country as the land began to glow with the light of Love and Truth that was finding its way into the culture through the glow of the golden pebble.

PREPARATION: *Review Part Three of your Fairy Tale. Decide whether you would like to stay in the context of your Fairy Tale or shift to the context of your own life. Then with your Personal Shield, Power Object, and journal nearby, sit or recline comfortably, take a deep breath, and close your eyes.*

As you tune in to your breathing, listen for your inhalation and your exhalation. Notice how your belly and chest fill . . . and empty. Your breath becomes slow and deep. Tensions release as your mind and body relax more completely.

Bring Part Three of your Fairy Tale back to mind. Tune in to the most dominant positive feeling. Locate the part of your body in which you are most strongly aware of this feeling. As it absorbs your attention, further observe the way your body reacts to it. Experience this feeling through your breathing, muscle tension, and temperature. Allow your breathing to intensify this feeling. Find a word that describes the feeling.

You will be using this feeling to lead you five years into the future, to a scene where either your Fairy Tale character or you yourself have been living out of the new myth for a good while. Notice the flow of sensations that make up the feeling. Imagine that these sensations form a bridge that can carry you into the future. Stepping onto this bridge, you are safe and comfortable as you move forward. You come to a scene from the future. You see yourself or your Fairy Tale character living according to the new myth. The scene becomes more vivid with each of your next three breaths. Observe the scene carefully, noting the setting, the people, and the action.

When you are ready, take another deep breath and return to your ordinary waking consciousness, refreshed, relaxed, and alert.

Under the heading "Fairy Tale Sequel," record this story in your journal. Frank's Sequel was about his own life:

The first thing I see is children, playful and full of fresh energy. The children run up to me full of excitement and curiosity. I have no concern about taking the time to speak with them and play with them. Nor am I stopped by any shyness. I know how to open my heart and let the energy flow. Later, I am in a hut transacting some business. The same openness and vigor are there in my dealings. I can play hard and I can work playfully. Suddenly Diane is there. We have grown closer and have much more fun together. We take a walk in the woods. I have learned to see and deeply feel the miracles of life that teem in the forest. We show each other intricate root patterns and speculate later on how they developed. She takes my hand and gently places it on some lush moss. I take my finger, wet now with dew, and moisten her lips. I'm very much in love.

SESSION 3:
A Contract for Living Your New Mythology

PURPOSE: *To specify and implement changes that firmly establish your new myth in your daily life*

An old adage suggests, "If you don't change your direction, you may wind up where you are headed." The challenge at this point in the program is to change your direction according to the wisdom of your new myth. William James counseled, "If we wish to conquer undesirable emotional tendencies in ourselves, we must assiduously, and in the first instance cold-bloodedly, go through the *outward* motions of those contrary dispositions we prefer to cultivate."[3] One of the most reinforcing sources of support for implementing new modes of thought and behavior is to establish accountability with someone who cares about you.

Identify a person, perhaps someone who participated in your "public ritual," and request that the person establish with you (and in subsequent weeks assist you in reviewing and revising) a contract that specifies the steps you will take that week to bring the vision of your new myth into your life. The person (or persons) will help you review your progress, serve as a sounding board, and assist you in planning your next steps on a continuing basis. As an alternative, you could go through the following instructions using your Inner Shaman or your journal as a surrogate partner. At first Frank was going to ask his wife to be his partner, but he decided that because she was already such a key figure in the areas he wished to change, it would be better to be accountable to someone else. It happened that a colleague who had recently joined a men's group was discussing many issues that were similar to those Frank was exploring, and he readily agreed to assist Frank with his contract.

Behavioral contracts are used to specify new behaviors that are associated with desired goals. They are statements of specific, measurable actions that are steps toward manifesting an intention. Behavioral contracts provide reinforcement for learning these behaviors and for making them habitual. In the behavioral contract, accountability becomes a form of support. In the following ritual, you will create a behavioral contract. The contract will specify the actions you plan to take as you begin to implement your new myth. Later you will review your experiences in attempting to fulfill the contract. At that point, you will consider what you learned from your efforts and how you might best revise the contract.

A behavioral contract should propel you into the challenges of the new myth without overwhelming you with unreasonable aspirations. After discussing with your partner the possible actions you might take, label a new page of your journal "My Contract" and put the date at the top of the page. Alternatively, photocopy or write into your journal the sample contract on page 239. Each point in your contract should be specific, stating, if possible, where, how, with whom, and when you will carry out the action: "I will have spoken with Mario, Susanne, and the guy from the historical society by Tuesday to identify at least three potential volunteer activities that would be satisfying and intellectually stimulating." Putting specifics in your contract provides you and your partner with criteria for evaluating the results of your efforts. While your behavioral contract may specify any areas you choose, we particularly recommend that you focus on three topics that have already been covered: a daily personal ritual, monitoring your self-statements so your new myth is better supported and your old myth is less frequently activated, and making changes in your outer life so your new myth is better reinforced.

In her contract, Meg identified several areas of focus, including monitoring her self-judgments, allowing more vulnerability with others, initiating more intimate and risky conversation with her friends, and listening patiently to other people's points of view. When she and her partner met a week later, Meg recounted her progress in taking these steps and reported a welcome shift in her relationships. Meg and her partner met once a week for two months. At each meeting they reviewed her successes, discussed areas of difficulty in carrying out the contract, and revised the contract for the following week. By the end of the second month, Meg felt that her new myth—"Serenity is gained through loving, thoughtful action"—had become conscious and accessible to her in many of the same areas of her life in which the isolation and defensiveness of the old myth had caused problems.

With your behavioral contract partner, review the experiences you have had to this point with your daily ritual. What has been valuable, and what has not been useful? Devise, with your partner, a personal ritual you are willing to carry out each day that will consistently reinforce your new myth in your subtle body and in your behavior. Frank enjoyed his morning stretching ritual but also found that it became mechanical when he did it every day. He decided that he would do the stretching ritual on his days off. On the way to work, he would contemplate his heart image and bring its energy to the spirit of his work and to the decisions he would be making that day.

Review with your partner the list of self-statements that support your old and new myths. Add to your contract what you will do to continue to recognize and tag the old and promote the new. You might, for instance, use the thought-stopping technique described earlier, place notes in your living quarters, or make the temporal tap one of your daily rituals.

Frank was determined to stop a pattern of piling one project on top of another in a way that crowded out any sense of accomplishment and pleasure. He identified the end points of various projects, and when he reached them he would monitor the inner voice that automatically directed him to the next task at hand. He listed several simple rewards, ranging from taking a brief walk to watching a video to taking a day off from work, and whenever he reached an end point he would instruct himself to stop and treat himself to one of the activities on that list. He also decided that he needed his partner's help in monitoring the self-statements he would use to evaluate his success with his behavioral contract. He agreed to measure his progress in the first week in terms of any new experiences that felt good to him, and he pledged to interrupt any thoughts about how much more he might have accomplished.

In addition to your daily personal ritual and self-statements, review your List of Reinforcers with your partner. Assess what you have learned from your initial attempts to shift the positive and negative reinforcers that affect your new myth. With your partner, decide what other actions would strengthen one or more of the promoting forces and minimize or eliminate one or more of the inhibiting forces. Some features will seem easier to change and are therefore good initial targets. Others that are not as accessible may come later. Start with one or two areas. Describe a first step in bringing about a change. Because the contract will be updated on a regular basis, you need specify only initial steps that can be accomplished within a short period of time.

A final focus for your contract is to plan a specific activity for the week, in which you flex the muscles of your new myth. We suggest that this activity push you just a bit beyond your comfort zone.

When/Where/With Whom is the next accountability meeting:

1. My daily personal ritual:

2. Old-myth and new-myth self-statements I will write, prominently display, memorize, *and* use with the thought-stopping technique or a related method during this time period:

3. At least one change I will bring about in my environment so it will better support my new myth *and* specific, measurable steps I will take toward bringing about that change(s) during this time period:

4. One new behavior I will carry out during this time period that is an expression of my new myth that pushes me beyond my comfort zone:

By the time you and your partner have created your contract, you will have identified several activities you plan to initiate. Your behavioral contract will specify concrete actions you can accomplish in the immediate future. Name names, indicate the number of times you will carry out an action, describe anticipated situations. Be so specific that when you and your partner review the plans, it will be clear which goals you accomplished. In making your contract, you and your partner should be particularly cautious about specifying steps that are too ambitious. Avoid setting yourself up for failure. Anticipate obstacles to fulfilling the contract successfully, and make plans about how to respond to those obstacles when you encounter them. Arrange to meet with your partner again after about a week.

In addition to her daily ritual and a commitment, each week, to change the placement of her notes with the word *Locate* so their impact would remain fresh, Ann specified several other activities for the first week of her contract. She contracted to take every afternoon that week to be with her eight-year-old son. She contracted to have one or more evenings that week of deep intimacy with her partner, and to remain available for the hour they already typically spent in the mornings centering with each other and doing inner work. She contracted to spend only the time she genuinely wanted to spend with guests who were coming that week to stay with her. She contracted to say no to the six lunch invitations waiting for her that she didn't want to accept. And she contracted to spend one morning that week getting back to writing her musical.

One of Frank's goals was to spend more time with his wife, whom he saw as the person most able to provide effective support for his new myth. He decided his first step that week would be to bring his wife to a restaurant for a leisurely breakfast on her day off, even though that meant he would be late for work. Shortly afterward, he had an opportunity to take more substantial action. He had been working two years to secure an account that would be very challenging to manage, extremely demanding, but that would pay well and offer high prestige. He had been ready to jump at the opportunity for a long time. But when he received the contract, he was reluctant to sign it. He felt he was about to sign away all of the promises he had recently made to himself. He decided to wait a few days and live with the implications of taking the project. He talked the issue over with his partner, the colleague in the men's group. They came up with what seemed to Frank to be a radical idea: He referred the account to the most prestigious investment firm in the area. The fact that he was in a position to make that referral was a boost for his reputation and his standing in the professional community, so the move was not without some practical benefits. More important, in terms of his new mythology, it was a significant affirmation of his intention to bring more peace and intimacy into his life.

Reviewing Your Contract. Plan your first review meeting with your partner so it will involve ceremony—perhaps through the sharing of food or a special atmosphere. The goal will be to review your attempts to support your new myth and assess what can be learned from any obstacles that emerged. Consider which items from your contract you attempted to carry out and what resulted. What do these results suggest about revising your contract the following week? Review the total process. Was the contract too ambitious? Not challenging enough? Were you motivated to carry it out? Did you and your partner correctly anticipate and plan for obstacles? Finally, remain alert to how the old myth may itself have influenced the way you attempted to change it.

One of the most informative ways to understand a personal myth is to try to change it and carefully watch what happens. The process of creating an active feedback loop between your lived mythology and your attempts to transform it can be enhanced by a classic social science method called *action research*.[4] This method might be employed, for instance, in helping a community group translate its goals and values into effective measures. Action research generally begins with a systematic assessment of a situation that needs to be changed. The central concept in action research is that ongoing feedback is critical for mobilizing effective activity. Constructively changing a social system is not seen as a one-shot endeavor. Even the most carefully considered efforts are best viewed as practical experiments that produce information that can be used in planning subsequent action. In this way, an ongoing feedback loop is established: plans are made, action is taken, results are analyzed, and new plans are formulated. Outcomes are valued according to the learning they produce as well as the actual changes they accomplish.

You can use the basic principles of this method as you implement your new myth, adopting it in each of your review sessions with your partner. After carefully defining precisely what changes are desired, action research proceeds through five basic stages:[5]

1. fact-finding to assess possibilities for change and obstacles to change;
2. planning specific actions to bring about the desired change;
3. carrying out the plan;
4. evaluating the results of the actions that were taken;
5. feeding this information back to the individuals concerned, in order to begin another round of the cycle.

By the time you meet with your partner to review your progress, you already will have completed the first three of these steps. The action research model provides a framework for assessing what has occurred and deciding what to do next. If you were unable to carry out parts of your contract, consider whether they were untenable because the new myth is not quite fitting for you, because obstacles in your environment were more intransigent than you anticipated, or because you set too ambitious a goal for a single week. Attempts at changing an established system are not expected to go exactly as planned, and the results of such efforts are used to gather new information. Future attempts can thus be revised and made more effective. It will likely be necessary to adjust the vision of your new myth from one meeting with your partner to the next. These are natural and expected corrections, and the action research model can help you monitor areas where such changes are required.

Frank's old myth caused him to be overly ambitious in envisioning his goals, and his contract was no exception. As he pushed toward meeting its terms, he found himself starting to approach the activities with a sense of drudgery. His plan to measure his progress according to small increments got lost in the shuffle. He was gaining little creative insight, and he was discouraged by the time of the first review. His partner, however, pointed out the way his old myth was trapping him and helped Frank recognize the pattern, see the irony in it, and ease back into the program. Noting how his self-discipline was stifling his passion even in this attempt to rekindle that passion, Frank revised his contract. He developed an image where he would "use my mind as a machete to carefully clear away the weeds in my life that are crowding out my passion, but I will not get so obsessed with clearing the weeds that there is no time to enjoy the garden." His second contract included fewer assignments and required that he devote specified periods of time to savor the successful completion of each item.

With your partner, review your experiences while carrying out your initial contract and, on the basis of your new insights, create a second contract. Again, be as specific as possible in describing each task you agree to undertake, and decide when you will hold your next meeting. The action research model keeps your awareness attuned to your mythology as you express it in the world, and it fosters ongoing monitoring and adjustments. Ann reflected on her experiences five weeks after making her initial contract:

I am learning how very difficult it is for me to maintain a sense of structure in my life. I found it easy to do those things that were single events, such as the Public Ritual and setting aside a morning to work on my musical. But I had great difficulty maintaining those things that required ongoing effort.

However, I have noted that although I might forget what was in my contract, and even forget to look at it, when I finally returned to it, I discovered that the very act of creating it had made a difference. I have been spending more time with my son. I did cancel the lunch appointments that I had agreed to cancel. I have been more careful with my time and was comfortable leaving houseguests to care for themselves. While I was not meticulous to the letter of my contract, I think it had a substantial subliminal impact on me.

Continue the process of meeting with your partner or reflecting in your journal about your contract on a weekly basis for as long as focusing attention on implementing your new myth seems useful. Some people become discouraged at this point because they find it more difficult to fulfill the contract than they had anticipated. Also, because human hope springs eternal, many people make contracts that are overly ambitious. Rather than affirming, "I won't lose my temper ever again," or, "I won't criticize my wife anymore," such lofty intentions can be "chunked down" into statements such as "I will notice when my temper is rising and take three deep breaths," or "When I start to criticize my wife, I will pause and consider what motivated her action." Ask your partner to help you affirm the steps you have taken and with you to use the action research perspective for revising your contract so it will correspond more closely with what you are actually capable of accomplishing.

Keep in mind that it is easier to articulate a new myth than it is to live it. We've not yet found a person who couldn't conceptualize a new mythology which, to some degree, resolved underlying mythic conflict. You may, like Frank, know that if you stop being a workaholic, your marriage will improve. That is basically an intellectual task. Integrating the new myth into your life, however, is a task that challenges your total being; it may push the limits of your environment, and it is likely to require sustained effort, experimentation, and awareness. Nonetheless, even if you are just beginning to achieve changes in the desired directions, you are already living with a greater awareness of the mythic dimension of your inner life. Do not allow the complexities of implementing mythic changes in your outer life to obscure the importance of the inner changes you have already initiated.

A Next-Step Dream

PURPOSE: *To invite your dreams to offer you further direction for your mythology's evolution as you complete this program*

Your personal mythology will never stop evolving. We suggest that you invite a dream that shows you a next step for remaining aware and active in the process of bringing the energy of your new myth into your life. Before falling asleep, take a few deep breaths, think about your new myth and your efforts to live according to it, and in your journal slowly and mindfully write a statement such as: "I will sleep soundly and peacefully while having a dream that tells me about a next step in the evolution of my personal mythology. When I awake, I will recall my dream." Then, with deliberation, repeat several times before falling asleep, "I will have a meaningful dream, and I will remember it." Immediately upon waking, record and explore your dream. You can usefully repeat this process whenever you want to refresh and deepen your conscious relationship with your guiding mythology. Ann's dream:

I dreamed I was in a loving relationship with a pop star, even though I am much older than he is. I felt a tremendous compassion for him. The true delicacy of his spirit, the rare fragility of his talent.

There were several older women, and it was clear they wanted something from him. They had invited him to stay the night in an old mansion. He was anxious, and I told him I would watch over him. I overheard a conversation in which the women were discussing something that felt wicked. I knew that he <u>was</u> in serious danger. I went to my friend and told him to come upstairs with me and pretend that we were retiring for the night. We passed the women, who tried to talk us into staying downstairs. I spoke very clearly that it was time for us to go. Not wanting to create suspicion as to their true motives, they allowed us to pass.

We began climbing the stairs. They were huge and seemed to spiral on forever. We finally got to the top and I found a door that led into a tiny room. It could hold only a small bed. He curled up on it and said he was very tired. I could feel that the walls began to contract in on us. Just before the door closed, I grabbed my friend's hand and pulled him to safety. We next found a door that led into a huge room that had been used as a dance studio. I said, "That's more like it. They are frightened of your dancing. We will be safe here." I held him close to me and began to gently sing in his ear. Although he was still afraid, we began to move together.

Suddenly, I was no longer in the attic, but riding a beautiful black horse across a field. I was dressed in silver armor with a sword in my hand. We were heading for a town that I could see in the distance. I felt tremendous joy. I had no idea what was waiting for me there, but I felt a sense of confidence that I could handle it when I got there. I awoke.

This dream seemed to be telling me that I can trust my new myth. I think that the pop star represented my old myth: kind, gifted, yet endangered. I, in the dream, am my counter-myth, able to see and speak the truth and therefore protect what is fragile and unsure.

When we finally came to the dance studio, the new myth was activated. We began to make something beautiful together, creative yet also safe. We became one.

When I found myself riding the horse in flexible, shiny armor, it was an expression of what is possible for me at this time: to ride the power of my instinctual nature, protected and empowered with clarity, beauty, and a sense of purpose. Being able to wield the sword of truth, I need not fear entering the realm of commerce, business, facts, and figures, as represented by the town at the bottom of the hill. I have what is needed to find my way safely and surely through that domain.

I awoke from the dream feeling excited about getting to work on a creative project. It is time for me to venture out, knowing I will have the strength and clarity to find my way through the world of business to better support bringing my creativity into the world.

A CLOSING

This is the final chapter that is organized around a set of personal rituals. Week 12 offers a conceptual framework for the immense challenge of living creatively and effectively in a culture whose guiding myths are frayed, tattered, and crying for rejuvenation. We would like to close this part of the program by reflecting on what it has offered and what it cannot offer.

"All important decisions," psychiatrist Sheldon Kopp has observed, "are made on the basis of insufficient data."[6] Day by day, we wind our way through the world compelled to make—without enough information—the choices that shape our lives.

Your guiding mythology organizes the information you do have and shows you how to use it. An astute mythology is worth a thousand facts. The program you are now completing has been helping you cultivate an astute mythology, a guiding perspective that is increasingly independent of limiting myths from your childhood and your culture.

Recall the research discussed in Week 9 indicating that the stronger its biological basis, the harder a psychological condition will be to change. Psychotherapeutic techniques have, however, been developed for correcting an array of conditions where biology is clearly implicated. While this is not the place to discuss the merits and abuses of psychiatric medication, there is no question that in cases such as schizophrenia and severe chronic depression, approaches that intervene directly at the level of the person's biochemistry should be seriously considered. A variety of less intrusive procedures have also been developed for physiologically releasing deeply entrenched patterns.

For instance, interventions focusing on the breath[7] or the body's deep tissue and musculature[8] are believed to soften long-standing psychological defenses that are embedded in the body, freeing the part of the personality that has been trapped beneath those defenses. Interventions that focus on a person's eye movements[9] or use hypnosis or biofeedback are believed to be capable of reprocessing disturbing thoughts and memories resulting from stress or trauma. Interventions that focus on the relationship between a therapist and client are believed to have an impact on the psychodynamic bedrock of the personality. Interventions that focus on the person as an energy system[10] are believed to have an impact on the subtle foundations of physical existence.

Maintaining, applying, and revising your mythology is as unending a task as that of the paint crew of the Golden Gate Bridge, whose job is never completed. We view the personal mythology program as an overture for bringing a mythic eye to the choices you make. While we have ushered you along a highly structured path marked by the personal rituals, you have in the process surveyed the territory of your personal mythology, and now that you know how to enter it, you can dig into it as deeply as you are inclined.

When we see people privately, the activities are often invented session by session. We do not attempt to guide people through the thirty-two personal rituals presented here (although our clients often do work through the book at home). Rather, we follow the spontaneity of the encounter. Yet even without the personal rituals, the five basic stages remain. That sequence of tasks seems built into the psyche. The rituals presented in this book have been structured with the intention of guiding you through each of the stages gently, harmoniously, and productively.

You may go through the program any number of times, and you will find ways to streamline and customize the approach as you become more familiar with the methods. It is not necessary, for instance, to create a new Personal Shield or autobiography each time you explore a mythic conflict. On the other hand, it may be useful to repeat some of the specific rituals many times, such as the dialogue between your old-myth and counter-myth characters or the meetings with your Inner Shaman or Power Object. The personal rituals are simply devices for turning inward and establishing a harmony between your efforts and the natural processes by which your mythology develops. The more you use these methods, the more you will understand the principles behind them and be able to adapt them as you periodically focus on your guiding mythology.

People who have gone through our workshops or the earlier edition of this book more than once have had vastly different experiences each time. Specific personal rituals can also continue to serve as useful tools after you have completed the program. Some people return to earlier stages of the program or specific rituals to rework matters that were not resolved the first time through and that are interfering with efforts to implement their new myth. Personal rituals such as "Healing an Ancient Wound," "Saying Good-bye to an Antiquated Myth," "Transforming Obstacles into Opportunities," and "Rewriting History Through the Emotionally Corrective Daydream" may be particularly useful in such instances.

Whatever the specific intervention, whether a personal ritual presented in this book, a tested psychotherapeutic technique, an understanding of your evolving mythology establishes its context. While certain ingrained patterns, particularly those with strong physiological underpinnings, are not likely to be changed dramatically through any preconfigured psychological procedures, the program you have just completed provides a perspective on your psychosocial and spiritual development that is relevant for more specialized change efforts, and its systematic set of personal rituals can itself initiate changes at many levels of your life.

Your Evolving Mythology

❧

While in the life of the human race the mythical is an early and primitive stage, in the life of the individual it is a late and mature one. What is gained is an insight into the higher truth depicted in the actual, a smiling knowledge of the eternal, the ever-being and authentic.

—Thomas Mann[1]

As people grow older and wiser, Mann is suggesting, they tend to experience the world from a larger perspective and to think in ways that begin to resemble more the nature-oriented primeval myths of earlier cultures than the nature-alien technological myths that are so dominant today. In the program you have just completed, you cultivated a mythological perspective, reaching toward a higher order of understanding about your world and your place in it. By bringing the harmful effects of antiquated personal myths into your awareness, you were also gathering strength and courage to live more fully from the depths of your being.

In this chapter, we shift our focus from the personal rituals to a presentation designed to leave you with a solid conceptual framework for understanding your evolving mythology. Developing such understanding inspires a more mythically attuned life and will support the new directions in your personal mythology that you have been envisioning throughout the program.

A Model of Personal Myth-Making

Dan McAdams has investigated personal myths and personality formation using research procedures such as comparing standardized psychological test results with the stories people tell about their lives. "To create a personal myth," he observes, "is to fashion a history of the self."[2] The self of contemporary Western cultures is *made,* not given. The enterprise of creating one's sense of self has shifted substantially in the past two hundred years,[3] and modern individuals are finding the experience of individual selfhood increasingly challenging and problematic.[4] Not only are kings, queens, chiefs, shamans, priests, and priestesses expected to be involved in a significant *self*-defining project; all contemporary individuals are required to find their unique identities in ordinary life, and they are held responsible for the selves they create. The modern self is required to construct a meaningful context to justify its way of being, so self-narratives, or personal mythologies, have become increasingly important in the individual's psychology. With the breakdown of traditional external sources of moral authority, the self itself is for many considered the most trustworthy moral compass.

In his empirical studies of the personal myths of thousands of individuals, McAdams has identified two basic themes: *love* and *power.*[5] Guiding myths about love are concerned with intimacy, interdependence, responsibility, and care. Guiding myths about power are concerned with achievement, independence, mastery, and justice. A person's mythology also has a characteristic disposition, its "narrative tone."[6] Within the first two years of life, the *narrative tone* of a child's guiding mythology is usually set. This tone reflects the child's underlying faith about whether or not the world is good and one's place within it is secure, and it colors subsequent beliefs and attitudes. Some guiding mythologies are characterized by optimism and hope, others by mistrust and resignation. But the person's mythology also continues to develop across the years. During periods of transition, McAdams observes, people may question their deepest assumptions and "recast the myth to embody new plots and characters and to emphasize different scenes from the past and different expectations for the future."[7]

In addition to McAdams's research on personal myths, a number of scientifically grounded psychological models overlap with our mythological formulation, including David Elkind's "personal fables,"[8] Seymour Epstein's "self-theory,"[9] Gary Gregg's "self-representations,"[10] Hubert Hermans's "dialogical self,"[11] Robert

Kegan's "evolving self,"[12] Silvan Tompkins's "nuclear themes,"[13] and George Kelly's pioneering "personal construct psychology."[14] Personal myths, by whatever name they are called, have been systematically investigated, and we will draw on this body of research in laying out a framework that we hope you will find useful as you continue to participate consciously and actively in the evolution of your own mythology.

Personal Theories of Reality. The findings of a research program conducted by psychologist Seymour Epstein at the University of Massachusetts are particularly revealing for understanding personal myths and how they develop. Just as scientists use theories to organize their findings and plan new experiments, Epstein notes, "people need theories to organize their experience, anticipate events, and direct their behavior in everyday life."[15] He refers to these internalized systems of information as personal, implicit (understood though not directly expressed) *theories of reality.* These personal theories contain postulates or generalizations about yourself, about your world, and about the relationship between the two.

Your personal theory of reality, or what we have been referring to as your personal mythology, is made up largely of postulates you derived from emotionally significant experiences, developed in the course of living your life, usually formed apart from your conscious attention. Such postulates, which are both descriptive and instructive, form the basis of the "self-statements" you examined in the program. *Descriptive postulates* are descriptions of your environment and of yourself, such as "Father beats me when I show anger" or "People readily trust me." *Motivational postulates* are instructions about what you must do to obtain what you desire and to avoid what you fear, such as "I will hide my anger so Father won't beat me" and "I will use people's trust to get them to do what I want."

Postulates tend to be organized like nested cubes. "I am a good carpenter" is an example of a *low-order postulate,* a small cube. *High-order postulates,* the larger cubes that surround the small, include "I am a good worker," "I am a competent person," and "I am a worthy person." Each of these four postulates is more general and less specific than its predecessor. The higher order a postulate, the more difficult it is to change, and the greater the number of low-order postulates that are affected when it does change.

Epstein explains that self-esteem is among the most ingrained postulates in a personal theory of reality.[16] As one of the highest-order postulates in your guiding mythology, it is extremely resistant to enduring change. When it does change, however, profound shifts are brought about throughout your entire mythology. When your sense of self-worth significantly increases or decreases, your view of your capabilities, your shortcomings, your mistakes, and your opportunities shift with it. Epstein has identified four high-order postulates that affect the tone as well as the more specific postulates of an individual's personal theory of reality:

1. the degree to which the world is viewed as benign versus malevolent;
2. the degree to which the world is viewed as meaningful (including predictable, controllable, and just) versus chaotic;
3. the degree to which others are viewed as a source of support and happiness rather than as a source of insecurity and unhappiness;
4. the degree to which the self is viewed as worthy (including capable, good, and lovable) rather than the opposite.[17]

These postulates are based, respectively, on four fundamental needs that jointly influence thought and behavior: the needs to sustain a favorable pleasure–pain balance, to assimilate the data of reality into a relatively stable conceptual system, to maintain relatedness, and to enhance self-esteem.[18] Your personal mythology functions to achieve compromise and balance among these four basic needs.

Here is an example, from Stanley Krippner's life, of how a relatively low-order descriptive postulate nearly caused him to turn away from what proved to be among the most important formative influences on his career. Stan has always been a bit of an iconoclast. By the time he was in college, he sadly concluded, "I inadvertently antagonize people I would like to get to know better." He also developed a strategy, a motivational postulate, for such situations: "When I do antagonize someone, I immediately back off so as to not antagonize them further." These postulates were put to a test when Stan, a graduate student at the time, met the renowned psychologist Gardner Murphy. Dr. Murphy seemed to take a strong and immediate liking to Stan, and he remarked that Stan might want to work with him as a graduate assistant at the University of Hawaii that summer. This response abruptly challenged Stan's descriptive postulate. Stan corresponded with Dr. Murphy, but nothing was finalized.

Several months later, Stan attended a conference where Dr. Murphy was one of the keynote speakers. Early in the conference, Stan saw the distinguished psychologist walking toward him in a hallway. Stan called out, "Hello, Dr. Murphy!" Murphy turned and walked in the opposite direction. Stan wasn't sure what he had done or said in one of his letters to antagonize Dr. Murphy, but according to his descriptive postulate, he must have done something wrong, and apparently it was quite memorable. With his descriptive postulate affirmed, his motivational postulate told him to stay out of Dr. Murphy's sight. But by the end of the lecture, he had challenged both postulates, speculating that perhaps Dr. Murphy had been preoccupied or was nearsighted. Stan forced himself to wait his turn in line after the lecture to greet the celebrated professor. Immediately upon seeing Stan, Dr. Murphy greeted him warmly and renewed his offer. Stan's summer in Hawaii was life-changing, setting him on a course that would shape his career. Had he not challenged his postulates, that sequence of events would not have occurred.

Conscious and Preconscious Information-Processing. Personal myths operate simultaneously in the two separate information-processing systems identified by Epstein,[19] one based on *rational,* analytic logic and more available to conscious awareness, the other more *intuitive* and less conscious. The rational system is better integrated and is organized according to the rules of conventional logic. The intuitive system is more affective and holistic, and its concepts are related to one another more loosely, via association. Through mechanisms such as psychological conditioning, the intuitive system can process information automatically, rapidly, and efficiently, yet at its higher reaches it can abstract and generalize, through the use of metaphor and narrative. It is ordinarily experienced passively and outside of awareness rather than actively and consciously. It utilizes private language that tends to be habitual and automated.

You are usually unaware of the self-talk in your intuitive system, but you can, with varying degrees of effort, become conscious of it. The intuitive system often uses imagery and private symbols representing more elaborated verbalizations that have faded with time. Their meanings become encoded in a private, preconscious shorthand. One of the major adaptive characteristics of the intuitive system is its ability to make quick assessments and promote decisive action. The rational system can sometimes override the influence of the intuitive system, as evidenced through "resolutions of conflicts between the heart and the mind in favor of the mind."[20] Significantly, Epstein observes, "it is when the conflict is not recognized that the [intuitive] system is most apt to dominate and influence the rational system unreasonably."

How Personal Theories of Reality Change. When an emotionally significant experience is inconsistent with your personal mythology, the inconsistency can be denied, it can be distorted through the use of psychological defense mechanisms, or it can effect a change in the personal theory.[21] Such change can expand your guiding myths, making them more flexible and creating a better fit with experience. A personal myth is challenged when experiences that do not correspond with its postulates are encountered. You can respond to such contradictions in two basic ways: distort the input or alter the myth.

Jean Piaget used the term *assimilation* to describe the filtering or modification of perceptions, and he used the term *accommodation* to describe the modification of internal theories to fit new experiences.[22] Faced with a refuting experience, a personal myth is changed so it corresponds with what is perceived, or perceptions are distorted to match the myth. If your spouse justifiably complains that you need to be more conscious of your health, you can grumble about your nagging mate (assimilating the discordant information into your existing mythology) or get on with the business of taking better care of yourself (accommodating the discordant information by letting it influence your guiding mythology).

Assimilation accounts for the way old myths are maintained amid contradictory experiences. Accommodation accounts for how they are elaborated and refined. A point can be reached, however, at which a personal myth has been so thoroughly revised that it becomes more or less, in Piaget's words, "worn out." A limit to the input that can be accommodated may be reached, beyond which "the cycle forming the scheme would rupture."[23] Experiences that do not match the myth then become more likely to exceed what Piaget called the internal scheme's *accommodation capacity*. This is the point where your old myth is beyond repair.

The breakdown of a long-standing personal myth is usually followed by a period of disorder and disequilibrium, as you no doubt recognized when you created your Personal Shield and completed other personal rituals that made you look at your past through a mythic lens. Psychologists have frequently observed that human development follows a classic dialectic "thesis-antithesis-synthesis" pattern,[24] and the evolution of a new mythology can be understood as a dialectical process. After the prevailing myth (*thesis*) has become outdated or otherwise dysfunctional, the psyche typically generates a counter-myth (*antithesis*) in an effort to compensate for the dysfunction of the prevailing myth.

The formation of a counter-myth often involves a creative excursion into a way of understanding reality that brings your storehouse of experience into a fresh gestalt, a new and more compelling motif, highlighting previously unseen possibilities and transcending previously unassailable limitations. The conflict between the old myth and the counter-myth is engaged in both the conscious and the preconscious systems of information processing. It is oriented toward a *synthesis* that incorporates the most advantageous elements of the old myth, which is tried and familiar, and of the counter-myth, which though often inspirational is untested and unrefined. In the third stage of the program, you promoted a dialectic, reaching for a synthesis between your prevailing myth and the counter-myth that was challenging it. In the fourth stage you refined this synthesis, and you are now in the fifth stage, translating this new mythology into your life.

A Summary. Personal myths are composed of a blend of descriptive (or explanatory) postulates and instructive (or motivational) postulates about yourself, your world, and the relationship between the two. They are organized hierarchically and in a manner that tends to promote compromise and balance in the fulfillment of your basic needs. Lower-order personal myths, such as the belief that mastering a particular area of knowledge will improve your professional success, are quite specific and can usually be changed without jeopardizing your personality structure. Changes in higher-order personal myths (such as those governing your sense of safety in the world, worthiness, relatedness to others, and purpose in life) may, however, be destabilizing because they are broad generalizations that are central to your entire scheme of reality.

Personal myths operate within both the rational system of information processing, which is largely conscious, and the intuitive system, which is largely preconscious. A given myth may function primarily within the preconscious system, as may be the case with a disowned "shadow" aspect of the psyche. Or it may function primarily within the rational system, such as in the case of a deliberately constructed "false self" that is only weakly connected to the deeper, preconscious system. But in the coding of a long-standing personal myth, the systems usually complement each other. Consciously participating in the natural dialectic between long-standing and emerging personal myths can lead to both a more rapid synthesis and a more favorable new myth.

THE SOURCE OF YOUR PERSONAL MYTHOLOGY

While myth-making is a way of grappling with life's most profound and ethereal questions, it begins in the chemistry of your brain. You can think mythically because your brain chemically codes events and then uses imagery and narrative to process this coded experience. The most obvious sources of your guiding mythology are your *biology,* your *personal experiences,* and your *culture.*

Biology. The biological sources of your personal mythology include your physiology, temperamental disposition, and other genetic givens, as well as changes in your biochemistry caused by learning, diet, exercise, stress, and other interactions with your environment. Your brain is constantly making sense of experiences, establishing meanings, and planning behavior—even while you sleep. Dreams are tales told by the brain when signals from the brain stem, fired randomly to discharge the electrical buildup from the day's activities, are woven into a more or less continual narrative.[25] That the images, feelings, and sensations composing the raw materials of a dream are haphazardly evoked via random electrical discharges accounts for the bizarre nature of dreams, yet existing memories, beliefs, needs, and fears are coherently woven into the story. Your brain is a remarkably gifted storyteller.

Your personal myths are also tales spun by your brain. Your brain is continually weaving your memories, beliefs, needs, and fears with new experiences, creating a preconscious narrative that organizes your perceptions and feelings, establishes their meaning, and directs your action.

The brain has a special module, the *interpreter*,[26] which instantly constructs explanations of why behaviors occur. The interpreter system was discovered as neurologists were treating people whose corpus callosum, the communication link between the brain's right and left hemispheres, had been severed through an injury or as a result of a surgical procedure to alleviate a life-threatening condition such as severe epilepsy. Even though the two sides of the brain were now acting independently, the left hemisphere, which is more language-oriented, would consistently interpret actions produced by the right hemisphere.

For instance, after a quick presentation of the written command "Laugh" only to the patient's typically obedient right hemisphere (by showing the command only to the left eye, which is governed by the right side of the brain), laughter was often produced. The left side of the patient's brain would of course know laughter was occurring, but not knowing the stimulus, would invent an explanation. When a researcher asked one patient why he was laughing, he replied: "You guys come up and test us every month. What a way to make a living!"[27]

The interpreter system is continually filling in the unavoidable gaps in your knowledge with speculation that *feels* like truth. This merry-go-round of unconscious assumptions explains people's certainty concerning things about which they know very little. Your interpreter system plays a central role in the formation of your beliefs, and it is continually providing explanations as you encounter new experiences.

The interpreter system also seems endowed with an endless ability to test and retest the mental constructs it generates. Generating and testing beliefs about oneself and one's world are integral parts of myth-making. Once they are established, however, personal myths tend to remain relatively stable, even after life experiences that would seem to contradict their premises. As neuropsychologists have observed, the brain tends to evaluate evidence concerning established beliefs in a manner that reinforces the belief.[28] Personal myths typically operate according to this self-fulfilling logic.

The interpreter system functions primarily in your brain's left hemisphere (if you are right-handed), and its activities are largely verbal. Other thought processes, however, occur without the use of language. The neurologist Antonio Damasio has described a *nonverbal* "internal narrative."[29] It takes care of things "behind the scenes," and you are largely unaware of this ongoing narration concerning your well-being. Your attention may be far away while your internal narrative instructs you to scratch an itch, chew your food, or put out the trash. This internal narrative can also govern much more complex activities. Without the use of words, for instance, you can envision the consequences of a behavior, conceive of alternative strategies, and plan a course of action for attaining the best of your imagined scenarios.[30] The foundations of myth-making run far deeper than language.

As your brain creates explanations and envisions courses of action, networks of neurons are linked and begin to operate as the units that encode such beliefs and plans. Through repetition, these networks become more stable and connect with other networks into increasingly complex systems of explanation and guidance. Established networks of neurons maintain consistent patterns, yet like the film frames that make up a movie, each moment is also a new creation. Damasio explains, for instance, that one's sense of self is "a repeatedly reconstructed biological state,"[31] constructed moment by moment, from the ground up, "so continuously and consistently *re*constructed that the owner never knows it is being *re*made unless something goes wrong with the remaking."[32]

Your myths and your sense of self are usually familiar, following patterns that are characteristic of your ways of being in the world. They are the staples of your daily experience, the steadfast background, requiring relatively little conscious attention. Your brain can, however, cause your internal narrative to intrude into your awareness by coding its nonverbal storyline into vivid feelings, words, and images. If you are driving your car, totally absorbed in an audio thriller, and you hear the squeal of brakes from a truck coming toward you, the whole process of driving leaps from the background to the foreground of your awareness. You have, throughout the program, been drawing on this aptitude to make subconscious processes conscious as you examined guiding myths that usually organize your mental life without your notice.

Personal Experiences. Your unique experiences are another primary source of your personal myths. Just as your mythology shapes your experiences, your experiences shape your mythology; the influence works in both directions.

Every emotionally significant personal challenge and interpersonal encounter, particularly in your formative years, has an impact on your developing mythology. Since Freud, the influences of past experience on beliefs and personality have been a major focus of psychological thought, and this relationship was a central area of your investigation during the program.

Culture. Your culture's mythology is another source of your own evolving mythology that you have been reflecting on in this program. To a larger extent than might be intuitively obvious, your mythology is your culture's mythology in microcosm, with powerful influences such as the customs that enforce socialization, the reward systems that confer status, and media portrayals of the good, the bad, and the ugly continually infiltrating your psyche. The culture in which you were brought up provided the psychosocial ecology that selected and reinforced some directions for the evolution of your mythology and not others. The culture's impact on people's mythologies is, in fact, so pervasive and generally invisible to them that psychologist Charles Tart has referred to ordinary awareness as a "consensus trance."[33]

THE SPIRITUAL FOUNDATIONS OF YOUR PERSONAL MYTHOLOGY

The fourth source of your personal mythology is rooted in *transcendent* or *spiritual experiences*—those episodes, insights, dreams, and visions that have a numinous quality, deepen your values, expand your perspectives, and inspire your creativity. Some personality theorists, from Freud onward, have associated spirituality with psychopathology, yet psychological research has consistently identified correlations between "spirituality" and mental health.[34] For example, in one study, people reporting mystical experiences scored lower on psychopathology scales and higher on measures of psychological well-being than did people who did not report such experiences.[35]

William James's *The Varieties of Religious Experience,* published in 1901, is the landmark scientific investigation of reported encounters with the "reality of the unseen." James examines, for instance, the following account from psychiatrist R. M. Bucke:[36]

I was in a state of quiet, almost passive enjoyment. . . . All at once, without warning of any kind, I found myself wrapped in a flame-colored cloud. For an instant, I thought of fire, an immense conflagration somewhere close by in that great city; the next, I knew the fire was within myself. Directly afterward there came upon me a sense of exultation, of immense joyousness accompanied or immediately followed by an intellectual illumination impossible to describe. Among other things, I did not merely come to believe, but I saw that the universe is not composed of dead matter, but is, on the contrary, a living Presence; I became conscious in myself of eternal life. It was not a conviction that I would have eternal life, but a consciousness that I possessed eternal life then; I saw . . . that the foundation principle of the world, of all the worlds, is what we call love.

While personal myths usually evolve gradually, such "revelations" can shift a person's guiding mythology in a single stroke, and they are not uncommon during experiences involving nonordinary states of consciousness, whether spontaneous, as in "near-death" experiences,[37] or cultivated through a contemplative discipline such as meditation.[38] Beneath a wide array of symbolism and personal interpretations, a common core of meanings has been identified among the revelations reported by humanity's most esteemed sages, spiritual leaders, and moral exemplars. Aldous Huxley summarized the "Highest Common Factor"[39] in their teachings as the "Perennial Philosophy." The essence of these teachings is that beyond the world we can perceive with our senses is a deeper reality, a transcendent, ineffable Ground of Being that "cannot be directly and immediately apprehended except by those who have chosen to fulfill certain conditions, making themselves loving [and] pure in heart."[40]

This Perennial Philosophy, according to Ken Wilber, constitutes the esoteric core of Hinduism, Buddhism, Taoism, Sufism, Judaism, and Christian mysticism, "as well as being embraced, in whole or in part, by individual intellects ranging from Spinoza to Albert Einstein, Schopenhauer to Jung, William James to Plato. . . . It can happily coexist with, and certainly complement, the hard data of the pure sciences."[41] Psychologists investigating this territory have found support for the basic tenets of the Perennial Philosophy in the worldviews of psychologically advanced individuals. The "peak experiences" reported by many of Abraham Maslow's "self-actualizing" subjects, for instance, resulted in shifts of motivation toward what he termed the "values of Being," such as truth, love, goodness, justice, simplicity, and beauty.[42]

As William James observed, "Mystical states of a well-pronounced and emphatic nature . . . are as direct perception of fact for those who have them as any sensations ever were for us."[43] Intensive "peak," "mystical," "spiritual," "religious," "unitive," "transcendent," or "transpersonal" experiences can compellingly alter a person's mythology, and with it, basic beliefs, goals, and behavior. Because physical sensations and mystical perception often seem to contradict each other, such experiences teem with myth-stretching paradoxes. Spiritual encounters are grounded in the brain and the body, yet no other kind of experience seems more emphatically to transcend biology. Such encounters are shaped by personal philosophy, yet they have a remarkable capacity abruptly to transform personal beliefs, values, and habits. Spiritual encounters are also influenced by the beliefs of the broader culture, yet they often challenge prevailing norms and reveal horizons that transcend the culture's mythology.

Myth has traditionally addressed the spiritual realm, conveying, in the words of anthropologist Bronislaw Malinowski, "a primeval, greater, and more relevant reality."[44] Spiritual development can be described, without metaphysical speculation, as an enhanced attunement to the subtle patterns and hidden forces in nature that comprise the wider context of the human story. Rollo May defined human destiny as "the design of the universe speaking through the design of each one of us."[45] Your body was, ultimately, assembled from the earth's surface and atmosphere, according to laws of evolution that totally transcend your personal story. From the ground up, you are a product of the planet and the cosmos. All of the principles that govern them govern you. As decisively as you carry the genes of your parents, you carry the design of the universe. To reflect on this relationship is to reflect on the spiritual realm of existence; to perceive it through direct experience is to open to the deepest sources of your being.

PRINCIPLES BY WHICH
YOUR PERSONAL MYTHOLOGY EVOLVES

Your personal mythology evolves within a psychosocial ecology of mutation and selection. This ecology favors and sustains those "mutations" or innovations in your guiding myths that optimize your development as dictated by the needs of your psyche and the demands of your society. A boy who by temperament is highly introverted but whose only goal is to be student body president is headed for a mythic showdown. A girl who claims to talk to spirits may be rushed to a psychiatrist in the United States but exalted as a potential shaman in Bali.

In addition to the way your myths fit or do not fit your temperament and your culture, even the most "fit" guiding myths are required to evolve. As you have seen, personal myths that are appropriate and effective during one period of your life may be inappropriate or dysfunctional at another. As myths become outmoded, they fail to support your psychosocial and spiritual needs and potentials, and they begin to cause difficulties in your life. A shift to more advanced guiding myths is often required for you to continue to mature and successfully adapt to the challenges that life presents. The alchemical fire of life's adversities may indeed transform envy into empathy, resentment into gratitude, or self-indulgence into generosity.

The quality of the guiding myths offered by your culture, and the rites of passage your society provides or fails to provide for moving into them, may promote or inhibit the success of your transitions and growth. The following eight principles, on which the program you just completed is based, can offer conceptual handholds as your own personal mythology continues to evolve. These principles have been synthesized from the theory already presented and are further developed here, integrating findings from cognitive, developmental, and evolutionary psychology.[46]

1. During your lifetime, you will pass through a succession of guiding myths. The breakdown of old personal myths is a necessary and, ideally, a highly constructive aspect of human development. As you mature and as you face new circumstances, more advanced guiding myths are required. The symbol of a helix has been used to portray the way people perpetually return to face certain core issues from higher levels of development.[47] After having successfully accomplished the developmental tasks associated with a core theme—perhaps your relationship to authority or your ability to love—you may return to the identical issue at a later time and rework it from a higher level of maturation, a more advanced personal mythology. For instance, troubling feelings about a derisive parent, who perhaps died long before, may become a prominent area of distress after having for years remained in the background. Often a person will feel discouraged when difficult patterns reemerge that once seemed to have been worked through. By emotionally reworking such issues from a higher level of development, it is possible to change your relationship with your past in a way that empowers you, and such issues may provide the clay as you form a more advanced mythology.

2. To emerge from being psychologically embedded in one guiding myth and move to a new myth requires a shift in your sense of self. The self has been compared to a multistory building composed of a *deep structure* (your given nature) and *surface structures* (culturally molded aspects of your identity).[48] Each floor of the building is part of its deep structure, while the furniture, tables, and chairs *on* each floor compose its surface structures. Psychological development occurs as your identification moves from one floor up to the next. This requires that you detach from your identification with the existing floor, and the mythology appropriate for it, and form a new identification with the next floor and the mythology appropriate there. Just as the tulip is latent in the bulb, the deep structures of your consciousness exist as potentials waiting, from the beginning of your life, to unfold. The challenges involved in each transition will, for a period, dominate your psychological life. With each successive level of consciousness, a new mythology appropriate to that level emerges.

3. Conflicts—both in your inner life and in external circumstances—are natural markers of these times of transition. When an emotionally significant experience is inconsistent with your guiding mythology, you may deny, distort, or otherwise distance yourself from the experience. The self-deception involved in maintaining a myth that is failing creates internal conflict that can show up in your feelings, thoughts, actions, dreams, daydreams, or the circumstances you create in the world. To move to a more advanced mythology, however, involves renouncing the old myth and recognizing that what you had known as yourself is yourself no longer.[49] Ann found it extraordinarily difficult to set boundaries that might cause her to appear unsupportive to someone she cared for. Such shifts in identity may involve a loss that is strongly resisted and deeply mourned. Treating such losses as markers of transition, rather than reflexively resisting them, will help you understand what is happening at such times and mobilize yourself more effectively for resolving the underlying conflict.

4. On one side of the underlying mythic conflict will typically be a personal myth that has become self-limiting but that once served a constructive function in your development. The basic postulates in your personal mythology are generalizations that were originally derived from emotionally significant experiences.[50] Because they were constructed early in your life, they are seminal in the development of subsequent guiding myths. Unless a given experience is of unusual significance, it is not likely in itself to affect a core guiding myth. Psychological defenses may also prevent you from recognizing features of your experience that are incompatible with a core myth, even as that myth becomes less capable of providing you with effective guidance. The greater the anxiety attached to an area of life with which a personal myth must cope, the more the myth is apt to take on an inflexible, driven quality; it becomes highly resistant to change. In exploring the roots of a dysfunctional myth early in the program, you became better able to connect current difficulties with past experiences. The old myth is best examined not only for its dysfunction but also for the constructive role it played at an earlier time. This reveals the needs the emergent myth will have to address as well as previous strategies for meeting them. By understanding how the old myth developed and once served legitimate needs, you become more able to embrace the valid guidance it still holds even while rooting out its dysfunction.

5. On the other side of the conflict will be an emerging counter-myth that serves as a force toward expanding your perceptions, self-concept, worldview, and awareness of options in the very areas the old myth is limiting you. Latent qualities not supported by old myths will naturally push toward expression, and they are often symbolized in the emergence of a counter-myth that is revealed first in dreams and other portals into unconscious processes. Counter-myths are woven from this developmental push, from a reservoir of unconscious primal impulses, from the accumulation of life experiences, from a readiness to accept more advanced myths of the culture, and from creative new perceptions that may be revealed in a transcendent experience. How did your counter-myth come into your awareness as you moved through the program? Counter myths are best understood as creative leaps in your psyche's problem-solving activities, but they typically lack real-world utility. Their origins are often in experiences that threaten the stability of your guiding mythology, and they may be encoded outside your awareness.[51] Still, counter-myths serve as a force to integrate unrecognized traits into your personality and to sustain qualities you have suppressed under the constraints of the old myth.

6. While this conflict may be painful and disruptive, a natural, though often unconscious, mobilization toward a resolution spontaneously occurs, a dialectic pushing toward a new myth that ideally synthesizes the most adaptive and developmentally progressive qualities of your old myth and of your counter-myth. One of the tasks of your personal mythology is to foster the fulfillment of your basic needs in a harmonious rather than conflictual manner.[52] While conflict inevitably arises between guiding myths and between guiding myths and experience, the psyche exhibits a basic striving for unity and coherence. As you have seen, this natural process occurs as a dialectic—a subterranean thesis–antithesis struggle between an old myth and a counter-myth—each vying to structure your perceptions, feelings, thoughts, and behavior. Although much of the dialectic occurs outside awareness and without volition, people tend to identify *consciously* more fully with one of the myths, or some of its elements, than with the other. By bringing the dialectic into awareness, you are empowered to work through the conflict as an internal challenge rather than condemned to act it out unawares and at your peril.

7. During this process, previously unresolved mythic conflicts will tend to reemerge—with the potential of either interfering with the resolution of your current developmental task or opening the way to deeper levels of

resolution in your mythology. Moving up the developmental helix, issues that previously seemed resolved may reemerge, inviting new solutions from a developmentally more advanced vantage point. Each new stage of psychological development finds its necessary preconditions in a previous stage that was achieved with at least some minimal degree of adequacy.[53] Thoughts and memories that can be neither assimilated nor ignored, however, "keep reemerging in abortive attempts to be incorporated."[54] When a woman was unable at an earlier age successfully to meet the requirements of a particular developmental task, such as reconciling herself to having been brought up by a loving yet abusive parent, that issue tends to play a thematic role in the resolution of subsequent mythic conflicts. A loving but abusive spouse may be chosen unconsciously in order to replay and perhaps rework the inner drama. Procedures that use guided imagination can bring you back experientially to a period when your development was arrested and provide this younger "self" with an emotionally corrective rite of passage that leads to the next developmental tier and into an expanded personal mythology (recall, for instance, the personal ritual "Rewriting History Through the Emotionally Corrective Daydream").

8. When you have successfully formulated a new guiding myth, reconciling it with your existing life structure becomes a vital task in your ongoing development. Long-standing myths tend to die hard. However dysfunctional they may be, they are also deeply embedded in your lifestyle and habits of thought and behavior. Marching even to an inspiring new myth may require substantial focus and commitment. As you move from being immersed in the issues of one stage of psychological development to the next, the *content* of your concerns can change dramatically. The process described by the first seven principles above, in which you shift your self-identification from one level of consciousness to a more advanced level, can be described as a *transformation* of consciousness (corresponding with the first four stages of the personal mythology program).[55] This eighth principle can be thought of as a *translation,* where you bring your life into harmony with that level of consciousness (corresponding with the final stage of the program). In the metaphor of a building, transformation involves a move to a new floor; translation involves rearranging the furnishings on that floor.[56] Even as a higher level of consciousness emerges, its more advanced mythology must also be "translated" into the particulars of daily life.

PASSAGES TOWARD A RENEWED MYTHOLOGY

Erik Erikson identified eight stages in the human life cycle, each characterized by a core task or psychosocial crisis. In infancy, the core issue involves basic trust versus mistrust. By young adulthood, it is intimacy versus isolation, and by old age, it is integrity versus despair.[57] Erikson has mapped and eloquently described many of the key issues that emerge as a person's mythology evolves across the lifespan. Our program, on the other hand, and the principles described above, focus on the underlying dynamics that occur as an outmoded personal myth is challenged by new mythic impulses, regardless of the season of the person's life.

The personal rituals presented in this program guided you through a five-stage process that parallels the developmental tasks that emerge when an existing myth is in transformation. To review the process:

1. You began by recognizing an area of difficulty in your life and identifying underlying conflict between a prevailing myth and an emerging counter-myth that was challenging it (Weeks 1 through 3).

2. You traced the roots of the prevailing myth to experiences from your past and attuned yourself to the forces summoning the counter-myth (Weeks 4 and 5).

3. You worked toward a resolution of their conflict, a dialectical synthesis that embodied the most vital elements of both the old myth and the counter-myth, and you articulated it as a new unifying myth (Weeks 6 and 7).

4. You refined this new myth until you could reasonably make a commitment to it (Weeks 8 and 9).

5. You directed your will toward translating this new myth into the particulars of your life (Weeks 10 and 11), and here you are developing a conceptual framework that will support the ongoing evolution of your guiding mythology (Week 12).

In the course of ordinary development, people move through these basic stages, again and again, naturally and spontaneously. Bringing your conscious and deliberate attention to the process enriches each passage and serves vital functions that cultural rituals and rites no longer adequately address. Mindfully weaving a carefully reformulated mythology into the fabric of your life is a concentrated act of personal empowerment.

One of the exciting developments in psychology over the past few decades has been the "cognitive revolution," whereby the beliefs, feelings, and thought patterns associated with various psychological difficulties, dysfunctional behaviors, and personality disorders have been carefully mapped. Core beliefs for people with obsessive-compulsive personality disorders, for instance, might include: "I need to be in complete control of my emotions" and "If I don't perform at the highest level, I will fail"; for people with passive-aggressive personality disorders, a core belief might be: "I have to resist the domination of authorities but at the same time maintain their approval and acceptance." [58] Such beliefs are the expression of deeper personal myths, and to place them in that context establishes a larger, holistic perspective that incorporates the biological, biographical, cultural, and spiritual dimensions of personality dynamics.

Psychologists who have examined the territory we are referring to as "personal myth" have introduced concepts such as "cognitive structures," "personal constructs," "implicit theories," "themata," "scripts," and "schema." We have attempted to formulate the personal mythology model to address a number of problems that have proven difficult for traditional psychological models. Among the strengths of personal mythology over other terms are (1) the fundamental connection between myth and spirituality, as described earlier; (2) the natural bridge between personal and cultural myths; (3) the supposition inherent to the model that any conception of reality is relative; (4) the nonpejorative nature of the model; and (5) its user-friendly character.

Early theories of personality, with their focus on internal processes, have often failed to account adequately for social and cultural influences on human development. Because personal myths and cultural myths are fundamentally interconnected, the relationship of psyche and society flows naturally into the personal mythology framework. A model that, at its base, recognizes the relative, metaphorical nature of any construction of reality is attuned also to the fundamental tenet of "postmodern" thought (and the essential insight of modern physics) that all knowledge is fluctuating rather than fixed, local rather than universal. [59] Any personal map of reality is a psychosocial construction, [60] an innovation created jointly by the person and the culture, an interpretation of experience, an act of myth-making.

Another issue that clinical psychology and psychiatry have had to wrestle with involves the caustic implications, when attempting to assist a person on the arduous journey toward a fulfilling existence, of being historically rooted in a medical model based on the concepts of *illness* and *treatment*. Professional helpers who think a person "has to be sick to get better" tend to find pathology in the inner turmoil that inevitably accompanies personal and spiritual evolution. As Abraham Maslow observed, "If your only tool is a hammer, you treat everything like a nail." A perspective recognizing that periodic mythic crises are part of the journey provides a dignified, nonpejorative, more shamanistic alternative to the medical model for conceiving of expert intervention in a person's psychological development. In addition, as we hope you have discovered for yourself, the personal mythology model is user-friendly enough that people can quickly grasp the idea that their lives are shaped by their personal myths, yet as they become more skilled in working with their myths, they enter more deeply into the concept's significance and find that they grow with it.

We have often been asked why we place mythology at the heart of our model of psychological and spiritual development when the term has been so denigrated in the culture. Since the mid-1970s, we have been responding by inviting the questioner to suggest a better term for describing the core of *psychologically constructed reality* that implicitly embraces the spiritual dimension of human experience and the essential relationship between psyche and society in a nonpejorative and user-friendly manner. We have yet to hear of one.

CONCLUSION: BRINGING A MYTHIC PERSPECTIVE TO A WORLD IN DISTRESS

As we prepare to write this conclusion, we take a break and walk out under the trees and stars. We open ourselves to the beauty that surrounds us, breathe it in, and acknowledge in gratitude the good fortune we each enjoy. We state an intention, and it feels like a prayer: "May these words make a difference." We have for many years been refining a vision of how our five-stage model and a mythological perspective could be of service to a world in distress. We want to close by suggesting that an understanding of the way your own personal mythology functions and evolves can better equip you to participate meaningfully in the development of the collective mythology that is steering humanity into the future.

Interviewed about his misfortune and his courage after an equestrian accident left him paralyzed from the neck down, actor Christopher Reeve brightly responded, "I've always played the hand I've been dealt." Depending on how we play it, those of us on the planet at the threshold of the new millennium have been dealt a hand that can make us the generation that prematurely ended humanity's occupancy of the most hospitable known habitat in the universe, or we can become the generation that realized the potential for human consciousness to become a constructive force in the earth's evolution—as the locus of consciousness extends from individual brains to a global culture networked by electronic synapses.[61]

The principles you have explored regarding your own mythology can be refocused onto a global canvas that urgently calls for a reorientation of the personal and cultural myths shaping humanity's fate. Organizational psychologist Anne Dosher describes a "reflexive relationship" between the myths of individuals and the myths of organizations and community groups.[62] In her consultations, she adapts to social concerns principles that parallel the five-stage sequence we have identified for working with personal myths.

Dosher attunes the leadership in a community organization to the group's operating mythology and teaches ways of assessing the practical consequences of that mythology. She uncovers links between the organization's myths and the personal myths of its early founders. She helps the organization's members acknowledge and celebrate these mythic roots, and sometimes ritualistically bid them farewell. The informal rewards and negative sanctions that reflect the organization's myths are delineated, and the fit between its myths and the personal myths of its members is examined. Dosher also identifies competing myths—within the organization and between the organization and the broader culture. Such conflicts are often at the basis of organizational crisis. If the organization can grasp the mythological dimension of the crisis and respond constructively, it shifts the fulcrum toward the possibilities of emerging revitalized and capable of creatively and realistically envisioning a vital future.

Dosher's interventions frequently include ritual, as when "the shadow sides of living myths are codified, recorded and ceremoniously burned as a way of 'exorcising' dysfunction."[63] Her approach parallels our five-stage model for working with the individual's mythology, in that she (1) identifies the myths operating in areas of organizational difficulty; (2) traces the historical roots of prevailing myths and recognizes emerging myths; (3) mediates the dialectic between competing mythologies; (4) assists the organization in refining new mythic images that will constructively shift its direction; and (5) helps the organization implement those images.

Social action that effectively promotes a new guiding myth contains at least three elements. It *embeds and multiplies images of the new myth within the culture,* as in education, art, and the use of media. It *directly and concretely incorporates the myth's vision into social reality,* as with specific reforms, model programs, and impassioned causes. Effective social action also *creates changes in social conditions so the new myth is more effectively reinforced.* For instance, new social policies, new funding priorities, new institutional designs, and new standards of progress could be established, such as the suggestion by a growing number of economists that the Gross National Product is a deeply flawed gauge and that we need measures that factor in such quality-of-life indicators as levels of literacy, infant mortality, crowding, access to clean water, and homelessness.[64] Refining and multiplying constructive mythic images that are attuned to the requirements of the times, incorporating them into social reality, and reinforcing them with decisive shifts in social policy constitute the mythological challenge confronting humankind at the threshold of the new millennium.

Evil triumphs, Edmund Burke observed, when good people stand by and do nothing. One of us (David Feinstein) recalls a day in high school when a rather plain-looking girl dropped her lunch tray in the dining area, loudly, and the contents of her purse scattered, widely. The entire school stopped munching for a millisecond of piercing silence, followed by derisive laughter and snickering as the girl's face took on deepening shades of crimson. In an instant, Paul Furukawa was on his knees helping her clean the mess and scoop her belongings back into her purse. With an embracing smile, he stepped into the line of ridicule and joined her. Everyone stopped laughing. David reflects: "Paul, wherever you now may be, with that action you indelibly demonstrated to at least one person the difference between *having* good intentions and *acting on* good intentions. I was myself laughed at a lot in those years, tall, lanky, uncoordinated, painfully shy. I did not laugh that day in the dining area; I died inside for this blushing, bespectacled stranger. But I took no action. Paul Furukawa, of Japanese-American descent in a largely white suburban high school, did. Paul later became our student body president."

The crush of destructive trends around the globe seems to many irreversible; good people do stand by and do nothing, and evil does flourish. The entire global response to the ecological crisis is perhaps akin to that of a two-pack-a-day smoker who cuts down to one and a half packs after being diagnosed with lung cancer, while increasing sugar and fat intake to quell the anxiety. Collectively we are barely responding to the advancing pestilence that confronts us, yet if the globe were seen as an organism, it is still within the realm of a good physician, the domain of human choice, the purview of a unifying new myth, to reverse the disease. And if we are each a cell in the global brain, we each can envision a level of action that is personally appropriate.[65]

The collective actions that would promote a sustainable future are complex and interconnected, but they can also be specified. Whatever the fresh guiding visions gestating in the culture's mythic underworld as the auspicious mythic possibilities of shared planetary consciousness come into view, they obviously will not come into being if humankind does not survive to give birth to them. The first order of business in taking action that might promote a viable global culture is to reorient our collective mythology so it supports a sustainable future. Sustainability has become the overarching requirement, superseding all other political positions. While a myth that focuses only on sustainability is not adequate to inspire a vibrant future, a critical mass of lived myths that do not adequately address the need for sustainability will preclude any future at all. Social policy that supports sustainability would face squarely the fact of the earth's dwindling resources and inspire humankind to conserve them wisely and apportion them justly. As the deep conflicts out of which such policy might evolve continue to broil, it is too early to predict how they will be reconciled, but many of the criteria for refining a mythic vision you considered during the program— such as its need to balance flexibility with commitment and promote learned optimism over learned helplessness—may prove crucial ingredients.

The handwriting is on the habitat regarding many of the actions required for a sustainable future. Such actions would create incentives to curb the population explosion. They would engender strong family cohesion and family-oriented values. They would inhibit conspicuous consumption. They would develop alternative fuels. They would root out the complex conditions widening the gap between rich and poor that makes class warfare a tangible threat. They would retrain the unemployed and underemployed. They would impede the diffusion of lethal weapons and militaristic adventures. They would decisively allocate resources for AIDS prevention and other forms of responsibility for personal health. They would encourage ecology-friendly business ventures. They would promote literacy and champion education. And they would enhance the self-determination of local communities.

Solutions to each of these challenges are within the reach of our collective will, but the optimism that would inspire the tenacious effort required to find and implement them does not come easily in today's world. In *Revolution of the Heart,* a generally optimistic book, Bill Shore admits that his optimism "may be nothing more than a faith in biology over experience. If compassion, common sense, and even self-interest don't work, perhaps biology will. If there is one thing that unites our species—black or white, rich or poor—it's the biological instinct to preserve and protect our offspring, to keep them safe, to leave their generation better off than ours."[66] But even if the juice is there, an impassioned cause still needs a guiding vision, a compelling myth that directs it toward effective action.

Amid even the crumbling social structures that besiege us, enormously thoughtful and creative visions for action are being articulated. Compatible mythic images that promote a promising future for humanity are arising in every society on the planet. The 1995 report of the independent, international, UN-endorsed Commission on Global Governance identified specific, achievable recommendations for promoting international security, enhancing global cooperation, managing economic interdependence, and strengthening the rule of law worldwide.[67] The report concludes that we unequivocally have the capacity to create "better global governance—better management of survival, better ways of sharing diversity, better ways of living together in the global neighbourhood that is our human homeland. . . . There is only a question of the will to take that action."[68] In brief, new myths that would foster humanity's survival are being articulated; the tools for actualizing them are available; the outcome is still in our collective hands. Will we find the will to act, and will we act in time?

Personal and collective myths decisively influence a people's ability to muster their will effectively. One of David Feinstein's core guiding myths as he was growing up was "Try, try again" (that is undoubtedly why there is a second edition of this book). He comments: "I grew up believing strongly in the *force of will,* the ability to pull oneself up by one's bootstraps, the power we all have to influence our fate. I suspect that one of my greatest assets as a therapist is in the bedrock knowledge that I have mindfully and willfully changed numerous self-defeating patterns in my own personality and mythology. Over the years, I have also come to appreciate the *force of destiny.* Good, conscious, smart-living people, particularly when they have an unfortunate genetic quirk, do get cancer. Some of the most important events in my life, both fortuitous and sad, seemed guided by a larger hand. Destiny, for instance, apparently kept placing my wife and me in each other's path, no matter how hard we tried to get away from each other. Now a third, wildcard explanation seems necessary to me in trying to understand what happens in the world. I think there is also the *force of chance,* a macro-version of the Heisenberg uncertainty principle. Good people are cut down in the prime of life by drunk drivers. Not destiny, nor logic, nor karma, nor 'God needs them in heaven' provides a satisfying explanation for this apparent randomness. Chance, fate, and will are each forces shaping our journey into the future. I still tend, however, to keep most of my attention on the *force of will*. It is the domain where my mind and my myths can most definitively make a difference, as can yours."

The mythology supported by your actions, large and small, will ultimately be the mark you leave on the world. Each of us is challenged to direct our strength, wisdom, and will toward creating a contemporary, unifying mythic vision within ourselves, our families, our organizations, our nation, the world. And as we reconcile logic with intuition, ego with shadow, old myths with new, material concerns with spiritual, and our personal well-being with the collective, we also pave the way for a world steeped in contradictions to move forward adaptively, humanely, hopefully. Blessings.

Deepening Your Experience

❧

The task is to go deeply as possible into the darkness . . . and to emerge on the other side with permission to name one's reality from one's own point of view.

—Anthea Francine[1]

Participating consciously and creatively in the evolution of your personal mythology requires time, focused concentration, and a willingness to explore material that may be uncomfortable. A number of suggestions based on our experience with people facing obstacles when they attempt to work with their personal myths, and the strategies they have found to be successful, are offered here for deepening your experience with the program.

Creating a Sacred Space. Be mindful of the setting you choose for your inner work. Seek a comfortable and inspiring atmosphere that protects you from distractions such as television, telephone, and the call of workaday concerns. Use focused intention to create an energy field that surrounds, protects, and sacralizes the spot where you will be working, whether in an easy chair, on a couch, at a desk, from pillows on the floor, in a meadow, or by a stream. Some people have built altars in the corner of a crowded living room. Treat your work space with reverence. Embellish it with inspirational prompts.

Inspirational Prompts. Candles, incense, chimes, flowers, other objects from nature, and inspirational works of art, literature, or music can also sacralize the atmosphere of your work space. Besides setting a mood, an inspiring object can be a talisman that focuses your mind and uplifts your spirit. Particularly if you are feeling resistant to continuing the work or if the program becomes uncomfortably intense, directing your attention toward inspiring materials can give you refuge; yet you will still be maintaining a habit of focused inner work. If you find yourself resisting a personal ritual, it may be wise to take a recess and use an inspirational object as a bridge to help you turn inward. One woman reported that when she felt bogged down, she could renew her enthusiasm for the program by browsing through an 1893 edition of Walt Whitman's poetry given to her by her grandfather. A man who was inclined to become lost in a welter of words found it grounding to contemplate a stunning polished stone his daughter had given him. When your attention begins to wander, experiment with immersing yourself in an object or a sound you find beautiful. Locate the part of yourself that resonates with it, and follow that resonance to renewed contact with your own depths.

Retreats. Many of the world's great religious leaders received their inspiration while in solitude, often in the desert or mountains. Inspiration can come when you remove yourself, psychologically as well as physically, from life's ongoing stresses and concerns and create a conducive environment. A weekend retreat to a mountain cabin, seaside campsite, or comfortable hotel could provide a fertile setting for immersing yourself in the program.

Speaking Your Inner Experiences. If you have trouble concentrating during the guided imagery journeys, your concentration will improve markedly if you tell your experience to a partner as it is occurring, or, if you are listening to the tape, if you speak your experience into a second tape recorder. This not only will keep you alert and on track during the inner experience but also will make it easier to recall the details later.

Building Habit Patterns That Support Self-Exploration. Your efforts in the program can also be enhanced by establishing habits not unlike those required to maintain a regular practice of exercise, meditation, yoga, or any similar discipline. Habits of thinking, such as curiosity and keen observation, and habits of doing, such as reflecting in a journal and working with dreams, can be cultivated. While you cannot necessarily receive profound insights on demand, you can marshal your will toward creating the time and the conditions that support effective inner work. Regularly stepping out of the stresses that normally occupy your mind and into a consistent routine for contemplation and self-exploration establishes a container you will be able to rely on for deep psychological exploration.

Staying Physically Vibrant. When you are weary or run-down, the energy available to you will not take you to your creative edge. Rest, good nutrition, and exercise are the first order of business for self-improvement. The relationship between physical exercise and mental health is well established,[2] and strenuous physical activity can induce nonordinary states of consciousness, such as the "runner's high," that bypass ordinary thinking habits, increase creative thought and perception, and open you to fresh experience and insight. Swimming, jogging, dancing, bouncing on a trampoline, or another properly paced aerobic exercise after a sedentary day at work or intensive focus on your inner work can sharpen you for the mental effort required by this program.

Working with Others. Other people can lend a different perspective and greater objectivity. They may recognize your blind spots—dysfunctional strategies that are invisible to you even as they inhibit your development. The program may be used alone, with a partner, as the focal point of a personal mythology study group, under the supervision of a therapist, or as the basis for clinicians or other qualified leaders to design their own personal mythology classes and workshops. Working with others can help you tap into the healing qualities of relationship and community. If you make yourself accountable to another person, you are also more likely to confront your resistances directly than unknowingly to allow them to sabotage your efforts.

We have received appreciative reports from "leaderless" women's groups, men's groups, adult children of alcoholics groups, and various other self-help groups who have used the first edition of this book and the prerecorded tapes to lead their members in exploring their guiding mythologies. When we work with a group, we usually divide it into subgroups of three or four people. Guided imagery instructions are given to the entire group as participants go through the experience simultaneously but individually. They then discuss in their small support group what occurred and explore its deeper meanings. Other personal rituals, such as the Fairy Tales and the dialogues between characters representing an old myth and a counter-myth, are performed in front of the subgroup. Discussions in the large group, where people can relate their most significant insights, bring another level of reinforcement and instruction as people share their discoveries. Exploring your personal mythology with others can intensify the potency of the program and provide significant support and perspective.

If you work with another person, begin by reaching an agreement on ground rules, such as honoring one another's privacy by maintaining strict confidentiality and respecting each other's personal defenses. This is not a time to "play therapist" in the sense of probing for hidden feelings or dark secrets the other may be avoiding, offering uninvited interpretations of the meaning of the other's experiences, or giving advice. When you challenge your established patterns of thought and behavior, you are making yourself deeply vulnerable. The first response you need from another is support and acceptance. If you are planning to conduct the program with a partner or a group, the most sensible posture is to agree to listen receptively to one another's experiences, offer supportive nonjudgmental comments, and provide an active sounding board. Maintaining the balance of engaging in mutual problem-solving and not becoming intrusive can be enhanced by discussing (prior to the program) the kind of support you want from your partner or group and building in a feedback mechanism (e.g., "After every third personal ritual, we will reflect and comment on how well we are assisting one another") so you can let it be known if you are getting what you need.

An Attitude Toward Resistance. The same resistance that may seem such an obstacle to personal development may also serve as a powerful teacher. Recognize that resistance is natural in the face of change. It is one of the ways you maintain your equilibrium. When resistance appears, it is often with good reason. We encourage you to respect any resistance you encounter in your work with the program and to approach it with an attitude of curiosity and the sense that if you can penetrate to its core, you will gain greater self-understanding. Perhaps you approach a particular ritual with dread. Perhaps you find yourself frittering away time you have set aside for the program. Perhaps you keep losing your journal. Such unintentional responses can provide you with information about a part of yourself that has been outside your awareness.

Take time to listen to your resistance. Reflect on it in your journal. Use one of the techniques you learned during the first week of the program, such as consulting your Inner Shaman about your resistance or incubating a dream that focuses on it. You may discover that the program is challenging life patterns that hold symbolic meaning you have not yet recognized. You may discover you are pushing yourself too hard in the program, or simply that you need more time to relax rather than to undertake another concentrated task. Listening to what the resistance is attempting to tell you can reveal new understandings that ultimately enhance the program. By using resistance as a gauge that points to areas of your life that are in need of greater attention, it becomes a teacher rather than a tyrant.

Intensifying Inner Rituals Through Progressive Relaxation. The imagery rituals in the program generally begin with a brief induction for tuning inward, relaxing, opening heart and mind, and invoking the support and blessings of an inner wise person who personifies your inner wisdom. You can deepen your experience with any of the inwardly focused rituals by preceding it with a practice you may already know for relaxing deeply or by using the following progressive relaxation procedure,[3] which you would need to tape, have read to you, or learn thoroughly. Leave generous pauses between instructions. Begin by sitting or reclining in a safe, secluded space where you are unlikely to be interrupted. Make the conditions pleasant for yourself.

Settle in comfortably. You are warm, secure, and well supported. Thank your body for its hard work and good service. Find the parts of your body that need special attention, healing, or rest. Picture a warm, wise hand filled with a fragrant ointment gently touching and acknowledging those parts. Focus your attention and sense the melting, calming relaxation that comes into those sore and tired places.

All is well with you as you set off on this journey of self-discovery. You are always able to move and adjust yourself, yawning and stretching, rearranging until your body is peaceful and satisfied. Use any sounds in the environment as a reminder to bring your attention back to these instructions.

Your facial muscles—forehead, eyes, cheeks, mouth, and jaw—yield to gravity by softening and melting. Blood flows freely through your skin, tingling your scalp and enlivening your face. At your own pace, breathe deeply seven times, exhaling completely. Be aware of your entire head—face, scalp, eyes, ears, mouth, jaw. You are vitally alive and relaxed.

Your neck, the bridge between your head and body, has worked hard and welcomes this peaceful time. The heavy load is at rest, and nothing is demanded of your neck or throat. You are grateful for the air and nourishment they have carried for you. The healing hand sensitively massages your neck and its muscles. You sigh, content. Take seven deep breaths, at your own tempo, becoming increasingly aware of softening your throat and neck.

Your chest, ribs, back, spine, shoulders, lungs, and heart are working together to bring breath into you as they have all of your life. Focus on each—ribs all the way around, back, spine, shoulders, lungs, heart—as you find the tired places. Take seven good breaths, at your own pace, exhaling completely and resting between inhalations. With each breath you are increasingly aware of the healing hand, which again finds the wounded, weary parts, nourishing them with tender touch. Be generous with yourself, allowing time for the healing to happen.

Your pelvis, hips, buttocks, genitals, belly, muscles, and deep organs deserve the attention you are giving them. Sense their needs and strength. Give thanks for their good service. With seven breaths, as before, feel the warmth as the wonderful, loving hand heals your hurts and soothes your restlessness.

Your arms, hands, legs, and feet are ready to rest and be appreciated. You will move your awareness to the muscles and joints of each, opening and freeing them in turn. One by one, discover and thank the muscles and joints in your arms, hands, legs, and feet. The healing hand will touch away your pains as you take seven deep breaths, exhaling your tiredness, hurt, and disillusion.

With each of the next ten suggestions, you will become more able to relax and move into the experience in front of you. You are always free to return to ordinary consciousness simply by opening your eyes and exhaling deeply, and you are just as free to explore the extraordinary landscape of your unconscious. You will recall all you need of this experience, and you will emerge from it with insight and power. This is your mythology, entirely your own creation.

One, you are able to focus fully on the instructions. You are conscious, alert, and curious.

Two, your body remembers the healing it has received and sinks pleasurably into full relaxation.

Three, your breathing deepens as your lungs become quieter and more efficient. Your chest rises and falls in gentle rhythm. The air moves softly through your nose and throat.

Four, your heart pumps at a peaceful, efficient rate, sending oxygen and nutrients to every part of your body. Trace this flow with a vivid sensation of refreshment reaching every cell.

Five, your deep organs—heart, stomach, liver, kidneys, and the others—have silently served you, and you are grateful as you visualize and sense their response to your attention.

Six, your buttocks, genitals, and belly are butter soft. Deliciously comfortable. How good you feel!

Seven, your thighs, calves, ankles, and leg joints are heavy and happy, relieved of effort and demand.

Eight, your head, face, neck, and shoulders are contented and easy, feeling good.

Nine, deeply relaxed, you feel the comfortable sensations of warmth and heaviness within you and a pleasant tingling on your skin.

Ten, fully relaxed, your body is vital and comfortable. Your best energy is available for the journey of self-discovery you have begun.

Progressive relaxation slows your metabolism, quiets your mind, increases your receptivity, and deepens the guided imagery experience that will follow it. By practicing this technique regularly, you will also be developing the ability to reach a deeply relaxed and peaceful state at will.

Working with Your Dreams

Can we transform dreamwork from a therapeutically valuable operation in the hands of specialists to a universally accessible experience that is available to anyone who wishes to take the time and trouble to learn how to go about it?

—Montague Ullman[1]

With the publication of *The Interpretation of Dreams* at the turn of the century, Sigmund Freud brought the mystery of dreaming into the reach of scientific investigation. While he believed that the meaning of a dream is often well concealed, he considered dreams to be "the royal road to the unconscious." Carl Jung insisted that, although dreams must be probed for their deeper meanings, their symbolism is typically produced to reveal insights rather than to conceal information from the dreamer. As a result, Jung went beyond Freud in having his clients write down their dreams and in asking them to play a central role in dream interpretation. Alfred Adler stressed the continuity between dream life and waking life, providing a perspective that made dream content particularly meaningful and useful for the dreamer.

A number of excellent books are available that provide detailed guidance for examining your dream life, such as *Breakthrough Dreaming* (Gayle Delaney), *Crisis Dreaming* (Rosalind Cartwright and Lynne Lamberg), *Dream Power* (Ann Faraday), *The Dream Workbook* (Robert Langs), *Dreamworking* (Stanley Krippner and

Joseph Dillard), *Our Dreaming Mind* (Robert Van de Castle), and *Working with Dreams* (Montague Ullman and Nan Zimmerman).[2] We have attempted to summarize here a few of the most useful ideas and methods we have found for working with your dreams and understanding them in the context of your personal mythology.

Psychologist Gayle Delaney has articulated two basic assumptions that can serve as useful guidelines in thinking about your own dreams:

1. Dreams have a point, a message intended to be grasped by the waking mind and used for the benefit of the dreamer.
2. The dreamer, upon awakening, has all the information necessary to understand the dream.[3]

If you regularly examine your dreams, you will find them so consistently innovative and often enough so profound that you might wonder if an anonymous playwright is working overtime in some hidden recess of your being. Psychologist Ann Faraday has compared the dreaming mind to a movie director who focuses on elements of "waking life that need more attention than we have given them [and who reflects] on them *in depth* by composing stories in which flashbacks, cartoon-style pictures, and all kinds of other devices are used to express what we are feeling deep down inside about ourselves, other people, and the quality of our lives."[4]

Your dreams comment not only on your psychological life but also on the state of your physical body. Jung once made an accurate diagnosis of a cerebrospinal condition—based solely on the content of a single dream—that so impressed the attending physician, T. M. Davie, that Davie concluded a published report of the case with the assertion: "Dreams . . . do not merely provide information on the psychological situation, but may disclose the presence of organic disorder and even denote its precise location."[5] As psychologist Patricia Garfield has observed: "Your dreams can help keep you healthy, warn you when you are at risk, diagnose incipient physical problems, support you during physical crises, forecast your recuperation, suggest treatment, heal your body, and signal your return to wellness."[6]

MYTH-MAKING ACTIVITY THROUGH
THE WINDOW OF YOUR DREAMS

Aristotle observed that one of the most important abilities for skillfully interpreting dreams is "the faculty of observing resemblances." [7] We have repeatedly been struck with resemblances between our clients' dreams and the focused work they were doing with the personal mythology at the time. While dream symbolism is so multilayered, mysterious, and inherently ambiguous that it lends itself to an almost endless variety of interpretations (an old quip among therapists is that people seeing Freudian analysts have Freudian dreams, and people seeing Jungian analysts have Jungian dreams), we have informally collected dream data over the years that suggest that dreams can be usefully classified according to their function in promoting one of the five tasks or stages by which we believe personal myths naturally develop and around which this program has been organized. [8]

Some dreams highlight an underlying conflict between a prevailing myth and a counter-myth that is challenging it (Stage 1). Some dreams attempt to buttress the old myth, perhaps bringing to your attention early experiences that caused you to form it; other dreams may attune you to the forces that are evoking your counter-myth (Stage 2). Some dreams work toward a natural dialectic between your old myth and your counter-myth, pushing toward a resolution of their conflict (Stage 3). Some dreams focus on the new myth that emerged from this resolution, refining and applauding it, and generating in you a commitment to live according to the myth's premises and instructions (Stage 4). Some dreams are oriented toward translating your new myth into the particulars of your life (Stage 5).

A woman had a recurrent dream about crossing a bridge that was in a forest. This was the only scene in the dream, but it was accompanied by a feeling of enormous frustration. She was asked to imagine that she was having the dream again. This time, however, she was told to "redream" the dream from the point of view of the bridge. She closed her eyes, relaxed, imagined she was the bridge, and was soon sobbing. She explained that her initial reaction was one of great satisfaction because she was helping people get from one part of the woods to another. But then, as people kept walking over her, she felt old and creaky, as if she were going to collapse and break apart. Then she realized that she really was the bridge. The bridge represented the way she was always serving her husband, waiting on her children, caring for her aged parents, and doing little for herself. She was living according to the dictates of a personal myth that had her reflexively serving others, underfoot, unaware, and unappreciated. She realized that if she kept on in this way, she was going to creak and fall apart.

This dream helped the woman recognize trouble that was brewing for her because of her unquestioned compliance to an image of the role of wife and mother that she had held since childhood. By dramatizing this core guiding myth in a manner that highlighted the harm it was causing her, the dream suggested the importance of revising the myth. Dreams may support or challenge a prevailing myth, foster or inhibit a counter-myth, or focus on conflict between the two. When a personal myth is placing you in harm's way, or when daytime experiences are inconsistent with the myth, your dreams may work to adjust the myth (by accommodating it to the discordant experience), or they may distort or reinterpret (assimilate) the experience to fit the myth better. You can more fully understand your personal mythology through the lens of your dreams, and you can more fully understand your dreams through the lens of your personal mythology.

Strong parallels can be identified between this framework and the research findings of psychologist Rosalind Cartwright, who identified a nightly pattern in which the initial dreams tend to review unresolved concerns from the day. Next are dreams that consider scenes from the past in which analogous problems have previously been confronted. Then come wish-oriented dreams in which there is a sense that the conflict has been resolved. The final dreams attempt to integrate the various elements of this dream sequence into a viable resolution of the conflict.[9] Dreams serve to mediate between your daily experiences and your underlying myths, and working with your dreams is a way to discover changes in your mythology that are occurring outside your awareness.

SUGGESTIONS FOR REMEMBERING YOUR DREAMS

Most people have four or five periods of dreaming every night. Some spontaneously remember one or two of these dreams almost every morning. Most do not. A few simple techniques can assist recall. Just before falling asleep, breathe deeply, relax, and with deliberation repeat several times: "I will remember a dream when I wake up." Keep a tape recorder or a pen and paper beside your bed. Record your dreams immediately upon waking. You can copy your dreams into your journal later, but the first draft upon waking is often so disorganized and barely legible that you may not want it in your journal. In addition, later copying your dreams into your journal can be part of the process of deepening your relationship with the dream. When psychotherapy clients record their dreams on tape or on pieces of paper and then transcribe these reports into their journal each week just prior to their therapy session, they are frequently amazed to realize that they have totally forgotten many—in some cases, more than half—of the dreams they had recorded.

Dreams are often fragile and transitory, and people sometimes lose the dream by leaving even a few minutes between waking and recording it. If you wake without recalling a dream, you might shift your body into the position it was in when you awoke—and presumably in which you had your final dream. Or you might remain alert during the morning because a trivial incident or association can take you back to a dream. Even if you can remember only a single fragment, or a fleeting feeling with which you awaken, record it. Sometimes the process of simply starting to write or speak the dream expands your initial glimpse into a much more complete recollection. There is a saying that a dream is like a tiger—if you catch even a trace of it, you have it by the tail and can pull it into view, stripe by stripe. It may take several days of giving yourself the recommended instructions before you start recalling your dreams. Do not become discouraged. The program is designed so that your dreams are a supplementary rather than a central focus of the work. Also, as you repeat this process for several nights, you will be developing habit patterns that support dream recall.

We will mention two additional methods that can help you remember your dreams, although they are more intrusive. While alcohol and most drugs tend to reduce dreaming, some people claim to have found that their dream recall is enhanced by the ingestion of certain herbal teas and other natural substances. Vitamin B-6, for instance, sometimes appears to facilitate dream recall. If there are no medical contraindications to your using B-6, occasionally taking between 50 mg and 250 mg with dinner may facilitate dream recall. Another technique is to set a gentle alarm clock to go off early so you will be more likely to awake mid-dream and also have additional time to work with your dreams. Although these are not recommended as regular practices, they may be useful on occasion. Even if you do not recall a dream on a particular morning, your attempt may foster new insight. Often people will ask for a dream that clarifies a certain issue, and they will wake up not with a dream but with a new take on the problem. Rather than be disappointed or self-critical if you do not remember your dreams, simply set aside a few protected minutes upon waking and remain alert for whatever comes. Nor should you be concerned if the meaning of a particular dream is not initially clear to you. Several useful techniques for dream exploration follow, and others can be found in the recommended readings.

WAYS OF WORKING WITH YOUR DREAMS

Jung commented that "if we meditate on a dream sufficiently long and thoroughly, if we carry it around with us and turn it over and over, something almost always comes of it."[10] Keeping your attention focused on a dream is likely to induce a greater understanding of its meaning. The techniques offered here are, in a sense, ways of creatively turning the dream "over and over." The oldest and most frequently used method of working with dreams is simply to repeat the dream to yourself or to tell it to another person. Recording your dreams serves a similar function. Eight additional methods for working with your dreams follow.

Review via Dream Elements. Some researchers have identified the categories of dream content.[11] One way of attending to a dream is to review it in terms of these categories. This process often helps the dreamer see new relationships among parts of the dream and may also bring additional aspects of the dream into memory. Eight common dream elements are:

> *Characters* (friends, famous people, strangers, mythical creatures)
> *Activities* (what the characters are doing: running, eating, watching TV, sewing)
> *Settings* (your home, nineteenth-century France, midnight, outer space)
> *Objects* (clothing, weapons, computers, buildings)
> *Nature* (trees, birds, stars, water)
> *Sensations* (warmth, sound, smells, tastes)
> *Emotions* (anger, love, fear, loneliness)
> *Modifiers* (small, pretty, purple, old, tall)

While no single dream is likely to have all eight categories represented in it, this list may remind you of important aspects of the dream. Also, if you record your dreams on a regular basis, you may find that certain elements regularly repeat themselves, revealing patterns that you can explore just as you would explore an individual dream symbol.

Identify with One of the Elements. Many clinicians who work with dreams believe that each image represents an aspect of the dreamer. The woman who "became" the bridge was using an approach to working with dreams that is based on this assumption. In this technique, you select a tangible element from the dream—usually one that is particularly puzzling, troubling, or ominous—and identify with that person, place, thing, quality, or activity. In identifying with a dream element, you "redream" the dream as that element. If a bear rug in the dream puzzles you, close your eyes and imagine you are having the dream again. But this time, imagine that you are the bear rug. What is the rug thinking and feeling as the dream proceeds? Perhaps your rug will feel stepped on and ignored. Or perhaps your rug is a resource that can transform itself into the living animal when you have a need for strength. This method can be enhanced by taking on the dream symbol in your body, physically assuming a posture that represents the symbol. Then redream the dream while in this position.

Role-play a Dream Element. Another method of examining a dream symbol is to role play it, using the technique called creative projection, introduced during Week 2. If you were exploring the bear rug, you would put yourself into the role of the rug and literally act out the dream, giving the rug a voice and gestures and, in your imagination, interacting with other elements as the dream proceeds. As you enact the plot of the dream, also follow your inclinations toward examining other dream elements. For instance, after finishing the dream as you dreamed it, you can extend the role-playing. The element with which you are identifying can have an imaginary dialogue with another dream element. The bear rug, for instance, might begin such a dialogue by asking the room in which it is placed, "Why are you so cold?" You would then "become" the room, answer, and proceed with a dialogue between them.

Free Associate to a Dream Element. You can identify your spontaneous associations to a particular dream image by saying or writing down everything that occurs to you when you bring the image to mind. Perhaps you dreamed about a robot. As quickly as you can, list all of your associations with "robot"—for example, "mechanical, efficient, futuristic, cold, programmed." You may come to understand some of these associations in the context of the entire dream, the context of recent events in your life, or the context of your evolving mythology. If you are working with a partner, you might have your partner ask you a series of "naive" questions. For example, imagine that your partner has just arrived from another culture and needs to have everything explained. Your partner could ask such questions as, "What is a robot?" If the answer is "A mechanical person," your partner might ask, "What do you mean by 'mechanical'?" Have your partner continue the process, moving so rapidly that you will need to express yourself spontaneously, without the opportunity to plan your responses. Another variation of this approach is to imagine that you are interviewing the dream element. You can ask the bear rug or the robot what it is doing in your dream and what it is trying to tell you, and then in your imagination have the dream element answer.

Vital Focus. With this technique, you redream the dream in your imagination, as if you were watching a motion picture. As you go along, however, you "freeze" the action at vital moments, for example where a scene changes, a new character appears, or the emotional tone shifts. Make a "still photograph" in your mind, or a short "film clip" of the scene. Scrutinize the scene, noting every detail you can, and then continue. This gives you a chance not only to focus on important points in the dream but also to enter the dream and sink into critical moments that might have escaped your notice on first recalling the dream.

Map the Dream in Your Body. Begin with the opening scene of the dream. If this scene lived in your body, where in your body would it be? Place the dream scene into this part of your body. Notice how your body responds. Does it want to become more open or closed? Does it grow hotter or colder? Does it react with fear, anger, sadness, pleasure? Let your body inform you about this opening scene of the dream. Then move to the next scene. What part of your body resonates with this scene? Again, explore the scene from your body's point of view. Continue until you reach the closing scene from your dream. When you are finished, you might want to "shake out" any unwanted emotional residue with strong exhalations and rapid free movements of your hands and body.

Extend the Dream. Sometimes you will wake up with a dream that feels unfinished or in some other way seems unresolved. To use this technique, again redream the dream in your imagination just as you remember it. Then carry the plot beyond the dream's actual stopping point. Extend the dream toward a new ending. For instance, you might have the bear rug become animated, leave the cold room, and discover what is beyond it.

Summarize the Dream as a Phrase or Sentence. You can sometimes get to the essence of a dream by summarizing it as a single statement, giving the dream a title, or identifying the underlying lesson of the dream by asking yourself, "What is this dream trying to tell me?" Another variation is to restate the theme of the dream at a higher level of abstraction. A dream about changing a lightbulb might be more abstractly stated as, "I was trying to fix something that sheds light on my life." The following formula can be useful. Begin a sentence with "This dream [or a particular segment or element of the dream] is about a . . ." and complete the sentence with a word such as "journey," "conflict," "lesson," "challenge," "attraction," "rejection," "birth," "death." Then reflect on the specific journey, conflict, lesson, challenge, attraction, rejection, birth, or death in your life about which the dream seems to be providing information.

Your dreams comment on the elaborate machinations of your mythological underworld in an intriguing blend of literal and symbolic language. Many psychologists believe that dreams are best understood as an unfolding of the movement of the psyche and should not be distorted by overly intellectual interpretations. Your work with your dreams need not be divorced from feeling or "all in your head." Several of the techniques presented here bring your body into the process, and most of them will arouse your intuition and emotions. While your dreams will not reveal an unambiguous picture of your personal mythology, they can provide enticing clues into its dynamics and fresh insights about the most important issues affecting your life.

If the Program Becomes Unsettling

When the time comes, we will have what we need to face our dragons, discover our treasures, and return to transform the kingdom.

—Carol Pearson[1]

A sensitive matter in presenting the potent inner rituals that compose this program is that any tool that is useful for psychological exploration can stir strong emotions or uncover dormant psychological problems. We have made every effort to present the program in such a manner that you can adjust it to your own needs and pace. The personal rituals presented here have been field-tested with several thousand people in our consultations, workshops, and seminars, and used by the many thousands who worked with the earlier edition of this book. In no instance have serious adverse effects been reported to us.

Most of the personal rituals presented in this book evolved, however, in face-to-face settings where interpersonal support is built in. If you should feel disturbed or unsettled as you proceed through the program, and if those feelings persist after you have utilized the suggestions given below, we strongly encourage you to elicit support from family and friends or seek professional assistance.

While some of the goals of this book parallel those of psychotherapy—such as increased insight, the resolution of inner conflicts, and decision making that is more psychologically informed—the program is not a substitute for psychotherapeutic treatment. In the face of emotional turmoil, persistent depression, an overwhelming life crisis, or recurrent patterns that prove to be destructive, psychotherapy—particularly with a qualified counselor who is at least as concerned with the larger personal journey as with symptoms—is one of the most trustworthy ways to gain access to the existing storehouse of behavioral science knowledge and technique for fostering healing and renewal. Psychotherapists today perform many of the functions that in earlier times were reserved for priests, priestesses, shamans, and other spiritual leaders.

Like many of our professional colleagues in psychology, we have been concerned about the simplistic promises of many "pop psych" books flooding the market since the 1960s. In designing this book, we have attempted to conform to the principles for self-help books set forth in the journal *Contemporary Psychology*.[2] We have worked with some ten thousand people in educational, clinical, and community settings, over a period of more than two decades, in developing and refining the program, and we have enlisted numerous additional participants specifically for reformulating and testing it in the self-guided format presented here. On the basis of these experiences, and given a reasonable understanding of the limitations of a self-help format, we believe it is responsible to suggest that you can gain valuable insight and bring about significant change in your guiding myths if you follow the program presented in this book. We have attempted to keep our writing consistent with the available research data about personal myths,[3] psychotherapy,[4] and the growing body of psychological findings on happiness and optimal functioning.[5]

Because many of the methods presented in this program are adapted from clinical practice, they may have a strong emotional impact. While they will not *cause* new emotional problems, any potent experience can bring underlying difficulties to the surface. Some people have repressed childhood traumas from the time of a horrifying experience onward. If repressed issues are on the verge of breaking through one's defenses, nearly any intense experience can trigger a reaction: seeing a powerful film, helping one's child through a difficult time, having an argument with a loved one, experiencing a volley of criticism from a friend, opening oneself to the deeper recesses of one's psyche by working with one's dreams, entering psychotherapy, attending an intensive "personal growth" workshop, or utilizing a program such as the one presented in this book.

In addition to the suggestions provided at various points in the text of the book, this Support Guide presents a variety of "psychological first-aid" measures you can take if your experience in the program becomes uncomfortable. In most cases, one or more of these will suffice. Prolonged upset, however, can also be an opportunity, an opening for a highly beneficial course of healing and growth facilitated by psychotherapy, a spiritual discipline, or other healing resource. If the program becomes upsetting, you may take any of these immediate steps:

Shift Your Focus. Simply put the book away and turn to a calming activity: listen to music, work in your garden, telephone a friend, take a walk, watch an entertaining video.

Honor Your Body. Give yourself rest. Eat wisely. Make choices that diminish stress. Involve yourself in an invigorating physical activity, such as swimming, running, dancing, biking, using exercise equipment, cleaning your house, or waxing your car. Regularly discharging pent-up or stagnant energies is an excellent form of emotional self care.

Quiet Your Mind. Meditate, practice yoga, or use a relaxation technique such as the one described in Support Guide 1. Along with the relaxation, you can experiment with imagery that takes you to a protected, beautiful, sacred place—a redwood grove, a mountain stream, a childhood hideaway—and cultivate your ability to go there in your mind whenever you feel the need for safety, sustenance, or renewal. Books that teach techniques for quieting a restless mind include *Being Peace* by Thich Nhat Hanh, *Wherever You Go, There You Are* by Jon Kabat-Zinn, *The Path of Insight Meditation* by Joseph Goldstein and Jack Kornfield, and *Beyond the Relaxation Response* by Herbert Benson.

Find Support from Another Person. Share intimately with someone who appreciates the task you have accepted and whom you can use as a sounding board. Knowing you are seen and valued in the darkest part of your struggle makes that struggle more endurable.

Tap into Mythic Resources. Visualize your Inner Shaman (introduced in Week 1) nurturing and advising you; use your Personal Shield for emotional and spiritual protection (as described at the end of Week 2); or immerse yourself in the mythic or spiritual wisdom of a tradition that draws you.

Be Patient with Yourself. Because the program is oriented toward identifying and changing areas of your personal mythology that are not serving you well, you are from the start exploring memories and feelings that are likely to be difficult and unpleasant. It is not necessarily bad to encounter challenging memories and frailties that had not previously been recognized. Although realistic adjustments to your self-concept may be of great value, we suggest that you frequently acknowledge to yourself that you have willingly entered a realm that holds difficult as well as inspiring material. Appreciate your courage. Abraham Maslow, one of the pioneers in bringing a spiritual perspective to scientific psychology, used to say, "Anything worth doing is worth doing poorly!" We are all beginners when we are learning something new. Newly conceived personal myths are likely to provoke discomfort even as they begin to improve your life.

Be Where Heaven Meets Earth. When emotional issues are stirred by deep personal work, as they tend to be, a "grounding" procedure can be extremely centering and reassuring. Standing or sitting with your feet firmly planted on the ground, imagine that your deep, slow inhalation is pulling the energies from the center of the earth, up your spine, and out the top of your head. Resonate consciously with these energies as they move through you. The earth, your ultimate support system, is referred to in many traditions as "The Mother" because all life springs from the earth. With each inhalation, feel or just imagine yourself being warmly touched and nourished by the energy coming up from the center of the earth. After several inhalations, accumulating in your body the energy and support of the earth, focus on your exhalation. With each deep, slow exhalation, pull the energy of the sky in through the top of your head, down your spine, and out your tailbone. The sky, with its air and stars and sun, brings to the earth the energies that impregnate and support life. It is often called "The Father." With each exhalation, feel or just imagine yourself being bathed in the energies that initiate and sustain life. After several exhalations, accumulating in your body the energy of the sky, breathe in the earth with each inhalation and the sky with each exhalation. Let their energies rendezvous and mingle within you. You are the container of their life-giving dance.[6]

Develop a Self-Affirming Perspective for Your Trials and Tribulations. For change to occur, the old, familiar mythic system must destabilize, and this is by its nature disorienting. If the program has evoked a memory or challenge that feels dismal or traumatic, the awareness that is upsetting you is still new. The creative responses you will eventually engage to meet it are still being mobilized. Also, keep in mind that not all of the "memories" people experience actually occurred (see discussion in Week 2). Give yourself time to adjust to new information. Affirm your faith, shift your perspective, call on your creativity, and find the humor, ironies, and lessons in the process. As Alan Watts observed,[7] if psychotherapy or personal growth becomes divorced from humor, something is terribly wrong. Watts described a group of Zen monks who consider their most important meditation to be a ten-minute session of hearty laughter before breakfast each morning, putting them into a flow with life's absurdities.

Release Your Stress.[8] This technique, which is used in Chinese medicine, is increasingly being adapted in settings ranging from emergency rooms to the Olympics. Its effect is to clear the meridians (the energy pathways on which acupuncture points are supposedly situated) of stress-related energy blockages. Experiment with this simple self-help procedure anytime the program brings up memories, thoughts, or feelings you find upsetting.

Keeping the troubling thought, emotion, or memory in your awareness, place the palm of one hand across your forehead. Place your other hand over the protrusion at the back of your head, just above the line of your ears. Gently hold your head between your hands as you continue to experience the emotion or memory. Continue for at least a minute. Most people have two points on their forehead that slightly protrude. These are called the frontal eminences. You will eventually feel a pulse on your hand emitted by your frontal eminences. This indicates that the blood supply that had been leaving your head and going to your limbs (the fight-or-flight mobilization of the stress-response syndrome) is returning to your head.

As you begin to relax, surrender into the calm. The bodily response to the stress will gradually diminish even as you keep the memory in your mind. Using this procedure repeatedly, with the same memory, has the effect of weakening the association between the memory and the stress response.

We have focused here on possible hazards of self-guided exploration and presented some basic psychological techniques for meeting them. We close by reemphasizing the potential benefits of actively working with your personal mythology. The emotional woundings that inner work may bring to the surface were, while beneath the surface, draining your vitality. By bringing them into your awareness, doorways open for healing them. With that healing, personal myths that had been defending against the wound can be transformed, freeing you to revel more fully in life's possibilities.

Notes

AN INVITATION

1. Joseph Campbell, *Creative Mythology,* vol. 4 of *The Masks of God* (New York: Viking, 1968), p. 4.

2. Sigmund Freud, *The Interpretation of Dreams* (London: Hogarth Press, 1955; first published 1900).

3. Charles Dickens, *A Christmas Carol* (New York: Macmillan, 1963), p. 34.

4. Joseph Campbell, *The Hero with a Thousand Faces,* 2d ed. (Princeton, NJ: Princeton University Press, 1949).

5. Jerome Bruner, *Actual Minds, Possible Worlds* (Cambridge, MA: Harvard University Press, 1986); Theodore R. Sarbin, ed., *Narrative Psychology: The Storied Nature of Human Conduct* (New York: Praeger, 1986).

6. Mircea Eliade, *Myth and Reality* (New York: Harper & Row, 1963), p. 6.

7. Ken Wilber, *No Boundary: Eastern and Western Approaches to Personal Growth* (Boulder, CO: Shambhala, 1981), p. 126.

Week 1

1. Erich Neumann, *The Origins and History of Consciousness,* trans. R. F. C. Hull (Princeton, NJ: Princeton University Press, 1970), p. 210.

2. David Feinstein and Stanley Krippner, "Personal Myths in the Family Way," in Steve A. Anderson and Dennis A. Bagarozzi, eds., *Family Myths: Psychotherapy Implications* (New York: Haworth, 1989), pp. 111–39.

3. This personal ritual is patterned after an exercise developed by Jean Houston.

4. Rollo May, *Love and Will* (New York: W. W. Norton, 1969), pp. 13–14.

5. Mircea Eliade, *Shamanism: Archaic Techniques of Ecstasy* (New York: Pantheon, 1964).

6. David Feinstein, "The Shaman Within: Cultivating a Sacred Personal Mythology," in Shirley Nicholson, ed., *Shamanism* (Wheaton, IL: Quest Books, 1987), pp. 267–79.

7. This case appears in David Feinstein, "Myth-Making in Psychological and Spiritual Development," *American Journal of Orthopsychiatry* (in press).

8. Guidelines for selecting such musical pieces are presented in Stanislav Grof, *The Adventure of Self-Discovery* (Albany: State University of New York Press, 1988), and Jean Houston, *The Search for the Beloved: Journeys in Sacred Psychology* (Los Angeles: Jeremy P. Tarcher, 1987).

9. Albert Upton, *Design for Thinking* (Stanford, CA: Stanford University Press, 1961), p. 11.

10. Joan Marler, "The Mythic Journey" (an interview with Joseph Campbell), *Yoga Journal,* November/December 1987, pp. 57–61.

11. Carl G. Jung, *Two Essays on Analytical Psychology,* trans. H. G. Baynes and C. F. Baynes (New York: Dodd, Mead, 1928).

Week 2

1. Linda Schierse Leonard, *Witness to the Fire: Creativity and the Veil of Addiction* (Boston: Shambhala, 1989), p. 14.

2. Dan P. McAdams, *The Stories We Live By: Personal Myths and the Making of the Self* (New York: William Morrow, 1993), p. 36.

3. Ibid.

4. Motifs from classical mythology have been used as frameworks for self-exploration in, for instance, Jean Houston's *The Hero and the Goddess: The Odyssey as Mystery and Initiation* (New York: Ballantine, 1992) and *The Passion of Isis and Osiris: A Union of Two Souls* (New York: Ballantine, 1995); Robert A. Johnson's trilogy *He, She, and We* (Harper & Row, 1974, 1976, and 1983); and Jean Shinoda Bolen's *Goddesses in Everywoman* and *Gods in Everyman* (Harper & Row, 1984 and 1989).

5. We are grateful to Melanie Morgan, one of Jean Houston's students, who uses the "Paradise/Paradise Lost" framework in her own personal mythology workshops.

6. The strengths and weaknesses of "ontogeny recapitulates phylogeny" explanations (i.e., the evolution of the collective is recapitulated in the development of the individual) are discussed by Ken Wilber, *Sex, Spirit, Ecology* (Boston: Shambhala, 1995), pp. 149–52.

7. Rollo May, *Love and Will* (New York: W. W. Norton, 1969), p. 281.

8. Daniel N. Stern, *The Interpersonal World of the Infant: A View from Psychoanalysis and Developmental Psychology* (New York: Basic Books, 1985).

9. Abraham H. Maslow, *The Farther Reaches of Human Nature* (New York: Viking, 1971), pp. 318–21.

10. The "notice breath; soften belly; open heart" meditation was taught to us by Stephen Levine.

11. Richard Ofshe, *Making Monsters: False Memories, Psychotherapy and Sexual Hysteria* (New York: Charles Scribner's Sons, 1994); Lenore Terr, *Unchained Memories: True Stories of Traumatic Memories, Lost and Found* (New York: Basic Books, 1995).

12. Elizabeth F. Loftus and Katherine Ketcham, *The Myth of Repressed Memory: False Memories and Allegations of Sexual Abuse* (New York: St. Martin's, 1994); Daniel L. Schacter, ed., *Memory Distortion: How Minds, Brains, and Societies Reconstruct the Past* (Cambridge, MA: Harvard University Press, 1995).

13. Terr, *Unchained Memories.*

14. This method is patterned after a Gestalt therapy technique developed by Fritz Perls. It is reminiscent of Carl Jung's technique of *active imagination*, combined with Jacob Moreno's *psychodrama*. Our colleague, Peg Elliott Mayo, one of Perls's students, dubbed the technique "creative projection," the term we use.

WEEK 3

1. Carl G. Jung, "The Theory of Psychoanalysis," in *Collected Works,* vol. 4, 2d ed., trans. R. F. C. Hull (Princeton, NJ: Princeton University Press, 1961; first published 1913), para. 451.

2. Martin E. P. Seligman, *Learned Optimism* (New York: Simon & Schuster, 1990), p. 8.

3. This case was first presented in David Feinstein, "Conflict over Childbearing and Tumors of the Female Reproductive System: Symbolism in Disease," *Somatics* 4, no. 1 (1982): 35–41.

4. Marion Woodman, *The Ravaged Bridegroom: Masculinity in Women* (Toronto: Inner City, 1990), p. 23.

5. Carlos Castaneda, *The Teachings of Don Juan: A Yaqui Way of Knowledge* (New York: Simon & Schuster, 1968), p. 107.

6. Jerome Bruner, "Myth and Identity," in Henry A. Murray, ed., *Myth and Myth-making* (Boston: Beacon, 1960), p. 286.

7. Henry A. Murray, "American Icarus," in Arthur Burton and Robert E. Harris, eds., *Clinical Studies of Personality* (New York: Harper & Row, 1955), pp. 615–41.

8. Abraham H. Maslow, *The Farther Reaches of Human Nature* (New York: Viking, 1971).

9. Daniel Goleman and Joel Gurin, eds., *Mind Body Medicine: How to Use Your Mind for Better Health* (Yonkers, NY: Consumer Reports, 1993).

10. John Watkins, "The Affect Bridge: A Hypno-Analytic Technique," *International Journal of Clinical and Experimental Hypnosis* 19 (1971): 21–27.

WEEK 4

1. Jean Shinoda Bolen, *Goddesses in Everywoman* (Harper & Row, 1984), p. 294.

2. Cited in Allan B. Chinen, *Once upon a Midlife: Classic Stories and Mythic Tales to Illuminate the Middle Years* (New York: Jeremy P. Tarcher/Putnam, 1992), p. 2.

3. Anthea Francine, *Envisioning Theology: An Autobiographical Account of Personal Symbolic Journeying as a Source of Revelation* (Master's thesis, Berkeley, CA: Pacific School of Religion, June 1983), p. 77.

4. Richard Gardner, *Therapeutic Communication with Children: The Mutual-Storytelling Technique* (New York: Science House, 1971).

5. The focusing instructions given here constitute the tip of the iceberg of Eugene Gendlin's *Focusing* (New York: Bantam, 1978).

6. Jean Houston, *The Search for the Beloved: Journeys in Sacred Psychology* (Los Angeles: Jeremy P. Tarcher, 1987), pp. 104–05.

7. Ibid., p. 105.

8. Peg Elliott Mayo, "The Alchemy of Transmuting Grief to Creativity," in David Feinstein and Peg Elliott Mayo, *Rituals for Living and Dying* (San Francisco: HarperCollins, 1990), pp. 132–72.

WEEK 5

1. Jean Houston, *A Mythic Life: Learning to Live Our Greater Story* (San Francisco: HarperCollins, 1996), p. 6.

2. Robert Jay Lifton, *The Protean Self: Human Resilience in an Age of Fragmentation* (New York: Basic Books, 1993).

3. Ibid., p. 1.

4. Ibid., p. 14.

5. Ibid., p. 28.

6. Ibid., p. 6.

WEEK 6

1. Clarissa Pinkola Estés, *Women Who Run with the Wolves: Myths and Stories of the Wild Woman Archetype* (New York: Ballantine, 1992), p. 414.

2. Rollo May, "The Problem of Evil: An Open Letter to Carl Rogers," *Journal of Humanistic Psychology* 22, no. 3 (1982): 10–21.

3. Ibid., p. 11.

4. Erich Neumann, *Depth Psychology and a New Ethic,* trans. Eugene Rolfe (New York: Harper & Row, 1969), p. 147.

5. Ibid., p. 138.

6. Cited in Connie Zweig and Jeremiah Abrams, eds., *Meeting the Shadow: The Dark Side of Human Nature* (Los Angeles: Jeremy P. Tarcher, 1991), p. 4.

7. Wendell Berry's verse is cited in Zweig and Abrams, *Meeting the Shadow,* p. 305.

8. Roberto Assagioli, *Psychosynthesis* (New York: Random House, 1965).

9. Ralph Metzner, "Alchemy and Personal Transformation," *The Laughing Man* 2, no. 4 (1981): 55.

WEEK 7

1. Ken Wilber, *The Atman Project: A Transpersonal View of Human Development* (Wheaton, IL: Quest Books, 1980), p. 80.

2. Richard Cavendish, *An Illustrated Encyclopedia of Mythology* (New York: Crescent, 1980), p. 11.

3. Colin Martindale, *Cognition and Consciousness* (Homewood, IL: Dorsey, 1981).

4. William Blake, cited in Charles Hampden-Turner, *Maps of the Mind* (London: Mitchell Beazley, 1981), p. 98.

WEEK 8

1. Joanna Rogers Macy, *Despair and Empowerment in the Nuclear Age* (Philadelphia: New Society, 1983), p. 136.

2. David C. McClelland, *Human Motivation* (Glenview, IL: Scott, Foresman, 1985).

3. David G. Myers, *The Pursuit of Happiness* (New York: Avalon, 1993).

4. Ibid., p. 108.

5. Ibid.

6. Angus Campbell, *The Sense of Well-Being in America* (New York: McGraw-Hill, 1981), pp. 218–19.

7. Martin E. P. Seligman, *Learned Optimism* (New York: Simon & Schuster, 1990).

8. Ibid.

9. Ibid., p. 288.

10. Dan P. McAdams, *Stories We Live By: Personal Myths and the Making of the Self* (New York: William Morrow, 1993), pp. 110–13.

11. Ibid., p. 111.

12. Ibid., p. 113.

WEEK 9

1. Stanislav Grof, *The Holotropic Mind* (San Francisco: HarperCollins, 1992), p. 156.

2. Michael J. Mahoney, *Human Change Processes: The Scientific Foundations of Psychotherapy* (New York: Basic Books, 1991), p. 269.

3. Ibid., pp. 258–66.

4. Martin E. P. Seligman, *What You Can Change and What You Can't* (New York: Ballantine, 1993), pp. 17, 29.

5. Ibid.

6. Ibid.

7. William Irwin Thompson, *Passages About Earth: An Exploration of the New Planetary Culture* (New York: Harper & Row, 1974), p. 174.

8. Linda Schierse Leonard, *Witness to the Fire: Creativity and the Veil of Addiction* (Boston: Shambhala, 1990), p. 323.

WEEK 10

1. Rupert Sheldrake, *The Presence of the Past: Morphic Resonance and the Habits of Nature* (New York: Random House, 1988), p. 173.

2. Supporting research is cited in David Feinstein, "At Play in the Fields of the Mind: Personal Myths as Fields of Information" (monograph, Ashland, OR: Innersource, 1996).

3. Roger D. Nelson, G. Johnston Bradish, York H. Dobyns, Brenda J. Dunne, and Robert G. Jahn, "FieldREG Anomalies in Group Situations," *Journal of Scientific Exploration* 10, no. 1 (1996): 111–41.

4. Dean I. Radin, Jannine M. Rebman, and Maikwe P. Cross, "Anomalous Organization of Random Events by Group Consciousness: Two Exploratory Experiments," *Journal of Scientific Exploration* 10 (1996): 143–68.

5. For a more detailed discussion of the relationship between fields and personal myths, see Feinstein, "At Play in the Fields of the Mind."

6. Benjamin Libet, "A Testable Field Theory of Mind-Brain Interaction," *Journal of Consciousness Studies* 1, no. 1 (1994): 119; Karl H. Pribram, *Languages of the Brain* (Englewood Cliffs, NJ: Prentice-Hall, 1971).

7. David Bohm, *Quantum Theory* (London: Constable, 1951); William A. Tiller, "What Are Subtle Energies?" *Journal of Scientific Exploration* 7 (1993): 293–304.

8. Robert G. Jahn and Brenda J. Dunne, *Margins of Reality: The Role of Consciousness in the Physical World* (New York: Harcourt Brace, 1988).

9. Virginia A. Larson, "An Exploration of Psychotherapeutic Resonance," *Psychotherapy* 24 (1987): 323.

10. Sheldrake, *The Presence of the Past;* Paul Weiss, *Principles of Development* (New York: Holt, 1939).

11. Valerie Hunt, *Infinite Mind: The Science of Human Vibrations* (Malibu, CA: Malibu Publishing, 1995).

12. Donna Eden, *Weaving the Energies, Setting the Field: An Introduction to Energy Medicine* (Ashland, OR: Innersource, 1996).

13. Ervin Laszlo, *The Interconnected Universe: Conceptual Foundations of Transdisciplinary Unified Theory* (River Edge, NJ: World Scientific, 1995).

14. Rupert Sheldrake, *A New Science of Life: The Hypothesis of Formative Causation* (Los Angeles: Jeremy P. Tarcher, 1981); *The Presence of the Past.*

15. Sheldrake, *The Presence of the Past.*

16. Ibid., p. 264.

17. Douglas M. Stokes, Review of *Research in Parapsychology 1991,* in *Journal of Parapsychology* 59 (1995): 173.

18. Rupert Sheldrake, *Seven Experiments That Could Change the World* (New York: Riverhead, 1995).

19. K. Schmidt-Koenig and H. J. Schlichte, "Homing in Pigeons with Impaired Vision," *Proceedings of the National Academy of Sciences* (USA) 69 (1972): 2446–47.

20. B. R. Moore, "Magnetic Fields and Orientation in Homing Pigeons: Experiments of the Late W. T. Keeton," *Proceedings of the National Academy of Sciences* (USA) 85 (1988): 4907–09.

21. Sheldrake, *The Presence of the Past,* p. 151.

22. Jeanne Achterberg, *Imagery in Healing: Shamanism and Modern Medicine* (Boston: New Science Library, 1985), p. 3.

23. John Predebon and Sean B. Docker, "Free-Throw Shooting Performance as a Function of Preshot Routines," *Perceptual & Motor Skills* 75 (1992): 167–71.

24. Susan M. Drake, "Guided Imagery and Education: Theory, Practice and Experience," *Journal of Mental Imagery* 20 (1996): 1–58.

25. Michael Murphy, *The Future of the Body* (Los Angeles: Jeremy P. Tarcher, 1992).

26. Jean Houston, *The Possible Human* (Los Angeles: Jeremy P. Tarcher, 1982), p. 11.

27. Mark S. Rider and Jeanne Achterberg, "Effect of Music-assisted Imagery on Neutrophils and Lymphocytes," *Biofeedback and Self-Regulation* 14, no. 3 (1989): 247–57.

28. This exercise, which comes out of the work of Moshe Feldenkrais, was taught to us by Ilana Rubenfeld.

29. The temporal tap is described and a neurological rationale is provided in David S. Walther, *Applied Kinesiology* (Pueblo, CO: Systems DC, 1976), pp. 261–63.

WEEK 11

1. Stephen Larsen, *The Shaman's Doorway: Opening the Mythic Imagination to Contemporary Consciousness* (New York: Harper & Row, 1976), p. 4.

2. Steven R. Covey, *Reflections for Highly Effective People,* audiotape (New York: Simon & Schuster, 1994).

3. William James, cited in David G. Myers, *The Pursuit of Happiness* (New York: Avalon, 1992), p. 126.

4. Kurt Lewin, *Resolving Social Conflict* (New York: Harper, 1948).

5. Ibid.

6. Sheldon B. Kopp, *If You Meet the Buddha on the Road, Kill Him!: The Pilgrimage of Psychotherapy Patients* (Palo Alto, CA: Science and Behavior Books, 1972), p. 166.

7. Stanislav Grof, *The Adventure of Self-Discovery* (Albany: State University of New York Press, 1988); Gay Hendricks and Kathlyn Hendricks, *At the Speed of Life: A New Approach to Personal Change through Body-Centered Therapy* (New York: Bantam, 1993); Jack L. Rosenberg and Marjorie L. Rand, *Body, Self, and Soul: Sustaining Integration* (Atlanta: Humanics, 1985).

8. Thomas Hanna, *Somatics: Reawakening the Mind's Control of Movement, Flexibility, and Health* (Reading, MA: Addison-Wesley, 1988).

9. Francine Shapiro, *Eye Movement Desensitization and Reprocessing* (New York: Guilford, 1995).

10. Donna Eden, *Weaving the Energies, Setting the Field: An Introduction to Energy Medicine* (Ashland, OR: Innersource, 1996).

WEEK 12

1. Thomas Mann, "Freud and the Future" (speech delivered in celebration of Freud's eightieth birthday, on May 9, 1936, in Vienna, in which Mann described what he called the "lived myth"), excerpted in Henry A. Murray, ed., *Myth and Mythmaking* (Boston: Beacon, 1968), pp. 371–72.

2. Dan P. McAdams, *Stories We Live By: Personal Myths and the Making of the Self* (New York: William Morrow, 1993), p. 102.

3. Roy F. Baumeister, *Identity: Cultural Change and the Struggle for Self* (New York: Oxford University Press, 1986).

4. This discussion of the "contemporary self" follows Dan P. McAdams, "Personality, Modernity, and the Storied Self: A Contemporary Framework for Studying Persons," *Psychological Inquiry* 7, no. 4 (1996): 295–321.

5. McAdams, *Stories We Live By.*

6. Ibid., p. 47.

7. Ibid., p. 109.

8. David Elkind, *Children and Adolescents: Interpretive Essays on Jean Piaget,* 3d ed. (New York: Oxford University Press, 1981).

9. Seymour Epstein, "Integration of the Cognitive and the Psychodynamic Unconscious," *American Psychologist* 49 (1994): 709–24.

10. Gary Gregg, *Self-Representation: Life Narrative Studies in Identity and Ideology* (Westport, CT: Greenwood, 1991).

11. Hubert Hermans, *The Dialogical Self: Meaning as Movement* (San Diego: Academic Press, 1993).

12. Robert Kegan, *The Evolving Self: Problem and Process in Human Development* (Cambridge, MA: Harvard University Press, 1982).

13. Silvan Tomkins, *Affect, Imagery, Consciousness: Cognition, Duplication, and Transformation of Information* (New York: Springer, 1992).

14. George Kelly, *The Psychology of Personal Constructs,* vols. 1 and 2 (New York: W. W. Norton, 1955).

15. Seymour Epstein, "The Unconscious, the Preconscious, and the Self-Concept," in Jerry Suls and Anthony G. Greenwald, eds., *Psychological Perspectives on the Self,* vol. 2 (Hillsdale, NJ: Lawrence Erlbaum Associates, 1983), p. 220.

16. Ibid.

17. Seymour Epstein, "Cognitive-Experiential Self-Theory: An Integrative Theory of Personality," in Rebecca C. Curtis, ed., *The Relational Self: Theoretical Convergences in Psychoanalysis and Social Psychology* (New York: Guilford, 1991), p. 118.

18. Ibid.

19. Epstein, "Integration of the Cognitive and the Psychodynamic Unconscious."

20. Ibid., p. 124.

21. Epstein, "The Unconscious, the Preconscious, and the Self-Concept."

22. Jean Piaget, *The Development of Thought: Equilibrium of Cognitive Structures* (New York: Viking, 1977).

23. Ibid., p. 33.

24. M. Basseches, *Dialectical Thinking and Adult Development* (Norwood, NJ: Ablex, 1984).

25. J. Allan Hobson, *The Dreaming Brain* (New York: Basic Books, 1988).

26. Michael Gazzaniga, *Nature's Mind: The Biological Roots of Thinking, Emotions, Sexuality, Language, and Intelligence* (New York: Basic Books, 1992).

27. Ibid., p. 126.

28. Ibid.

29. Antonio Damasio, *Descartes' Error: Emotion, Reason, and the Human Brain* (New York: Grosset/Putnam, 1994).

30. Ibid.

31. Ibid., pp. 226–27.

32. Ibid., p. 240.

33. Charles T. Tart, *Waking Up: Overcoming the Obstacles to Human Potential* (Boston: Shambhala, 1986), p. 85.

34. David Lukoff, Francis G. Lu, and Robert Turner, "Cultural Considerations in the Assessment and Treatment of Religious and Spiritual Problems," *Cultural Psychiatry* 18 (1995): 467–85.

35. Ralph W. Hood, "Differential Triggering of Mystical Experience as a Function of Self-Actualization," *Review of Religious Research* 18 (1974): 264–70; Nicholas P. Spanos and Patricia Moretti, "Correlates of Mystical and Diabolical Experiences in a Sample of Female University Students," *Journal of the Scientific Study of Religion* 27 (1988): 105–16.

36. R. M. Bucke, cited in William James, *The Varieties of Religious Experience* (New York: Crowell-Collier, 1961; original work published 1901), pp. 313–14.

37. David Raft and Jeffry Andresen, "Transformations in Self-Understanding after Near-Death Experiences," *Contemporary Psychoanalysis* 22 (1986): 319–46.

38. Charles N. Alexander, Maxwell V. Rainforth, and Paul Gelderloos, "Transcendental Meditation, Self-Actualization, and Psychological Health: A Conceptual Overview and Statistical Meta-Analysis," *Journal of Social Behavior and Personality* 6 (1991): 189–247.

39. Aldous Huxley, *The Perennial Philosophy* (New York: Harper & Row, 1945), p. vii; the term "Perennial Philosophy" was originally coined by the German philosopher Gottfried Leibniz (1646–1716).

40. Ibid., p. viii.

41. Ken Wilber, *Up from Eden* (Garden City, NY: Anchor/Doubleday, 1981), pp. 3–4.

42. Abraham H. Maslow, *Religions, Values, and Peak Experiences* (Columbus: Ohio State University Press, 1964).

43. James, *The Varieties of Religious Experience,* p. 332.

44. Bronislaw Malinowski, *Magic, Science and Religion* (Garden City, NY: Doubleday, 1954), p. 108.

45. Rollo May, *Freedom and Destiny* (New York: W. W. Norton, 1981), p. 90.

46. Further theory and references to research supporting these principles are presented in David Feinstein's "Myth-Making in Psychological and Spiritual Development," *American Journal of Orthopsychiatry* (in press).

47. Kegan, *The Evolving Self,* p. 31.

48. Ken Wilber, *Sex, Ecology, Spirituality* (Boston: Shambhala, 1995), p. 61.

49. Kegan, *The Evolving Self,* p. 82.

50. Epstein, "Integration of the Cognitive and the Psychodynamic Unconscious."

51. Ibid.

52. Ibid., p. 716.

53. Kegan, *The Evolving Self,* p. 82.

54. Epstein, "Integration of the Cognitive and the Psychodynamic Unconscious," p. 717.

55. Wilber, *Sex, Ecology, Spirituality,* pp. 59–61.

56. Ibid., p. 61.

57. Erik H. Erikson, *Identity and the Life Cycle* (New York: W. W. Norton, 1980).

58. Aaron T. Beck and Arthur Freeman, *Cognitive Therapy of Personality Disorders* (New York: Guilford, 1990), pp. 360–61.

59. Stanley Krippner and Michael Winkler, "Postmodernity and Consciousness Studies," *Journal of Mind and Behavior* 16 (1995): 255–80.

60. Walter Truett Anderson, *Reality Isn't What It Used to Be* (San Francisco: HarperCollins, 1990); Robert A. Neimeyer and Michael J. Mahoney, *Constructivism in Psychotherapy* (Washington, DC: American Psychological Association, 1995).

61. Peter Russell, *The Global Brain Awakens: Our Next Evolutionary Leap* (Palo Alto, CA: Global Brain, 1995).

62. Anne W. Dosher, "Personal and Organizational Mythology: A Reflexive Reality," in Stanley Krippner, ed., *Into the Mythic Underworld* (special issue of *AHP Perspective,* San Francisco: Association for Humanistic Psychology, April 1982), pp. 11–12.

63. Ibid., p. 12.

64. Hazel Henderson, *Paradigms in Progress* (Indianapolis: Knowledge Systems, 1991).

65. Jeffrey Hollender, *How to Make the World a Better Place: 116 Ways You Can Make a Difference* (New York: W. W. Norton, 1995).

66. Bill Shore, *Revolution of the Heart* (New York: Riverhead, 1995), pp. 148–49.

67. Commission on Global Governance, *Our Global Neighborhood* (New York: Oxford University Press, 1995).

68. Ibid., p. xix.

SUPPORT GUIDE 1

1. Anthea Francine, *Envisioning Theology: An Autobiographical Account of Personal Symbolic Journeying as a Source of Revelation* (Master's thesis, Berkeley, CA: Pacific School of Religion, June 1983), p. 45.

2. Patricia A. Brill and Kenneth H. Cooper, "Physical Exercise and Mental Health," *National Forum* 73, no. 1 (1993): 44–45.

3. This procedure is patterned after Edmund Jacobsen's classic method of *Progressive Relaxation* (Chicago: University of Chicago Press, 1938).

1. Montague Ullman, "Dreams, the Dreamer, and Society," in Gayle Delaney, ed., *New Directions in Dream Interpretation* (Albany: State University of New York Press, 1993), pp. 11–40.

2. Gayle Delaney, *Breakthrough Dreaming* (New York: Bantam, 1991); Rosalind Cartwright and Lynne Lamberg, *Crisis Dreaming: Using Your Dreams to Solve Your Problems* (New York: HarperCollins, 1992); Ann Faraday, *Dream Power* (New York: Berkley, 1973); Robert Langs, *The Dream Workbook* (Brooklyn, NY: Alliance, 1994); Stanley Krippner and Joseph Dillard, *Dreamworking: How to Use Your Dreams for Creative Problem-Solving* (Buffalo, NY: Bearly, 1988); Robert L. Van de Castle, *Our Dreaming Mind* (New York: Random House, 1994); Montague Ullman, *Appreciating Dreams: A Group Approach* (Thousand Oaks, CA: Sage, 1996); Montague Ullman and Nan Zimmerman, *Working with Dreams* (Los Angeles: Jeremy P. Tarcher, 1985).

3. Gayle Delaney, "The Dream Interview," in Gayle Delaney, ed., *New Directions in Dream Interpretation* (Albany: State University of New York Press, 1993), pp. 198–99 (italics deleted).

4. Ann Faraday, *The Dream Game* (New York: Harper & Row, 1974), p. 4.

5. R. A. Lockhart, "Cancer in Myth and Dream," *Spring* (1978): 1–26.

6. Patricia L. Garfield, *The Healing Power of Dreams* (New York: Simon & Schuster, 1992), p. 19.

7. Delaney, "The Dream Interview," p. 195.

8. For further discussion of dreams and personal myths, see David Feinstein, "Myth-Making Activity through the Window of Your Dreams," in Stanley Krippner, ed., *Dreamtime and Dreamwork: Decoding the Language of the Night* (Los Angeles: Jeremy P. Tarcher, 1990), pp. 21–33.

9. Rosalind Cartwright, *Night Life: Explorations in Dreaming* (Englewood Cliffs, NJ: Prentice-Hall, 1977).

10. Carl G. Jung, "The Practice of Psychotherapy," in *Collected Works,* vol. 16, 2d ed., trans. R. F. C. Hull (Princeton, NJ: Princeton University Press, 1966), p. 42.

11. Calvin S. Hall and Robert L. Van de Castle, *The Content Analysis of Dreams* (New York: Appleton-Century-Crofts, 1966).

1. Carol S. Pearson, *Awakening the Heroes Within* (San Francisco: HarperCollins, 1991), p. 2.

2. Gerald M. Rosen, "Guidelines for the Review of Do-It-Yourself Treatment Books," *Contemporary Psychology* 26 (1981): 189–91.

3. David Feinstein, "Myth-Making in Psychological and Spiritual Development," *American Journal of Orthopsychiatry* (in press); Stanley Krippner and David Feinstein, "Psychotherapy in a Mythic Key: The Legacy of Carl Gustav Jung," in S. Lynn, ed., *Contemporary Psychotherapies* (Monterey, CA: Brooks/Cole, in press); Dan P. McAdams, *Stories We Live By: Personal Myths and the Making of the Self* (New York: William Morrow, 1993).

4. Alan E. Bergin and Sol I. Garfield, *Handbook of Psychotherapy and Behavioral Change,* 4th ed. (New York: John Wiley, 1994).

5. See, for example, Mihaly Csikszentmihalyi, *Flow: The Psychology of Optimal Experience* (New York: Harper & Row, 1990); Robert Jay Lifton, *The Protean Self: Human Resilience in an Age of Fragmentation* (New York: Basic Books, 1993); David G. Myers, *The Pursuit of Happiness* (New York: Avon, 1992); Martin E. P. Seligman, *Learned Optimism* (New York: Simon & Schuster, 1990).

6. A variation of this meditation was taught to us by Tiziana de Rovere.

7. Alan Watts, cited in Ann Faraday, *The Dream Game* (Harper & Row, 1974), p. xvii.

8. We are grateful to Donna Eden for teaching us this procedure.

Index